THE
NEW HARMONY
MOVEMENT

THE

NEW HARMONY

MOVEMENT

BY

GEORGE B. LOCKWOOD

[1905]

AUGUSTUS M. KELLEY · PUBLISHERS

NEW YORK 1970

First Published 1905

(New York: D. Appleton & Company, 1905)

Reprinted 1970 by

AUGUSTUS M. KELLEY · PUBLISHERS

REPRINTS OF ECONOMIC CLASSICS

New York New York 10001

.   .   .   .

I S B N   0 678 00667 9

L C N   68 56245

PRINTED IN THE UNITED STATES OF AMERICA
by SENTRY PRESS, NEW YORK, N. Y. 10019

COMMUNITY HOUSE No. 2.

Scene of the first successful American experiment in Pestalozzian education.

THE NEW HARMONY
MOVEMENT

BY

GEORGE B. LOCKWOOD

With the Collaboration of CHARLES A. PROSSER
in the preparation of the Educational Chapters

NEW YORK
D. APPLETON AND COMPANY
1905

INTRODUCTION

WHAT is called in this book the " New Harmony Movement " forms a noteworthy practical lesson in sociology—in that part of sociology which treats of the ISMS of that important science.

In the institutions of civilization we count four cardinal types—the family, civil society with its division of labor, the state, the church. The two extremes—the family and the church—give us, on the one hand, the first departure from the individual with his narrow experience, and on the other the arrival at the highest reenforcement by the race or the social whole. The family, although nearest to the unassisted individual, does not for that very reason permit much development of individuality. Its principle is obedience to elders, and especially to parents and naturally constituted guides. A high degree of self-activity and independence is not found possible in this institution, because blind obedience is irrational.

As compared with the family, civil society with its division of labor gives greater opportunity for the development of individuality. The individual through his vocation contributes something to supply the wants of his community. He makes some article or performs some function that is useful to the social whole, and thereby lays his community under obligation to him and gets recognition for his service. He has proved himself essential to the society in which he lives, and society hastens to set before him, for the supply of his own particular needs, the aggregate production of all the units of society. It does this through and by means of the market wherein his own product is measured with the products of others, and he gets a *quid pro quo*.

In civil society, therefore, the individual manifests his differences and idiosyncrasies, and gets them recognized and approved by the whole community. And, on the other hand, he gets his needs and wants, his defects and peculiarities, supplemented and provided for by his fellow men. Their capacities and idiosyncrasies make up for his deficiencies, just as he makes up for their deficiencies to the extent of his own real power. Hence society seems to be, in one respect, a larger individual, an institutional person; more perfect than the particular individual because it contains all the strengths united into one great social strength, the defects and weaknesses eliminated by mutual compensation.

The state is the individuality of this greater human self which comes to exist through the division of labor and the process of compensation. It subordinates the individual to the social will. And it does this not only in respect to the property and belongings of the individual, but in reference to his liberty and his very life itself. It uses the individual and his property to protect the life and property of the whole, but by this negative process it secures the positive result of the protection of life and liberty to all its citizens. The individual is reenforced by the strength of his whole nation, and thus achieves an individuality altogether transcendent as compared to that which he realized in the family, or even in his industrial vocation. We are ascending a ladder toward emancipation from natural limits, and toward achievement of a colossal individuality—family, industrial vocation, citizenship in a nation.

There is one step of higher emancipation. The three institutions just considered are worldly. The church is the other-worldly institution which has for its object emancipation from the thraldom of space and time by revealing to man his origin and his final purpose in the divine order of the universe. Man as a moral being belongs to an other-worldly realm. In the church he celebrates his discoveries of the divine order, and founds upon them a higher emancipation from the shortcomings and imperfections, the restraints and limitations, of mere nature.

These are the four rounds in the ladder of civilization. The mere individual outside of these four institutions of civilization exists in a state of rudimental freedom. A state of Robinson Crusoe isolation is the lowest order of rational life. Crusoe finds himself dependent on the products of nature for his food, clothing, and shelter, but is without organized means for the subjugation of nature. Hence he lives from hand to mouth and subject to all the vicissitudes that visit his habitat in and out of season. He exists also in a state of war, not only against natural forces but of one savage man against other savage men. Progress out of these evil conditions will demand social organization through the four institutions which we have been considering. These will emancipate his individuality and bring him beyond the stage of animal likes and dislikes to the stage in which is revealed to him deeper and deepest ideas of reason and higher and highest attainments of freedom and achievement.

By these institutions he will get command not only of bread for his body, but of high positions of influence and power among his fellow men; above this, he will attain insights into the science of nature and into the structure of the moral order of society; the gradual unfoldment of human nature in the history of civilizations; insights into the art and literature of the most gifted peoples. Reading all things in the light of the highest principle, he will receive what is better than bread, or than dominion over nature and man, or than insights into special realms of truth. Emerson, in his poem The Days, celebrates the gifts which the days bring to man:

> "To each they offer gifts after his will,
> Bread, kingdoms, stars, and sky that holds them all."

Emerson has indicated in his poem progressive steps of emancipation of individuality. Bread gives freedom from the wants of the body; kingdoms the sway over our environment of nature and human society—wealth and high station; stars the several insights and skills which give us a deeper self-knowledge and the artistic power needed for the poet and the sage; and "the sky that holds them all" is the religious view or philosophic view of the divine which is presupposed by all these gifts.

It happens that partial insights into the good and the evil of institutions create sects of reformers who seek to eradicate one institution by another. They would substitute civil society for the family and for the state. Communism or socialism undertakes to do this, and the failure of this view of the world is illustrated in a great variety of phases in the history of New Harmony, both in the experiment of the Rappites and in the longer and fuller experiment of Robert Owen and his successors.

The Rappites, as pointed out by the author of this history, were religious communists. Rapp himself was prophet, priest, and king. As is usual in this kind of communism, one prophet excludes all other prophets. He prevents his disciples from growing into prophets, or, indeed, from undertaking any original thinking or planning. Originality, if encouraged, would soon destroy the community. Morris Birkbeck is quoted as saying: "Strangers visit their establishment and retire from it full of admiration; but a slavish acquiescence, under a disgusting superstition, is so remarkable an ingredient in their character that it checks all desire of imitation."

With Rapp's community, the ideal disciple was an

obedient slave. Governed by a man who understood business, like Frederick Rapp, labor could be well organized
and the earnings could be accumulated in the strong chest
of the prophet and king. But in this case, the institution
which we have called civil society does not get established
in such a way as to develop individual freedom. The
Roman idea of property emancipates the individual from
the patriarchal ties of the family and develops individual
initiative, but New Harmony suppressed the individual
initiative and secured obedience to the priest and king.

Thus the church admitted civil society only in its
serfdom, and not in its freedom. But the church, in this
experiment, abolishes not only civil society in its aspect of
individual initiative, substituting the family principle of
patriarchal rule, but in turn it abolishes the family out-
right by introducing the principle of celibacy. And by
this it saws off the limb on which the whole community
depends. Moreover, such a community is incompatible
with the state except in its most rudimentary form of
the tribe. No neighboring town or county could trust
the New Harmony citizens in a political election because
they were puppets moved by a king inspired by other-
worldly interests and firmly keeping aloof from the interests of the county and the State of Indiana and the
nation. There was in store for this community, when
the Indiana Territory should become populous, an exter-
minating persecution at the hands of a mob like that
which drove Mormonism out of Nauvoo in later years.
Its return to Pennsylvania anticipated the catastrophe.
Religious communism attacks family, civil society, and
state in the developed form which these institutions take
on in modern civilization.

The second form of community, that of Mr. Owen,
which came to be established at New Harmony, was in
some respects the opposite of the religious community that
had preceded it. It established itself in the name of a

civil society more or less opposed to the family, more or less opposed to the state, and, above all, opposed to the church. The strict regulations penetrating to the private life of the Owenite communist remind us of the Rappite community of the prophet and priest, and so also does the control of labor by a one-man power and the covering of all production into the common storehouses, and in this it contradicted the ideal of the civil community, smothered individual initiative and arrested the training of the population into civil freedom. Owen might desire to have original initiative develop in the individuals of his community. And his establishment of common-school education shows that he was almost entirely unconscious of the meaning of the division of labor as a function of the institution of civil society. He seemed to think that not only could the laborer forswear self-activity in planning as well as executing, but even could be aroused by school education without the danger of feeling the absolute need for the exercise of original initiative in his trade and vocation.

Involved in this contradiction, his communistic experiment could not flourish, and did not flourish. The religious community, after the death of its prophet, gradually changed into a civil community.

The lesson forced on us by these two experiments is the necessity for each of the four institutions, and the limitation of each through the other. If, in the name of one of these institutions, an attempt is made to suppress another institution, the attempt destroys the whole experiment. For each institution, in order to be complete, demands the creation of the other institutions in their full development. If the dominant institution endeavors to create for itself the other institutions, it dwarfs them or mutilates them.

The lack of a religious faith in the Owen experiment made impossible on the part of the other citizens of Indiana the cooperation necessary for an influential citizenship in the State. The outside citizens could never forecast what practical cooperation in their policy might be secured from the Owen community. Hence they suspected even the best measures proposed by Robert Dale Owen in the constitutional convention and in the legislature. They were afraid that his well-known opinions regarding the church concealed some latent mischief which would come out as an injury to the commonwealth sooner or later if adopted, and hence arose some of the opposition against the legislation which he proposed in behalf of so good a cause as that of public free schools.

Public free schools have a tendency to develop the power of the boys and girls in the line of original initiative. The school enables them to see not only things as they are, but to compare them with the scientific and historical ideals of what they ought to be. They can see possibilities of the manufacture of useful machinery in beds of ore and forests of timber; they can see the possibility of mills for textile manufacture or for manufactures of hardware in the waterfalls of their rivers. Armed with science, the mind is able to make mechanic inventions. All classes of citizens gain in directive power by means of the studies of the school. But the citizens of Indiana looked upon the experiment of communism at New Harmony as in the direction of suppressing individual initiative and the substitution of a one-man power for independent ownership of real estate and personal property, and for independent freedom of choice.

If Robert Dale Owen had described the true effects of school education in the line of freedom of property and independent initiative, he would have recommended his scheme for free public schools more effectively than he was able to do as the representative of a communistic experiment, for his communism preached a silent lesson in contradiction to his plea for free schools. And his

xi

INTRODUCTION

opposition to the churches established in the several towns and villages of Indiana aroused that deepest and most bitter of all opposition, the opposition founded on divergence of theological views, divergence as to the fundamental view which one takes of the meaning of the world of nature and of human destiny. This hostility of the people of Indiana to measures which were really greatly for the benefit of the whole State is a very interesting feature in this history, and it is very clearly pointed out by the author in this book.

The work of Maclure in the school at New Harmony, and afterward as publicist, deserves study on its own account. He brought industrial instruction into his school, and laid so much stress on the mechanical features of education that he in a great measure neutralized the effect of the school on the characters of his pupils, for he more or less turned off the minds of his pupils from those studies which give original initiative, and turned them in the direction of matters of skill and routine practise. In these days of attempts in the direction of manual training and other industrial education, the experiment of Maclure and its results on the people of New Harmony deserve the most careful consideration. How much directive power came from his instruction in the way of industrial preparation? How much directive power in the way of enabling his pupils to understand and cooperate with their fellow men in other parts of Indiana and the United States in later life?

I am greatly impressed with the value of this work as a study for teachers everywhere, and would commend its careful study especially to the great storm-centers of social agitation, such as the cities of Chicago, Boston, and San Francisco, for example.

W. T. HARRIS.

WASHINGTON, D. C., *April 20, 1905.*

CONTENTS

xiii

CONTENTS

LIST OF ILLUSTRATIONS

LIST OF ILLUSTRATIONS

THE NEW HARMONY MOVEMENT

CHAPTER I

NEW HARMONY'S PLACE IN HISTORY

ON the Indiana side of the Wabash River, fifty-one miles above its mouth, the village of New Harmony lies within the shelter of a long range of encircling hills. In summer New Harmony's dooryards are shaded by a veritable forest of maple and gate trees, above which, here and there, rise the gables and dormer-windowed roofs of quaint buildings suggestive of another country and another century. The vandal hand of business enterprise has not been heavily laid upon this place, and thus it happens that the New Harmony of to-day bears everywhere the impress of its earlier and greater years. Houses reared by German communists in the second decade of the century, and in the twenties occupied by members of the Owenite communities, still stand in New Harmony's quiet streets. A large and handsomely housed public library, rich in the heritage of collections of books brought to the place by the scholars and *savants* of community days—more than this, the character of the present population, which includes a large number of the descendants of the Owenite communists— suggests a time when New Harmony was the promised land of Owenism—a social experiment-station toward which the eyes of the whole world were turned, and not in vain, if we take into account the several great movements

1

which in later years have made the New Harmony failure appear a wonderful success.

Parke Godwin, in his Popular View of Fourierism, divides social reformers into three classes of "architects of society," as he calls them: first, the pure theorists, who have contented themselves with picturing an ideal state of society, without suggesting a practical effort at its attainment, as Plato in the Republic, More in Utopia, Harrington in Oceana, and Campanella in City of the Sun; second, the practical architects, as the Rappites, Moravians, and Shakers, who, on religious rather than on economic grounds, have established societies in imitation of the supposed communism of the early Christians; third, the theoretico-practical architects, who have combined the enunciation of social theories with actual experiments, as Owen, Cabet, Fourier, and St. Simon.

By strange coincidence, New Harmony became the scene of the most notable experiments yet attempted by the "social architects" of two of these three classes. Among religious communists, the Rappites, founders of Harmony, have been most successful, and their residence in Indiana marked the high tide of their growth in wealth and numbers. There has not been another trial of philosophical communistic association so auspiciously undertaken, or so thoroughly carried to a conclusion, as that which Robert Owen inaugurated at New Harmony more than three-quarters of a century ago. Brook Farm has occupied a larger place in literature, but as a serious effort at solving the social problems of its time, it did not approach New Harmony in importance. To New Harmony, Brook Farm was as a playground to a workshop. Brook Farm afforded temporary amusement to a congenial coterie of literary celebrities who cherished romantic ideals in common, but it bequeathed little to the world except their individual contributions to the literature of that period. The New Harmony experiment was conducted in a less romantic

2

atmosphere, but it was more earnest, thorough, and satisfying, and to the modern student of sociology it is more significant as a social venture. As Owenism was the forerunner of Fourierism, so New Harmony was the forerunner of Brook Farm. As Brook Farm was the center of a group of Fourieristic phalansteres, or colonies, so New Harmony was the inspiration of a large number of Owenite experiments, scattered over so wide a range of territory that they assumed the proportions of a national movement. Robert Owen declared, Emerson says—and Owen is not the only witness to the fairness of his contention—that Fourier learned all he knew of communism from a study of Owenism. If this be true, Brook Farm was only a far-off reflection of the great experiment at New Harmony.

Notable as New Harmony was in its own time as the scene of an ambitious effort at social regeneration, the perspective of years is necessary to an adequate portrayal of its importance in American history. The death-bed of Robert Owen's " social system " became the birthplace of several distinct movements which have assumed great proportions since the story of the New Harmony communisms became a half-forgotten chapter in the history of social experiments. There the doctrine of universal elementary education at public expense, without regard to sex or sect, as a duty of the State, was first proclaimed in the Middle West, and through the labors of Robert Dale Owen, more than any other one man, this conception of the State's duty has found expression in a common-school system that is the glory of the Republic. Through William Maclure, Robert Owen, and Joseph Neef, Pestalozzi's pupil and the author of the first American works on the science of teaching, the Pestalozzian system of education, now everywhere predominant, was first successfully transplanted to this country. William Maclure's manual-training school at

New Harmony was the first of its kind in the United States, and through that institution and its popular publications, the idea of technical training was first widely disseminated in this country. The infant schools established at New Harmony by Robert Owen, "the father of infant education," and conducted throughout the lifetime of the communistic experiments, were the first of their kind in America. It was in the schools at New Harmony that the theory of equal educational privileges for the sexes was first put into practise, and through Robert Dale Owen, as author, agitator, and legislator, the New Harmony idea of "free, equal, and universal schools" exerted a determinative influence upon American institutional development. Through William Maclure, "the father of American geology," Thomas Say, "the father of American zoology," Constantine Rafinesque, the pioneer ichthyologist of the West, Charles Albert Lesueur, the first classifier of the fishes of the Great Lakes, Gerard Troost, one of the earliest American mineralogists, and the younger Owens, New Harmony became the greatest scientific center in America, and the first important scientific outpost in the West; there came such distinguished students as Sir Charles Lyell, Leo Lesquereux, Audubon, Prince Alexander Philip Maximilian and his company of scientists, F. B. Meek, and Dr. Elderhorst. New Harmony became the headquarters of the United States Geological Survey, with one of its own students, David Dale Owen, in charge; it was the site of a museum containing the remarkable collections of Say and Maclure, and of a scientific library unexcelled on the continent. One member of the New Harmony coterie of *savants*, William Maclure, was one of the founders of the Philadelphia Academy of Natural Sciences, another, Robert Dale Owen, became the legislative father of the Smithsonian Institution. It was in certain of the New Harmony communities that women were first given a voice and vote in local legislative assemblages, and there the doctrine of

4

equal political rights for all, without regard to sex or color, was first proclaimed by Frances Wright. Through this brilliant woman, too, New Harmony became one of the earliest centers of the abolition movement, and spoke forcibly through Robert Dale Owen to President Lincoln when emancipation hung in the balance. Through Robert Dale Owen, New Harmony impressed upon American law the modern conception of the legal rights of women, and in New Harmony was founded, by Frances Wright, what is known as the first woman's literary club in the United States. The New Harmony Thespian Society (1828–'75) was one of the earliest among American dramatic clubs. New Harmony in 1826 afforded the first known American example of prohibition of the liquor traffic by administrative edict. Through William Maclure New Harmony gave to the West a system of mechanics' libraries from which dates the beginning of general culture in more than a hundred and fifty western communities. Through Josiah Warren New Harmony originated a philosophy of individualism, a rebound from communism, which has had sufficient vitality to survive its author for nearly a half century and to impress itself indelibly upon modern economic thought; beyond this, it is claimed by credible authorities that from Josiah Warren, who founded the New Harmony " Time store," and originated a system of " labor notes," Robert Owen derived the central idea of the great labor cooperative societies of Great Britain, which constitute the most successful labor movement of the last century. Even the religious latitudinarianism of the New Harmony communists, so bitterly denounced in its own day, has served as a leaven of liberality in religious thought itself, until the narrow type of religion which the Owenites so steadfastly opposed has in large measure disappeared.

So it is that the little torch of learning long ago kindled in the wilderness, made New Harmony a center of light and leading while it was yet surrounded by " the trackless wild." But New Harmony's place in history has never been adequately appreciated, and it is worth while, in studying the Owenite communities, to trace to their source some of the movements which rose from the ruins of the " social system."

It seems proper to preface a history of the Owenite communities with a brief account of the German communistic colony which paved the way for Robert Owen's experiment at New Harmony, if it did not indirectly suggest it. While the Rappite *régime* is less interesting, and vastly less important, than the Owenite period, it affords a strong background for the later experiments, the failure of George Rapp's success standing out in vivid contrast to the success of Robert Owen's failure.

CHAPTER II

THE RISE OF THE RAPPITES

In slow succession there passed through the beautiful valley of the Wabash—described by Col. George Croghan as early as 1765, as "one of the finest countries in the world"—the roving Indian, the Jesuit missionary, the French trader, the British redcoat, the colonial soldier, and the American pioneer. But, strangest feature in all this strange procession of invaders, there entered the Wabash River one spring day in 1815, several boat-loads of Württemberg peasants. Eight hundred strong, clad in the garb of the Fatherland, this quaint company went ashore at a point near the site of the present village of New Harmony. They knelt on the bank about a patriarchal leader, and with song and prayer dedicated "Harmonie" to the uses of a Christian brotherhood. These were the Rappites —German peasants, primitive Christians, practical communists, and disciples of George Rapp. As an organized protest against the existing state of religion in Germany, they had left the shores of their Fatherland behind them ten years before.

During the seventeenth century the German prototype of Puritanism, called Pietism, had caused the flame of faith to burn brighter in the churches, through the ministrations of Spener, Gerhardt, Franke, Arndt, and other Wesleys and Whitfields of that revival movement. But in the eighteenth century, official religion again degenerated into "a multiplicity of meaningless ceremonies." The universities of Germany "became hotbeds of vice and infidelity." On the one hand there were in the ministry those who

7

guarded against their unbelief by the assumption of zealous bigotry and narrow biblical construction—on the other hand there were skeptics and rationalists filling pulpits and receiving the support of the church.

" The church now," says Hurst, " presented a most deplorable aspect. Philosophy had come, with its high-sounding terminology, and invaded the hallowed precincts of scriptural truth. Literature, with its captivating notes, had well-nigh destroyed what was left of the old Pietistic fervor. The songs of the church were no longer images of beauty, but ghastly, repulsive skeletons. The professor's chair was but little better than a heathen tripod. The pulpit became a rostrum, where the shepherdless masses were entertained with essays on such general terms as ' Human Dignity,' ' Truth,' and ' Light.' The peasantry received frequent and labored instruction on the raising of bees, cattle, and fruit. The poets of the day were publicly recited in the temples where the reformers had preached."

But in certain portions of Germany the people retained their former simplicity, and stoutly resisted the encroachments of what they considered wicked innovations. Especially was this true of southern Württemberg, where societies like the early Methodist organizations were formed for the conserving of piety, and a spirit of fanaticism was rampant which contrasted strangely with the rationalism prevalent elsewhere. There were frequent prophecies of the end of the world as a punishment for the sins of the people. One party of schismatics, called Separatists, disgusted with the new order of things, set out to found an asylum in Russian Tartary, near the Caspian Sea. Joseph Bimeler, at the head of a considerable following, denounced the state as " that great Babylon," and, with his associates, refused to pay taxes. Persecuted and frequently imprisoned, Bimeler finally led a colony out of Germany, and. on five thousand acres of land in Tuscarawas County, Ohio, founded " Zoar." Here this communistic society so pros-

pered that in less than fifty years its property was valued
at a million dollars.

Preceding and instigating this emigration, however, was
that of George Rapp and his followers, who sought the
religious freedom offered in the United States as early as
1803. George Rapp and Michael Hahn were zealous lay-
workers and leaders of Pietism in Württemberg at the end
of the eighteenth century. Rapp was a vine-dresser and
farmer of plebeian descent, and a man of unusual strength
of character. Born in 1757, he began to speak in his own
house when about thirty years of age, giving to his congregation, which gathered from miles around, the results of
years of reading and careful Bible study. Hahn was a
man of literary talent as well as an orator of great power.
He did not separate from the established church, but sought
to reform it from within. Rapp refused to cooperate with
what he considered a corrupt ecclesiastical institution, and
though he counseled strict obedience to the laws, which included payment of tithes to the church, neither he nor
his followers attended regular services. Hahn and Rapp,
therefore, no longer worked together, and Rapp, with the
following of three hundred families which his preaching
had attracted, was compelled to endure religious persecution of no gentle type.

At this time, as well as in later years, George Rapp
taught certain doctrines which were peculiarly his own.
Since the Rappites acknowledged no written creed, we must
accept his views as theirs. Rapp evolved a curious doctrine
concerning what he called "the dual nature of Adam."
He taught that Adam contained within his own person both
the sexual elements, reading literally, in confirmation of
this, Genesis i: 26-27: "And God said, let us make man in
our own image, after our own likeness, and let them have
dominion. So God created man in his own image, in the
image of God created he him: male and female created he
them." This Rapp held to mean that both the creator and

9

the created had this dual nature, and had Adam been allowed to remain in his original state, he would have begotten offspring without the aid of a female. But Adam became discontented, and God separated from his body the female part. This is the Rappite interpretation of the fall of man. From this Rapp concluded that the celibate state is more pleasing to God, and that in the "renewed" world man would be restored to the Adamic condition. After a period of religious excitement subsequent to the removal of the Rappites to America, marriage was renounced, and celibacy became a rule of community life. There is evidence that prior to this time Rapp had himself performed marriage ceremonies. Passages of Scripture quoted in support of celibacy were Matthew xxii: 30: "For in the resurrection they neither marry, nor are given in marriage, but are as the Angels of God in heaven." Matthew xix: 10–12, 22–30; I Corinthians vii: 7–8, 25–27 and 29; I Thessalonians iv: 3–5; Revelation xiv: 4. Rapp taught that the coming of Christ and the "renovation" of the world were near at hand. Father Rapp and many of his followers firmly believed that he would live to see the reappearance of Christ in the heavens, and that he would be permitted to present his followers to the Saviour. It is related that when Father Rapp was upon his death-bed, at the age of ninety years, his last words were: "If I did not know that the dear Lord meant that I should present you all to him, I should think my last moments come."

Of Jesus, Rapp taught that he was, like Adam, a dual being, and that he enjoined upon his followers a community of goods. In support of this position Rapp referred to Acts iv: 32, in which it is said of the early Christians: "And the multitude of them that believed were of one heart and of one soul: neither said any of them that aught of the things which he possessed was his own; but they had all things common." Total regeneration Rapp declared necessary to salvation. The sum and substance of

10

his creed of conduct was: Love to God above all, and to thy neighbor as thyself, without laying much stress on form, letter, or ceremony. Though Rapp believed in the doctrine of future rewards and punishments, he did not believe that this punishment would be eternal. " In some far distant geological cycle the universe of matter, which, like the universe of spirit, has been distorted and diseased through the fall, will be restored to its former beauty and happiness, and sin and suffering will finally be banished."

Before leaving Germany Rapp and a number of his followers had been brought before the king for the teaching of heretical doctrines and refusal to attend the services of the established church. The ruler, who happened to be a liberal man, inquired if Rapp and his associates were accustomed to obey the laws of the state. The accusers reluctantly admitted that they were. " Then let them believe as they please," said the king, and dismissed the prisoners. Petty persecution, however, did not cease with this display of royal clemency. " If we could only find a land where religious toleration is enjoyed," declared the Rappites, " we would wish to be there even if we might for a while have to live upon roots."

Thus, in 1803 George Rapp and several associates, including his adopted son, Frederick Rapp, had set out for the United States, for the purpose of locating a colony in the New World. They selected and bought a large tract of land near Zelienople, Pennsylvania, and in the following autumn, three ships, carrying one hundred and twenty-five families of the adherents of Rapp, had followed him to the land of religious liberty. About one-third of these joined one Haller in founding a settlement in Lycoming County, but six hundred members remained with Rapp and settled upon an estate of five thousand acres of unimproved land. They set to work, under the direction of Rapp, with such zeal that they soon made comfortable homes for the entire population.

11

In 1805 the " community of equality " was established. The agreement to which the members bound themselves specified:

1. All cash, land, and chattels of every member to be a free gift for the use and benefit of the community, and to be at the disposal of the superintendents as if the members had never possessed them; members pledge themselves to submit to the laws of the community, to show a ready obedience to the superintendents, to give the labor of their hands for the good of the community, and to hold their children to do the same.

2. George Rapp and his associates to give to each member such secular and religious education as would tend to his temporal welfare and eternal felicity, to supply to members all the necessaries of life, to support them and their widows and children alike in sickness, health, and old age.

3. In case of withdrawal, a member's money to be refunded to him without interest; if he had come in without capital such a sum to be awarded to him as his conduct as a member would justify. (This section was abrogated in 1808.)

One hundred and fifty acres of land were cleared the first year, and forty to fifty log houses erected, besides a large church, mills, and shops. The next year four hundred acres were cleared, a sawmill, tannery, storehouse and distillery erected, and a vineyard of several acres planted. The Rappites had six hundred bushels of surplus grain, and three thousand gallons of whisky, none of which they drank themselves, for it is a peculiar fact that while the Harmonists were long famous for the excellence of their distillery output, strict temperance was always a rule of their organization. Even the use of tobacco was forbidden.

The renunciation of the married state by the Rappites dates from 1807. Persons formerly married, of whom there was a large number in the community, were separated and placed in different establishments. No instance is recorded of marriage among the original Harmonists, excepting in a few cases where young people eloped and deserted the community. The acquiescence of the society in this rule reveals the supreme authority of George Rapp, who was revered as a prophet and a saint.

The remarkable prosperity of the community may be judged from a report of the products in 1809, four years after the removal to America. In that year they raised six thousand bushels of Indian corn, four thousand bushels of wheat, the same of rye, five thousand bushels of oats, ten thousand bushels of potatoes, and four thousand pounds of flax and hemp, besides other less important products. During this year they made their first woolen cloth spun by hand from yarn. In the following year the woolen factory was erected. The community now included about one hundred and forty families comprising seven or eight hundred persons. Two thousand acres of land were under cultivation, and there was a large surplus for sale. A visitor to the settlement at this time said: " We are struck with surprise and admiration at the astonishing progress in improvements and the establishment of manufactories which this little republic has made in five years. They have done more substantial good in the short period of five years than the same number of families, scattered about the country, have done in fifty. This arises from their unity and fraternal love, added to their uniform and persevering industry. They know no self-interest except that which adds to the interest and happiness of the whole community."

The Rappites soon realized the disadvantages of a situation twelve miles distant from navigation, and discovered the inadaptability of their land to fruit cultivation, in which they desired to engage extensively. It is also said that they desired a warmer climate. In 1813 Frederick Rapp was delegated to go farther West in search of a new home. Rapp traveled all over the territory bordering on the Ohio, and finally chose a beautiful tract of land on the Wabash River, a few miles above its mouth. In addition to twenty thousand acres of government land, he purchased several adjacent improved farms, a total of nearly thirty thousand acres.

The Harmonists sold their property in Pennsylvania, with all improvements, at a great sacrifice, for one hundred thousand dollars, and early in 1815 went down in boats and founded the village of " Harmonie," where a large advance party had begun the requisite clearing in the preceding June.

CHAPTER III

THE RAPPITES IN INDIANA

"When Rapp the Harmonist embargoed marriage
In his harmonious settlement which flourishes
Strangely enough as yet without miscarriage,   *   *   *
Why call'd he ' Harmony ' a state *sans* wedlock ?
Now here I've got the preacher at a dead lock.

" Because he either meant to sneer at harmony
Or marriage, by divorcing them thus oddly ;
But whether reverend Rapp learn'd this in Germany
Or not, 'tis said his sect is rich and godly,
Pious and pure, beyond what I can term any
Of ours.   *   *   *"
                                        —BYRON, Don Juan, Canto xv.

ALL that we know of the history of the Rappite community on the Wabash is gleaned from the accounts of travelers who visited the settlement, which immediately attracted wide attention in the West, and became the largest town in the territory of Indiana. The last of the thousand persons who were members of the original community died some years ago, and the Harmonists kept no record of their proceedings.

The Rappites found themselves pleasantly situated on the Wabash. The broad river which flowed before the town furnished power for a large grist-mill which they erected some miles below. Almost opposite the settlement lay an island of three thousand acres, affording excellent pasturage for their flocks. The great estate which they were to till was more fertile than the farms they had deserted, and the undulating hills which enclosed the river-bottom furnished ample territory for vineyards. Favor-

15

ably to Rapp's ideas, they were farther removed from ener-
vating contact with the outside world, and the simple peasants were here less liable to become dissatisfied with their
mode of life by the contemplation of that of others. There
was little in the hard lot of the pioneers who inhabited the
surrounding country to tempt the Rappites from their comfortable homes, and though the squatters regarded with
contempt the servile allegiance of the Harmonists to
Father Rapp, they must have envied them the oasis which
they soon created in the wilds of Indiana at a time when
the total population of the State was but a few thousand,
and the life of its settlers was one of constant hardship
and danger.

The Rappites soon discovered, however, that their new
home was not a serpentless Eden. The first breaking up
of the bottom ground released the germs of malaria, and
the death-rate was enormous during the first five years of
the settlement. While the ratio decreased in later years,
it is claimed by some authorities that the Rappites held to
a resolution made during the first year of their residence
in Indiana to remain only long enough to improve the land
sufficiently to make it salable. In the last year of their
residence on the Wabash, it was officially stated that but
two members of the community died—a surprisingly low
death-rate, showing the establishment of healthful conditions.

It was not long until Harmonie began to show evidences
of German thrift. Numerous log, frame, and brick buildings were erected, orchards and vineyards were planted.
Among the first buildings constructed was a large frame
church, having a belfry with a clock striking the hours
and quarters. This was replaced as a place of worship
in 1822 by a huge brick structure. One entire block was
given to manufacturing purposes, and among the buildings
were a cocoonery and silk-factory, a sawmill, brick-yard,
brewery, distillery, woolen mill, and an oil-mill. The power

16

GEORGE RAPP'S RESIDENCE AND GRANARY, OR FORT.

The house was later occupied by the Owens.

in several of the smaller manufacturing establishments was derived from a treadmill propelled by dogs. The brick dwelling-houses erected by the Rappites still stand as monuments to the faithful work of their sturdy builders. The frames were made of very heavy timbers, and the spaces between the weather-boarding and the plastering were filled with cement and brick. Four large buildings were erected to serve as community houses. What was known as "Number 1" has been torn down; "Number 2" is now a general store; on its south wall is an old-fashioned sundial which has been faithfully telling the time since community days. "Number 3," partially rebuilt, is used as a hotel, "The Tavern." "Number 4" has been converted into an opera-house. A large brick house was built as a residence for Father Rapp. Near it was a brick and stone structure used as a granary, and intended also for a fort or refuge for the population in case of invasion by the squatters, of whom the Rappites stood in much dread. This structure was provided with loopholes, and was so substantially built that its defense would have been easy. It was never used for other than peaceful purposes. It became in later years a museum and a woolen mill; now rapidly falling into decay, it is one of the picturesque features of New Harmony.

George Flower, one of the founders of an English settlement in Edwards County, Illinois, describes the village as he saw it in 1819. A large portion of the land included in the estate, he says, was of the best quality, between two and three thousand acres being under cultivation and fenced. The town consisted of several brick and frame two-story houses for the use of small families, all built after one model, with ample gardens, well fenced and neatly cultivated, and a vast number of log cabins, neatly kept. There were also five or six very large buildings, three stories high, which contained the community families, of sixty to eighty individuals each. Rapp had a brick mansion, a large building, with a granary of the most solid masonry, and a large brick church, itself a curiosity, the plan, it is said, having been given to Mr. Rapp in a dream. There were four entrances to the church, closed by folding doors; the doors were about one hundred and twenty feet from each other. The upper story was supported by twenty-eight pillars of walnut, cherry, and sassafras, the walnut pillars being six feet in circumference, and twenty-five feet high; the others were twenty-one feet high and of proportionate circumference; a surprisingly large building, Mr. Flower declared, for this country. William Herbert, a London traveler, writes of this church: " I can scarcely imagine myself to be in the wilds of Indiana, on the borders of the Wabash, while passing through the long and resounding aisles and surveying the stately colonnades of this church." There were shops for every occupation, Mr. Flower tells us, represented in the community, magnificent orchards of grafted fruit in full bearing, and extensive vineyards.

" This singular community of Germans," Mr. Flower writes, " had little or no communication with the outside world, except through the miller, the storekeeper, the tavern-keeper, and Mr. Rapp. All who went to Harmony, with surprise observed with what facility the necessaries of life were acquired and enjoyed by every member of Rapp's community. When compared with the privations and discomforts to which individual settlers were exposed in their backwoods experience, the contrast is very striking. The poor hunter that brought a bushel of corn to be ground, perhaps from a distance of ten miles, saw with wonder people as poor as himself inhabiting good houses, surrounded by pleasant gardens, completely clothed with garments of the best quality, supplied regularly with meal, meat, and fuel, without any apparent individual exertion, and he could not fail to contrast the comforts and conveniences surrounding the dwellings of the Harmonists with the dirt

18

and discomfort of his own log hut, and it opened to his mind a new train of thought. One of them said to me in his own simple language: 'I studies and I studies it,' an expression that depicts the feeling of every person that obtained a sight of Rapp's colony at Harmony."

At the time of the founding of the community in Pennsylvania, a record was made of the amount of property contributed by each member, and it was agreed that at the withdrawal of any member, this amount, or its equivalent, should be returned to him. In 1808, as before stated, this agreement was abrogated, and in 1818, after the removal of the Harmonists to Indiana, the record was destroyed, on motion of George Rapp, unanimously adopted by the society. With its consignment to the flames, the last tie which bound the Rappites to the system of individual property was dissolved.

We are not at a loss to explain the wonderful authority acquired by George Rapp as leader of the Harmonists. Nearly six feet in height, with patriarchal beard and stately walk, he commanded the reverence of the members of his sect as a prophet among them, while his cheerful and kindly manner, his sympathetic and plain-spoken way of talking over with the Harmonists their smallest trials, made him beloved as well. Father Rapp shrewdly maintained a nominal cabinet, or board of advisers, chosen from among the more intelligent members of the community, such as might be able to set up a rival leadership. He gained great prestige by playing on the superstitions of the peasantry. He professed to be guided on many occasions by communications received in visions, as noted by Flower, for instance, in building a great structure in the form of a Greek cross on plans supposed to have been handed down from heaven. Among other traditions of Rappite days still lingering in New Harmony is one concerning the existence of an underground passage connecting Father Rapp's cellar and the granary or fort. Through this passage, the story goes,

Father Rapp was accustomed to appear as from the ground, mystifying the simple workmen, and perhaps leading them to believe that their labors were constantly within the range of his observation. It is also said that Father Rapp entered his pulpit through a tunnel leading to the church porch from his house just across the road.

There still remains in New Harmony what is known as " Gabriel's Rock "—two limestone slabs, originally one stone, ten feet by five, and five inches thick. Upon one a square figure is traced, occupying the center, and upon the other appears, seemingly, the imprint of two feet—the print of the right foot being perfect, while the forepart of the left foot has disappeared. The tradition is that Father Rapp informed his followers that these were imprints of the feet of the Angel Gabriel, who had alighted upon earth to convey to the society a message from heaven. David Dale Owen concluded that the figures were chipped in the stone by Indians. Another theory is that the slab was hewn from the pictured rocks along the Mississippi, which was traversed by the Harmonist flatboats in the extension of their trade. H. R. Schoolcraft, the famous traveler and ethnologist, who visited Harmony in 1821, gives a labored description of the rock. " The impressions," he writes, " are to all appearances those of a man standing upright, the left foot a little forward, the heels turned inward. The distance between the heels by an exact measurement was six and a quarter inches; three and a half inches between the extremities of the great toes. By an accurate examination it will, however, be ascertained that they are not the impressions of feet accustomed to the use of European shoes, for the toes are pressed out and the foot is flat, as is observed in persons who walk barefoot. . . . The probability is that they were caused by the impression of an individual belonging to a race of men ignorant of the art of tanning hides, and that this took place in a much earlier age than the traditions of the present Indians.

This supposition is strengthened by the extraordinary size
of the feet. In another sense the imprints are strikingly
natural, since the muscles are represented with the mi-
nutest exactness and truth. This weakens the hypothesis
that they are examples of the sculpture of men living in
the remotest ages of this continent. Neither history nor
tradition gives us the slightest information of such a people, for it must be kept in mind that we have no proof that
the people who erected our remarkable western *tumuli* ever
had a knowledge even of masonry, much less sculpture, or
that they had invented the chisel, the knife, or the ax, other
than those made from porphyry, hornstone, or obsidian.
The medium length of the human male foot may be accepted as ten inches. The length of the footprint described
amounts to ten and a fourth inches, the breadth measured
over the toes in a right angle with the first line is four
inches, but the greatest spread of the base is four and a
half inches, which decreases at the heels to two and a half
inches. Directly before these impressions is a mark similar
to a scroll, of which the greatest length is two feet, seven
inches, and the greatest breadth twelve and a half inches.
The rock bearing these interesting impressions is of compact limestone, bluish gray in color." The Duke of Saxe-
Weimar, who visited New Harmony only two years after
the departure of the Harmonists, says: "This piece of
stone was hewed out of the rock near St. Louis and sold to
Mr. Rapp." This theory, therefore, seems to have the
weight of authority.

Father Rapp taught humility, simplicity, self-sacrifice,
neighborly love, regular and persevering industry, prayer,
and self-examination. He also demanded that each evening any one who had sinned during the day should come
to him and confess his transgression. No quarrels were
allowed to pass through the night uncompromised, the rule
which declares, "Let not the sun go down upon thy wrath,"
being literally enforced. Persons seeking admission to the

community were compelled to make full confession of their sins, this being considered requisite to the forgiveness of God.

Two periods of religious service were observed—one on Sunday, when two services and a Sunday-school were conducted, one on Thursday, when general services were held. In the church were two bells, one of which called the people to and from their daily labors, and another, said to have been the largest imported up to that time, marked the opening of religious services. Father Rapp presided and preached at all the religious gatherings of the community. For the purpose of making religious instruction more personal, the community was divided into classes according to sex and age. Four holidays were observed, Christmas, Easter Sunday, Pentecost, and Good Friday, besides three feast-days, February 15th, the anniversary of the founding of the society, Harvest Home, and an annual " Lord's Supper " in the autumn.

The day's work was conducted after a fixed routine. Between five and six the people rose, breakfasted between six and seven, lunched at nine, dined at twelve, ate an afternoon lunch (Vesperbrod) at three, and supped between six and seven. At nine o'clock the curfew-bell was rung. Women as well as men labored in the fields, as many as fifty sometimes being employed in a body, harvesting wheat or breaking flax in the streets. Often they marched to the fields to the music of a band which was one of the regular institutions of the community. On summer evenings this band, stationed in the public garden, discoursed the old German hymns while the women busied themselves with their housework, the stolid peasants dozed upon the door-steps, and the children shouted at play in the streets. It is said that this band often played upon the hillsides while the peasants labored in the valley. A hundred acres of wheat were harvested by the sickle in a day—a remarkable result for that time.

THE RAPPITES IN INDIANA

John Woods, a member of the settlement at English
Prairie, twenty miles from "Harmonie" on the Illinois
side of the Wabash, visited the Rappites in 1820. He says
that the value of their property was then estimated at a
million dollars. "Each lives in his own house," writes
Woods, "but all dine at one hour and take their meals in
the same manner." Woods says that the houses were dis-
tributed among the Harmonists by lot, but "though there
was of necessity much difference in the size and equipment
of the various buildings, there was no dissatisfaction or
disturbance over the apportionment." He declared them
to be a most industrious people, but said the greater part
of them were not very enlightened. "As I approached the
place in July, I met their plow-teams, sixteen in number,
just entering a field of wheat-stubble. I was much pleased
with their appearance." Woods counted eighty-seven
milch cows going to pasture, driven by a herdsman who,
according to another authority, lived in a house on wheels,
called "Noah's Ark." "The dress of the Harmonists,"
writes Woods, "is uncommonly plain, mostly of their own
manufacturing. The men wear jackets and pantaloons,
with a coarse hat; the women a kind of jacket and petti-
coat, with a skullcap and straw hat made in the factory
here. As this society do not marry, I presume they depend upon immigration from Germany to keep up their
numbers, as the Americans are not likely to join them;
most of them regard the Harmonists with jealousy on
account of their engrossing most of the business of this
part of the country." Woods's surmise as to the method
employed in keeping up the numbers was correct. In 1817
one hundred and fifty recruits from Würtemberg swelled
the membership.

Morris Birkbeck, an associate of the Flowers in the
Edwards County settlement, visited Harmony frequently,
and in his diary of August 3, 1817, gives the following
account of a short stay there: "When I arrived on Sunday

23

evening, all were at services. I found even the tavern deserted, and was compelled to call the keeper from the church in order to secure accommodations. Soon the entire body of people, which is about seven hundred, poured out of the church, and exhibited so much health, peace, and neatness that we could but exclaim: ' Surely, the institutions which produce so much happiness must have more of good than of evil in them,' and here I rest, not lowered in my abhorrence of the hypocrisy, if it be such, which governs the ignorant by nursing them in superstition, but inclined in charity to believe that the leaders are sincere.

"The colony is thrifty and useful to the community. The Harmonists set a good example in neatness and industry. Though the population is ignorant, it is advanced in the social scale perhaps a hundred years beyond their solitary neighbors.

"I am quite convinced that the association of numbers in the application of a good capital is sufficient to account for all that has been done, and the unnatural restraint which forms so prominent and revolting a feature of their institutions is prospective, rather than immediate, in its object.

"Strangers visit their establishment, and retire from it full of admiration, but a slavish acquiescence, under a disgusting superstition, is so remarkable an ingredient in their character that it checks all desire of imitation."

Connected with George Rapp in the leadership of the Harmonists was Frederick Rapp, who for many years served as manager of the business interests of the Rappites. Frederick Rapp was the adopted son of George Rapp, and a man of intelligence and education. He met a violent death in 1834, some allege at the instigation of George Rapp, incensed at his son's refusal to put away his wife. A more probable story is that he was fatally injured by a falling tree at Economy, Pennsylvania. Frederick Rapp contributed to the community most of its attractive features. By nature an artist, he was the originator of plans which made Harmony one of the most attractive villages in America. Had it not been for his influence upon George Rapp, amusements would have been few in the place, and the unrelieved monotony of the community might have impelled even the stolid Rappites to renounce their allegiance and seek happier homes.

While Father Rapp was king of the community Frederick Rapp was his secretary of state. Father Rapp controlled internal, Frederick Rapp external affairs. Through Frederick Rapp the community held business and political connection with the outside world. Frederick Rapp was a member of the convention which met under the famous elm at Corydon and framed the first constitution of Indiana, preliminary to the admission of the Territory to the Union. He was afterward a member of the State legislature. Among the important committees upon which he served was that which located the State capital at Indianapolis in 1820.

Under the younger Rapp's administration, Harmony became a garden of neatness and beauty in the wilderness. The gabled roofs of the buildings were lifted above the forest of black locust-trees which the Rappites seemed to love so well. The broad river, the vine-covered hills, the fertile valley with its peaceful town, the stately church and the fruitful orchards, furnished a scene of Arcadian beauty which seemed a vision of promise to the Owenite communists who succeeded to the ownership of the estate. In the language of Mr. John Holliday: "It would seem to the traveled visitor like some quaint German village, transported from the Neckar or the Rhine, and set down in this western waste like an Aladdin's palace." There were tables and benches in the orchards, and on each machine in the factories stood a vessel filled with flowers.

A work of art credited to Frederick Rapp still to be seen in New Harmony is the figure of a rose and the accompanying inscription carved upon stone to decorate the doorway of the Rappite church. The reference, Micah iv: 8, reads, in the Lutheran edition: " Unto thee shall come' the golden rose, the first dominion."

A short distance from the village was a famous horticultural design which visitors came miles to see. It remained as an object of curiosity during the years of the Owen settlement, but the only present reminder of its existence is a pleasant grove of locust-trees which marks the spot where it stood. A labyrinth of vines and shrubs was constructed about a summer-house, rough on the exterior, but beautifully furnished within. Robert Owen was told, on his first visit there, that this was the emblematic representation of the life the colonists had chosen. Robert Dale Owen says: " It contained many circuitous walks, enclosed by high hedges and bordered with flowering shrubbery. It was arranged with such intricacy that without some Dædalus to furnish a clew, one might walk for hours and fail to reach a building erected in the center. This was a temple of rough material, but covered with vines of grape and convolvulus, and its interior neatly fitted up and prettily furnished. Thus George Rapp had sought to shadow forth to his followers their final state of peace and harmony; and the rough exterior of the shrine, and the elegance displayed within, were to serve as types of toil and suffering succeeded by happy repose."

The Rappites carried out strictly in every-day life the moral laws and religious observances prescribed by Father Rapp. Any transgression of these regulations was punished, not by Father Rapp, but by a refusal of the remaining members of the society to associate with the wrongdoer until full forgiveness had been obtained. There is no account of a single infraction of the law of celibacy. In later years, elopements were not unknown, but the care with which the sexes were separated prevented a frequent repetition of the offense, and such transgressors were not again admitted to the society, except after the performance of prolonged penance. The character of Father Rapp has never been questioned, and his example went far toward insuring good conduct on the part of his followers. The reputation for honesty borne by the Rappites was one of the secrets of their commercial prosperity. Flour, woolen goods, or distillery products bearing the Harmony brand were known to be of the best quality, and this fact secured them trade from all parts of the country. Robert Owen said of them: "It is due to the society who formed this settlement to state that I have not yet met with more kind-hearted, temperate, and industrious citizens, nor found men more sincere, upright, and honest in all dealings, than the Harmonists."

The jealousy of neighbors and the natural hatred of the squatters for this simple sect led in the early years of the settlement to the circulation of reports injurious to their credit. It is related that when on one occasion Frederick Rapp made his regular trip to Pittsburg for supplies, he found himself denied credit by merchants of that city. In deep discouragement and humiliation, he went to the riverside to weep and pray. He was found there by a merchant, who was so touched by Rapp's dependence on prayer to release him from his troubles, that he offered him all the supplies he could transport in two four-horse wagons. The offer was accepted with thanksgiving, and in a short time the merchant was paid in full. Several years later this man was on the verge of financial embarrassment during a period of business depression. When the news reached the Harmonists, Frederick Rapp filled his saddle-bags with coin, and hastening to Pittsburg, saved their benefactor from bankruptcy.

The financial management of the society was always most careful. Mr. Arthur Dransfield, librarian of the working men's institute at New Harmony, has in his possession a letter from Frederick Rapp, concluding a transaction with William Maclure involving over one hundred thousand dollars, in which Rapp gives minute directions for the disposition of a balance of sixty-five cents due the society.

The moundless surface of the Rappite cemetery at New Harmony, which occupies the site of an old Indian bury-ing-ground, bears witness to the fact that the community was one of perfect equality. Old and young, high and low alike were at death laid to rest under the trees, with only the elders as witnesses. Before morning the place of burial had been sodded over, with nothing left to distin-guish the spot, although a plan indicating the site of each grave was retained.

Robert Dale Owen, in Threading My Way, gives us the last information we have of the Rappites in their In-diana home, describing them just as his father found them before their departure from the Wabash valley:

"Harmony was a marvelous experiment from a pecu-niary point of view, for at the time of their emigration from Germany, their property did not exceed twenty-five dollars a head, while in twenty-one years (i. e., in 1825), a fair estimate gave them two thousand dollars for each man, woman, and child, probably ten times the average wealth throughout the United States; for at that time each per-son in Indiana averaged but one hundred and fifty dollars' worth of property, and even in Massachusetts the average fell far short of three hundred dollars for each adult and child. Socially, however, it was doubtless a failure; as an ecclesiastical aristocracy, especially when it contravenes an important law of nature, must always be. Rapp was an absolute ruler, assuming to be such by virtue of a divine call, and it was said, probably with truth, that he desired to sell Harmony because life there was getting to be easy and quiet, with leisure for thought, and because he found it difficult to keep his people in order excepting during the bustle and hard work which attended a new settlement.

At all events, he commissioned Mr. Flower to offer the whole property for sale.

" When my father reached the place, he found among the Germans, its sole occupants, indications of plenty and material comfort, but with scarcely a touch of fancy or ornament, save the flowers in the gardens, and what was called the labyrinth.

" The toil and suffering had left their mark, however, on the grave, stolid, often sad German faces. They looked well fed, well clothed (so my father told me), and seemed free from anxiety. The animal had been sufficiently cared for, and that is a great deal in a world where millions can hardly keep the wolf from the door, drudge as they will; where hundreds of millions, manage as they may, live in daily uncertainty whether in the next week or month (chance of work or means of living failing), absolute penury may not fall to their lot. A shelter from life-wearing cares is something; but a temple typifies higher things —more than what we shall eat, and what we shall drink, and wherewithal we shall be clothed. Rapp's disciples had bought this dearly—at the expense of heart and soul. They purchased them by unquestioned submission to an autocrat who had been commissioned—perhaps as he really believed, certainly as he alleged—by God himself. He bade them do this and that, and they did it—commanded them to forego wedded life and all its incidents, and to this also they assented."

CHAPTER IV

THE RAPPITE HEGIRA

"In the twenty-fourth of May, 1824, we have departed. Lord, with thy great help and goodness, in body and soul protect us."—Inscription under a stairway in Community House No. 2, at New Harmony, left by one of the Rappites.

TEN years after the Rappite advance-guard reached "Harmonie," the Harmonists made way for the advance of a more interesting social experiment. The sale of the estate is curiously connected with the history of the famous English settlement in Edwards County, Illinois, established by Richard Flower on an estate of twenty thousand acres in 1818. Mr. Flower and his associates had intimate business relations with the Rappites, and frequently visited the Harmonist colony. In 1828, an effort was made to legalize slavery in Illinois, and in the front rank of the opposition were the English colonists in Edwards County, led by Richard Flower, and his son Edward, then a youth of eighteen. The antislavery campaign was successful, but the activity of the Flowers was so distasteful to those favorable to slavery, that attempts were made to assassinate the young man. His father deemed it prudent to take him to England to remain until the excitement should subside. Before leaving he was commissioned to sell the Harmonist property by Father Rapp, who offered him a commission of five thousand dollars. Edward Flower never returned to America, but achieved great prominence in England as a participant in several reform movements, notably the agitation for the abolition of the check-rein on horses. His daughter Sarah wrote the hymn, Nearer My God to Thee.

THE RAPPITE HEGIRA

During the Civil War Edward Flower took the platform in England in behalf of the Union cause.

The elder Flower visited New Lanark, and laid before Robert Owen the advantages of Harmony as a site for a communistic establishment in the New World, where Mr. Owen might work out in practise theories long promulgated by him. The sale was effected, the whole tract with all its improvements, and most of the valuable equipments, going for less than one hundred and fifty thousand dollars.

Strong reasons must have impelled Father Rapp in his desire to move the colony back to Pennsylvania, for this sale was made at a great sacrifice, though at a large advance over the original expenditure ten years before. Double the sum received would have been a modest estimate of the value of this princely estate and well-built town. Removal, too, meant the sacrifice of a trade extending all over the adjacent States, and down the Mississippi to New Orleans, as well as the abandonment of prosperous stores at Vincennes, Indiana, and Shawneetown, Illinois. Nordhoff catalogues the Rappites' reasons for leaving Indiana as fever, ague, unpleasant neighbors, and remoteness from business centers, from all of which causes they had indeed suffered. But fever and ague, according to the statements of the Harmonists themselves, had about disappeared in 1824, and the Rappites ought easily to have been able to defend themselves against the depredations of unorganized squatters. According to Dr. Schnack, one authority states that the Harmonist property had become involved, and that Rapp was compelled to sell; it is certain, however, that the Rappites had sufficient funds to redeem their property from any such complications, for within eight years after their return to Pennsylvania, they not only paid for their estate, and erected upon it the village of Economy, but were able to pay one hundred and five thousand dollars to a party of seceders. Another authority says: " I have been informed that Mr. Rapp adopted this plan in order to have the new deeds made out in his name, and thus hold possession of all the landed property, as well as the control of the funds for which Harmony was sold." There seems to be no evidence to corroborate this supposition. Doubtless the Harmonists found some difficulty in transporting supplies from Pittsburg, and Frederick Rapp realized that a better market for their products would be afforded in the East.

With the proceeds of the Harmony sale, an estate was purchased in Beaver County, Pennsylvania, eighteen miles below Pittsburg, on the Ohio River, not far from the site of their first settlement. A steamboat was built for the Rappites, and they ascended the Ohio in detachments. A village was built, and called Economy. In Economy the Harmonist society has remained, its uneventful history broken only by the great secession of 1831–'32, a brief account of which we obtain from Nordhoff's Communistic Societies of the United States:

" In 1831 there came to Economy a German adventurer, Bernhard Müller by name, who had assumed the title ' Graf,' or Count Maximilian de Leon, and had gathered a following of visionary Germans, whom he imposed, with himself, upon the Harmonists, on a pretense that he was a believer with them in religious matters." (Another authority states that Müller claimed to have come directly from Württemberg.) " He proved to be a wretched intriguer, who brought ruin on all those who connected themselves with him, and who began at once to make trouble in Economy. Having secured a lodgment, he began to announce strange doctrines; marriage, a livelier life, and other temptations to worldliness, and he finally succeeded in effecting a serious division, which, if it had not been prudently managed, might have destroyed the community. After bitter disputes, at last affairs came to such a pass, that a vote had to be taken in order to decide who were faithful to the old order, and to Rapp, and who were to

32

Count de Leon, before an agreement was reached." When the vote was taken, it was found that five hundred stood with Father Rapp, and two hundred and fifty with Count de Leon. When Father Rapp heard the result he quoted from the book of Revelation: " And the tail of the serpent drew the third part of the stars of heaven, and did cast them to earth."

" The end of the dispute," continued Nordhoff, " was an agreement, under which the society bound itself to pay to those who adhered to Count de Leon, one hundred and five thousand dollars in three instalments, all payable within twelve months; the other side agreeing on their part, to leave Economy within three months, taking with them only their clothing and household furniture, and relinquishing all claims upon the property of the society. This agreement was made in March, 1832, and Leon and his followers withdrew to Philipsburg, a village ten miles below Economy, on the other side of the river, where they bought eight hundred acres of land. Here they set up a society on communistic principles, but permitted marriage, and here they very quickly wasted the large sum of money they had received from the Rappites, and after a desperate and lawless attempt to extort more money from the Economy people, which was happily defeated, Count de Leon absconded with a few of his people in a boat to Alexandria, on the Red River, where he perished of cholera in 1832. Those he had deluded meantime divided the Philipsburg property among themselves, and set up each for himself, and a number afterward joined Dr. Keil in forming the Bethel community in Missouri."

Nordhoff points out the fact that the Harmonists had demonstrated in this transaction their great prosperity during the few years of their existence as a community. In twenty-seven years they had built three towns, and endured all the expense and loss of three removals, and yet they were able to produce this immense sum of ready cash. The

Harmonists, at the time of their removal from Indiana, were reported to be worth a million dollars, and New Harmony tradition has it that bullion was conveyed from Father Rapp's cellars in wagon-loads to the boat which conveyed the Rappites to Economy. "During this whole time, moreover," says Nordhoff, "they had lived a life of comfort and social order, such as few individual settlers in our Western States at that time could command."

George Rapp died on August 7, 1847, greatly mourned by his people. One of his last hours was spent in preaching to the Harmonist congregation from his death-bed, through the open window. Shortly before his death, he called the members to his bedside, one by one, where he bade them good-by and exhorted them to the perpetuation of the principles he had taught them. After his burial, the members again signed the agreement. R. L. Baker, long since dead, and Jacob Henrici, who died on Christmas morning, 1892, were elected to succeed him, ruling in conjunction with seven elders. Henrici was succeeded in the senior trusteeship by John Duss, a young man who had been educated in the schools of Economy, but drifted West in early manhood. In Missouri he became a school-teacher, a candidate for superintendent of public instruction, and owner of a cattle-ranch. Being called to Economy to take charge of the schools, he became successively elder, junior trustee and senior trustee and ruler of the society. Strangely enough, this successor to the authority of George Rapp is a married man with two children.

But for the executive ability of John Duss, it is generally agreed that the accumulations of the Rappites would have been entirely swept away. Large sums were lost through unfortunate investments, and the mills ceased to be profitable. Thirty years ago the wealth of the Rappites was variously estimated at from $10,000,000 to $30,000,-000, but when Trustee Duss succeeded to the management of the society's affairs, the community was found to be

34

almost bankrupt, with lawsuits on hand that threatened to wipe out the last vestige of the vast property. By careful administration of the affairs of the community, Mr. Duss succeeded in saving several hundred thousand dollars after clearing the society of debt.

The Rappite organization long since ceased to be a community and became a close corporation administered for the benefit of a dwindling membership. Having placed the affairs of the society on a safe financial basis, Trustee Duss removed to New York, where he devotes himself to music as leader of a celebrated concert orchestra. Mrs. Duss was left to manage the town of Economy. Only six members of the society remain, Mr. Duss and his wife and four others related to the family. Under court decisions, the litigation having been carried to the Supreme Court of the United States, Trustee Duss is empowered to wind up the affairs of the society, and with the passing of the property into individual hands, the organization will cease to exist even in name. In 1903, the Liberty Land Company, a syndicate of Pittsburg capitalists, purchased the entire Rappite estate of twenty-five hundred acres for a price said to be four million dollars, only three blocks in the town of Economy and some property in Beaver Falls being reserved. With these three blocks were retained the Rapp mansion and its gardens, the old music-hall and its quaint belfry, and the large barn for live stock. Before many years have passed the lands once tilled by the Rappites will be grown over with factories and homes, the last of those who lived and labored in the hope of realizing the communism of the early Christians will be laid to rest under the moundless greensward of the Rappite burying-ground, the last dollar of the millions heaped up through the patient labor of the stolid Harmonists will have passed to individual bank-accounts, and amid the smoke and noise of a Pennsylvania industrial center there will be no more to mark the spot where George Rapp preached to his simple followers the gospel of self-effacement, than remains in the quiet Economy churchyard to indicate the place where the Rappites laid their patriarchal leader to rest more than a half century ago.

.   .   .   .

With the other buildings conveyed to Robert Owen at New Harmony was the immense church of the Rappites. For a time after the dissolution of the Owenite communities, this building was partitioned off in rooms, but after William Maclure's death it was presented to St. Stephen's Episcopal Church. The east wing was for years used as a ballroom, and the room south for a theater, the walls being, according to Dr. Schnack, " beautifully frescoed and painted." Later a part of the building was used as a pork-packing establishment. In 1874 the Rappites sent Jonathan Lentz to New Harmony. He purchased the church building and the lot upon which it stood. Of the large building he tore down all but the east wing, using the brick to construct the wall which protects the Rappite cemetery to this day. This wall is one foot thick, five feet high, covered with a heavy limestone coping, and guarded by iron gates. The Harmonists gave the church lot, together with the remaining material and the wing standing, to the town of New Harmony. They also gave two thousand dollars of the sum necessary to construct the building which, until a few years ago, was occupied by the library of the working men's institute, and is now used as a public school. According to an inscription, this building was erected " In memory of the Harmony Society, founded by George Rapp, 1805." With this act of philanthropy, the connection of the Rappites with New Harmony ceased.

Thirty years ago, a writer in the Atlantic Monthly well foreshadowed the destiny of the Harmony Society. " It needs no second thought," he said, " to discern the end of Rapp's schemes. His single strength sustained the colony during his life, and since his death one or two strong wills

THE OLD FORT AS BUILT.
From a drawing by J. L. Parke.

have kept it from crumbling to pieces, and converted the
whole machinery of this system into a powerful money-
making agent. These men are the means by which it
keeps a hand on the world, on the market, perhaps I should
say. They are intelligent, able, honorable, too, we are glad
to know, for the sake of the quiet creatures drowsing away
their remnant of life, fat and contented, driving their plows
through the fields, or sitting on the stoops of the village
when evening comes. I wonder if they ever cast a furtive
glance at the world, and the life from which Rapp's edict
so early shut them out. When they finish working, one
by one, the great revenues of the society will probably fall
into the hands of two or three, and be returned into the
small currents of trade, according to the rapid sequence
which always follows the accretion of large properties in
this country."

From a sordid standpoint, at least, we may denominate
the Harmony Society a successful communism; its history
perhaps forms the nearest approach to a justification of
communistic association, but to what extent this justification continues is a question which can only be determined
by a careful analysis of the primary elements contributing
to this success. What may be said of the Harmony Society
in this connection may in large part be declared of all
religious communistic associations in America, which have
been the only successful attempts at community life.
" The temporary success of the Hernhutters, the Moravians,
the Shakers, and even the Rappites," says Miss Peabody,
in Christ's Idea of Society, " has cleared away difficulties
and solved problems of social science. It has been made
plain that the material goods of life are not to be sacrificed
in doing fuller justice to the social principles. It has been
proved that with the same degree of labor, there is no way
to compare with that of working in a community, banded
by some sufficient idea to animate the will of the laborers.
A greater quantity of wealth is procured with fewer hours

of toil, and without any degradation to the laborer. All these communities have demonstrated what the practical Dr. Franklin said, that if every one worked bodily three hours daily, there would be no necessity of any one's working more than three hours." Many economic ideas of the present day are based upon such suppositions regarding the success of cooperative labor like that of the Harmonists. Robert Owen received much of his communistic inspiration from the apparent success of the Rappites, and the origin of every American communism can be traced to a belief that these experiments have demonstrated the practicability of communistic principles. This success, in a great degree, however, seems to have sprung from favorable circumstances not the result of communistic association, while we may reasonably inquire if there has not been, indeed, a degradation of the laborer, and whether his life has not been even harder and more barren of compensating advantages than the life which the individual system would have offered him.

In the first place, the Rappites, the Shakers, the Amanaites, and in fact most of the communistic societies which have proved successful, secured advantages by the purchase of large tracts of wild land at a low price. The land held by the Harmonists in Indiana increased in value after their departure far more in proportion than did the wealth of the Rappites. They owned, before leaving Indiana, for instance, a considerable portion of the site of the city of Terre Haute, which George Rapp secured in foreclosing a mortgage of something over a thousand dollars. This new country, moreover, afforded an unusually profitable market for manufactured goods, since manufactures had then been little developed. The German peasants who made up the Harmony Society, and other successful religious communities, were thrifty and industrious. Moreover they worked, not three, but ten hours a day. The Harmonists were peculiarly prepared for their communistic state by their previous experiences in Germany. They had little of the American idea of liberty, and had endured such intolerance of private opinion and suppression of religious freedom that even the rigid discipline of the new society afforded relief. In their simplicity, these peasants were pleased and satisfied by the freedom from responsibility, and the good food and clothing which the community afforded them. The contemplation of the hard life of the pioneers about them made the community seem a haven of refuge. Their exclusive use of the German language furnished another barrier against the outside world. Celibacy was one secret of their material success. There were few children to rear and educate; this unproductive class of accessions was supplanted by the entrance of able-bodied men and women, many of whom added considerable wealth to that of the society. Celibacy has been a rule of practically every successful communism. We are frequently reminded of the Amana Society, in Iowa, as an example of communistic success under the family system. But while the wealth of the Harmonists twenty years after their removal to America was thirteen times as much per capita as the average in Indiana, and seven times that in Massachusetts, it is shown in Historical Monograph No. 1 (1890), of the University of Iowa, that the average per capita wealth of the Amana Society in 1890 was about ten per cent less than the average wealth in the State of Iowa: this after an American residence of nearly fifty years, with practically the same collateral advantages which contributed to the wealth of the Rappites. The Zoarites, a communistic society in Tuscarawas County, Ohio, which was until recent years successful, had permitted marriage after the year 1830, although they taught that the celibate state is more commendable, and that this teaching was observed is shown by the fact that they added only seventy-five to their original membership during the first fifty years of their residence in this country.

Peculiar reasons made possible the peaceful and prosperous association of the Harmonists. Among these conditions was ignorance in the masses, controlled by intelligence in a limited leadership. " Jacobi," says Noyes, " seems disposed to give special prominence to leadership as a cause of success. He evidently attributes the decline of the Beizelites, the Rappites, and the Zoarites to the old age and death of their founders." We must also remember the superstition which prevailed among the Rappites, cultivated and directed by a theocratic head; akin to this their belief in the near approach of the judgment-day, which made them careless of private effects.

We can not overestimate the importance of religion as a cohesive force in societies like that of the Harmonists. Upon religious grounds their community was founded; religion was the guiding principle of their daily lives. " Religion," says Horace Greeley in his Recollections of a Busy Life, " often makes practicable that which were else impossible, and divine love triumphs where human science is baffled. Thus I interpret the past successes and failures of socialism. . . . With a firm and deep religious basis, any socialistic scheme may succeed, though vicious in organization and at war with human nature; without a basis of religious sympathy and religious aspiration it will always be difficult, though I judge not impossible." " Communities based on religious views have generally succeeded," said Charles A. Dana, in the New York Sun of May 1, 1869. " The Shakers and the Oneida community are conspicuous illustrations of this fact, while the failure of the various attempts made by the disciples of Owen, Fourier, and others, who have not the support of religious fanaticism, proves that without this great force the most brilliant social theories are of little avail."

How far has the destruction of the family in the Rappite and other communities contributed to the possibility of individual effacement? Is the institution of marriage in

40

its present form based upon and a preserver of individualism? Is family life as now constituted a stumbling-block in the way of socialism, in so far as socialism proposes to broaden sympathy for the circumscribed family circle until it becomes sympathy for universal mankind? Advocates of communism have almost invariably proposed to destroy, change, or regulate the institution of marriage. Robert Owen declared that marriage based on the possession of private property was "one of the great trinity of evils which have cursed the world ever since the creation of man." The Oneida Perfectionists "proposed to abolish family ties by the institution of free love." The Zoarite elders opposed marriage "because it makes a division of interests among the brethren." Jacobi calls attention to the fact that in nearly all communistic associations attended by a degree of success, marriage is sacrificed for communism. John Humphrey Noyes cites an article by Charles Lane, a Fourierist, in the Dial of January, 1844, in which he says:

"The maternal instinct, as hitherto educated, has declared itself so strongly in favor of the separate fireside, that association, which appears so beautiful to the young and unattached soul, has yet accomplished little progress in the affections of that important section of the human race—the mothers. With fathers, the feeling in favor of the separate family is certainly less strong; but there is an indefinable tie, a sort of magnetic *rapport*, an invisible, inseverable umbilical cord between the mother and the child, which in most cases circumscribes her desires and aspirations for her own immediate family. All the accepted adages and wise saws of society, all the precepts of morality, all the sanctions of theology have for ages been employed to confirm this feeling. . . . The question of association and of marriage are one. If, as we have been popularly led to believe, the individual or separate family is the true order of Providence, then the associative life is

41

a false effort. If the associative life is true, then the separate family is a false arrangement. By the maternal feeling it seems to be decided that the coexistence of both is incompatible, is impossible. . . . That the affections can be divided, or bent with equal ardor on two objects so opposed as universal and individual love, may at least be rationally doubted. . . . The monasteries and convents which have existed in all ages have existed solely by the annihilation of that peculiar affection on which the separate family is based. . . . Spite of the speculations of hopeful bachelors and esthetic spinsters, there is somewhat in the marriage-bond which is found to counteract the universal nature of the affections, to a degree, tending at least to make the considerate pause before they assert that, by any social arrangements whatever, the two can be blended into one harmony. . . . It is only the determination to do what parents consider best for their families and themselves which renders the o'erpopulous world such a wilderness of selfhood as it is. Destroy this feeling, they say, and you prohibit every motive to exertion."

CHAPTER V

" As long as he was merely a philanthropist he was rewarded with nothing but applause, wealth, honor, and glory. He was the most popular man in Europe. Not only men of his own class, but statesmen and princes listened to him approvingly."—FREDERICK ENGELS.

" THE interest of the life of Robert Owen," as his friend and biographer, Lloyd Jones, has said, " lies not in the completeness of its success, but in its practical wisdom and devotion to principle." Yet, measured from a strictly practical standpoint, the work of Robert Owen has not been without its great results. Frederick Engels declares: " Every social movement, every real advance in England on behalf of the workers, links itself on to the name of Robert Owen." Robert Owen has been called " The Father of English Socialism." The great labor cooperative societies of Great Britain, which now number sixteen hundred, with two million registered members, and seven million patrons, doing an annual business of four hundred million dollars, have conferred inestimable benefits upon the working people of Great Britain. They are in large part a monument to Robert Owen's philanthropic labors. " His specific plans as a social reformer," writes Robert Dale Owen, " proved on the whole, and for the time, a failure, . . . yet, with such earnestness, such indomitable perseverance, and such devotion and love for his race, did he press, through half a century, his plans upon the public, and so much truth was there mixed with visionary expectation, that his name became known, and the

influence of his teachings has been more or less felt over
the civilized world. A failure in gross has been attended
by sterling incidental successes, and toward the great idea
of cooperation—quite impracticable as he conceived it—
there has been, ever since his death, very considerable advance made, and generally recognized by earnest men as
eminently useful and important."

A brief review of the social and industrial conditions
which gave occasion and purpose to the career of Robert
Owen is necessary to an understanding of his life and work.
The concluding years of the eighteenth century marked
the beginning of an industrial revolution. Human power
had received a magnificent impetus from an era of great
invention, but this increase of power brought in its immediate train serious results for the laboring classes of England. Machinery began to supplant manual labor so suddenly and so rapidly, especially in the great cotton
industry, that thousands of men, willing to labor, were deprived of employment. Factory-owners began to realize
immensely upon their investments. While their establishments were enlarged, wages were reduced, for not only were
the recently employed clamoring for work, but the rural
population was flocking by thousands to the factories on
account of the prevalent agricultural depression.

In many ways the whole population of England suffered
from this rapid transformation. The expense of machinery, and inability to compete with the greater facilities of
the large factories, caused the extinction of the smaller
establishments. As a result, the personal relation which
had formerly existed between employer and employee was
destroyed, to the infinite damage of the latter. Intoxi-
cated with the possibilities of wealth so suddenly opened
before them, the great factory-owners gave no heed to the
welfare of their thousands of employees. The workmen
were herded together in squalid and crowded quarters, with
none of the comforts or pleasures of wholesome home life.

No provisions were made for the education of children who were employed by thousands in the factories. The intellectual and moral results of such a system were deplorable. The English laboring classes, but a generation before happy, independent, and respected, became, in effect, slaves to their grasping employers. Everywhere in these large establishments ignorance and vice were prevalent to an alarming extent. Whereas the passage of an employee from a lower to a higher state could formerly be effected with little difficulty, under the new *régime* it became almost impossible. The majority of those engaged in manufacturing must, from the nature of things, remain laborers. It became more difficult to ascend the social ladder. The division of labor resulted in simplifying the task of each workman, making him a mere cog in a great machine, and thus rendering him more dependent. Luxury increased among the upper classes, and class feeling was developed. " The rich man," says one writer, " came to labor only for the increase of his capital, the poor man to satisfy the cravings of his stomach."

By strange coincidence, this enslavement of the English working classes came at a time when ideas of political freedom were everywhere in the ascendant. In France and in America old political institutions had been shattered, and flushed with their success, the people looked forward to the near approach of a social as well as a political millennium. They had looked upon monarchical institutions as the source of all inequalities of condition, and seemed to think that the disenthronement of royalty meant the end of all unhappiness and oppression. The Continent produced a school of philosophers who advocated a reorganized society based upon higher conceptions of public duty. In France, St. Simon, " representative of a discontented and impoverished aristocracy," was the first advocate of socialism. Fourier, an idealist, one of the middle class, and Babeuf, a social reconstructionist, were promulgating ideas of social regeneration against which the English Channel was no barrier.

"England," says Sidney Webb, a Fabian society socialist, "was covered with rotten survivals of bygone circumstances. The whole administration was an instrument for class domination and parasitic nurture. The progress of the industrial revolution was rapidly making obsolete all laws, customs, proverbs, maxims, and nursery tales: and the sudden increase of population was baffling all expectations and disconcerting all arrangements. At last . . . ' every man for himself and the devil take the hindmost' became the social creed of what was still believed to be a Christian nation."

"At this juncture," says Frederick Engels, "there came forward as a reformer a manufacturer twenty-nine years old, a man of almost sublime and childlike simplicity of character, and at the same time one of the few born leaders of men." Robert Owen was born of humble parentage at Newtown, Montgomeryshire, Wales, May 14, 1771. Though fond of learning, his schooling was quite limited, for when but ten years old he went to London to become an apprentice to a Stamford draper. Fortunately he found a well-selected library in the home of his employer, and five hours a day were regularly spent by the boy in eager reading. At the close of his apprenticeship, Robert Owen took service with Flint & Palmer, large retail drapers at London Bridge, where he received one hundred and twenty-five dollars a year and his board. Here he worked from fifteen to eighteen hours a day, and managed to save almost the whole of his salary, since during his whole lifetime, according to his own statement, he "never indulged an injurious or expensive habit." His next employer was a Mr. Satterfield, with whom he remained until he reached the age of eighteen.

Owen's first enterprise on his own account was a partnership with a wire-worker named Jones, who was inter-

ested in the new machines just invented for spinning cotton. Into this business Owen took five hundred dollars,
borrowed from his brother. The establishment was soon
employing forty men in the manufacture of spinning-ma-
chines. As Jones was not a partner to young Owen's taste,
he sold out for three of the " mules " which they were making. With this and other machinery, operated by three
men, Owen made fifteen hundred dollars as his first year's
profit.

Soon afterward Owen became superintendent of a Manchester cotton-mill owned by a Mr. Drinkwater. The
young man assumed the whole responsibility of managing
the factory, in which five hundred men were employed. So
successfully did he fill this position that the quality of
goods manufactured by the Drinkwater mill soon commanded a fifty per cent advance above regular prices. His
services were recognized by an increase of salary, and an
agreement of partnership with Mr. Drinkwater, which was
signed by Owen at the age of twenty. In 1791 Mr. Owen
used the first sea-island cotton brought into England
from America, which was soon to furnish a large proportion of the raw material used in English cotton-mills.
Soon after the partnership was formed, Mr. Drinkwater's
daughter was married to a wealthy cotton-manufacturer,
who desired to enter the partnership. On the first intima-
tion of this plan, young Owen burned up the agreement
with Mr. Drinkwater, and, though he remained in his position as superintendent until his successor could be secured,
he refused reemployment at any price.

During Mr. Owen's apprenticeship and his connection
with factory management, he was thrown into a daily contact with the toiling classes which was largely to influence
his conduct as an employer. He regarded with sorrow and
indignation the debased condition of the laboring people,
and with alarm the frequent riots indicative of the deep-
seated discontent prevailing in the factory towns. The

47

condition of the children employed in factories especially appealed to him. Denied a knowledge of even the elements of education, separated from all the influences of home which are so important a determinant of character, children of honest parents were forced to work side by side with those brought from the workhouses to labor at starvation wages. These children were habitually flogged and debarred from moral and religious instruction. In such squalid and vicious surroundings, they grew to a sour and debased maturity. Some employers attempted in a clumsy way to better these conditions, but such rare efforts were generally rendered useless by the ignorant sensitiveness of the poor. Though the factory act of Robert Peel (1802) limited the hours of labor to twelve, and provided for the elementary education of all apprentices, the provisions for the enforcement of this law were so feeble as to render it practically inoperative.

Robert Owen, soon after his release from the Drinkwater establishment, accepted an offer of partnership with Borrowdale & Atkinson, a wealthy and established firm. In this factory he superintended the manufacture and sale of yarn. During his connection with this concern he was elected a member of the Manchester literary and philosophical society, with which he maintained a conspicuous connection for many years. It was under the supervision of this society, at the instigation of Mr. Owen, that the investigations were carried on which formed the basis for Sir Robert Peel's later bills for the relief of the laboring classes.

Robert Owen's marriage was the culmination of a very business-like romance. While on a business trip to Glasgow, he met a Miss Dale, daughter of David Dale, owner of an extensive manufacturing establishment at New Lanark, Scotland. Something in Miss Dale's enthusiastic descriptions of this great factory, and doubtless something in the pleasure which he felt in her companionship, in-

48

duced him to make a trip to New Lanark on a visit to the
Dale establishment. Upon his return to Manchester, young
Owen wrote a proposal of marriage to Miss Dale. Her
acceptance was conditioned on the doubtful approval of her
father. The young manufacturer was too shrewd to plead
his own cause at once, unknown as he was, but trusted to
the results of a business venture to win the coveted consent. He again visited the factory, thoroughly investigated
its workings, returned to Manchester, and gained the consent of his partners to a project for purchasing the New
Lanark mills in connection with another firm in which he
had also become a partner. The bargain was soon concluded, the purchase price being three hundred thousand
dollars. His marriage with Miss Dale was soon arranged,
and the union seems to have been a most happy one,
though Miss Dale was a stanch Presbyterian in religious
doctrine, and Robert Owen was, to say the least, unorthodox in his views concerning religion.

On January 1, 1800, Robert Owen assumed control
of the New Lanark mills, and began his illustrious career
as a practical philanthropist. He found drunkenness, neglect of work, and theft common among the New Lanark
operatives, though Mr. Dale had been an employer more
than usually considerate. In the town of New Lanark
were thirteen or fourteen hundred families, and from four
to five hundred pauper children. The work which Robert
Owen accomplished in the training and development of
these miserable creatures into educated and contented men
and women gave to him and to New Lanark an international reputation. Representatives of royalty, philanthropists, and educators from all parts of Europe journeyed
thither to study the processes which Mr. Owen put in operation for the betterment of the working people in his mills.

Mr. Owen first sought out the recognized leaders among
his employees, and explained his plans to them. Though
these were first regarded with suspicion, the New Lanark

operatives soon began to realize his sincerity and to cooperate with him. Owen taught cleanly habits, and enforced them in the town with such rigor that there were frequent complaints from people with an aversion to soap and sanitation. He discouraged the credit system and established a store in which the people were furnished goods at cost, the saving being estimated at twenty per cent. He instituted a system of checks to detect pilfering, and opened a debit and credit account which at the end of each year served as a complete record of each workman's conduct, and as a guide in the promotion and increase of salaries of the more worthy. These were called " books of character."

In 1806 the United States placed an embargo on cotton, and Mr. Owen was afforded an opportunity to display his real feeling toward the people in his employ, and as Lloyd Jones says, " to make a complete conquest of their good-will." The advanced price of raw material crippled the English factories, and, among others, the New Lanark mills were compelled to close. To the surprise of the employees, their wages were continued in full during this suspension. Ever after this occurrence, Mr. Owen commanded the love and respect of the workmen of New Lanark.

Mr. Owen's partners, however, did not fully indorse such extraordinary consideration for the comfort of their employees, and while such plans were well enough as experiments in philanthropy, they did not regard them as business-like. It could not be alleged that Mr. Owen's management was unprofitable, since the mills, now beginning to be filled with a better educated, more capable and more willing class of employees, made money as never before. Mr. Owen would not consent to any change of policy, and was therefore compelled to form a new partnership and make a new purchase of the establishment, which now sold for four hundred and twenty thousand dollars. Mr. Owen proceeded with his work of establishing schools and improving the condition of the working people until the members of the new partnership in turn became dissatisfied, and finally forced the sale of the property at auction. Though Owen's enemies alleged that the value of the establishment had depreciated during his management, an exciting contest for its possession took place between the old partners and Mr. Owen, who had enlisted financial support from several wealthy Quakers. The property was finally sold to Mr. Owen for seven hundred and seventy thousand dollars. The employees at New Lanark had watched with anxious interest the progress of the sale, and when the news of Mr. Owen's success came, a general celebration was held. Mr. Owen rode through the streets in a carriage drawn by a long line of his workmen, and there was an illumination of the town and rejoicing among its people. When the books of the second copartnership were balanced, it was found that the profits of the four years, after setting aside five per cent interest for the capital employed, were eight hundred thousand dollars.

Mr. Owen was destined again to be embarrassed by troubles in the partnership. From the standard of belief held by his associates in business, Mr. Owen was heretical in his moral and religious teachings. In their eyes the games of the kindergarten were frivolous and vain. William Allen and others accused him of infidelity, and of promulgating such sentiments among the people of New Lanark. Though a committee under the chairmanship of the Duke of Kent, grandfather of the present King of England, acquitted him of the charge, everything possible was thrown in the way of the new schools. Mr. Owen was finally forced out of the New Lanark mills. From the beginning his management had been financially prosperous, and the community had been made by him one of the happiest and most orderly in England. The results of Robert Owen's work at New Lanark are summed up by an American traveler (Mr. Griscom), who stayed some time at the place: " There is not, I apprehend, to be found in any part of the world, a manufacturing community in which so much order, good government, tranquillity, and rational happiness prevail."

" Up to this time," says a biographer, " we see Robert Owen fighting with the difficulties by which he was immediately surrounded; reforming such abuses as were operating to the injury of the people; giving to them more comfort, more independence, more manliness, more hope; above all, gaining among them that confidence and cooperation which might enable him to work out the changes on which he relied for proving the practicability of reforms that might be applied to the rapidly growing cotton industry in all its branches throughout the kingdom."

CHAPTER VI

LABOR troubles which culminated in the riots of 1811
at last awakened the conscience of the English people, and
brought them face to face with the evil results of the
factory system. Robert Owen and his following of reformers began to be accorded a respectful hearing. Until the
dissatisfaction of the laboring classes found expression in
desperate crusades against machinery and the assumption
of a threatening attitude toward the employing classes, the
"poverty, degradation, deformity, ignorance, and premature death" suffered in the crowded factory settlements as
the result of overwork, scanty food, and unwholesome sani-
tary conditions, seemed to be regarded with carelessness.

Since 1803 Robert Owen had devoted a large portion of
his time to the consideration of the labor problem, and
upon this question wrote voluminously. The year 1815
was for him a period of great activity. He called a meeting
of factory-owners at Glasgow for the purpose of asking the
repeal of the revenue tariff on raw cotton, and considering
means of improving the condition of the working people.
The first suggestion was unanimously adopted; Owen's
motion regarding the second purpose did not even receive
a second. Mr. Owen flooded the kingdom with copies of
the address delivered by him at this session. In part he
had said:

"True, indeed, it is, that the main pillar and prop of
the political greatness and prosperity of our country is a

53

manufacture which, as now carried on, is destructive of the health, morals, and social comfort of the mass of the people engaged in it. It is only since the introduction of the cotton trade that children at an age before they had acquired strength or mental instruction, have been forced into cotton-mills, those receptacles, in too many instances, for living human skeletons, almost disrobed of intellect, where, as the business is often now conducted, they linger out a few years of miserable existence, acquiring every bad habit which they may disseminate throughout society. It is only since the introduction of this trade that children and even grown people were required to labor more than twelve hours in a day, not including the time allotted for meals. It is only since the introduction of this trade that the sole recreation of the laborer is to be found in the pot-house or gin-shop, and it is only since the introduction of this baneful trade that poverty, crime, and misery have made rapid and fearful strides throughout the community.

" Shall we then go unblushingly and ask the legislators of our country to pass legislative acts to sanction and increase this trade—to sign the death-warrants of the strength, morals, and happiness of thousands of our fellow creatures, and not attempt to propose corrections for the evils which it creates? If such shall be your determination, I, for one, will not join in the application—no, I will with all the faculties I possess oppose every attempt to extend a trade that, except in name, is more injurious to those employed in it than is the slavery in the West Indies to the poor negroes, for deeply as I am interested in the cotton-manufacture, highly as I value the extended political power of my country, yet knowing as I do from long experience both here and in England the miseries which this trade, as it is now conducted, inflicts on those to whom it gives employment, I do not hesitate to say: *Perish the cotton trade, perish even the political superiority of our country, if it depends on the cotton trade, rather than that they*

54

shall be upheld by the sacrifice of everything valuable in life."

During the next session of Parliament, Robert Owen was actively urging a bill stipulating that no child under ten years of age, or unable to read, should be employed in the factories, proposing the establishment of schools for their especial benefit where reading, writing, and arithmetic should be taught, and stipulating that the hours of work in mills, including two hours for meals and recreation, should not exceed twelve and a half a day. The bill also provided for more thorough methods of factory inspection by government agents. Nothing more significant of the devotion of Robert Owen to the welfare of the workers could be cited than the fact that he worked assiduously for the passage of this measure, not only in direct opposition to the wishes of his fellow manufacturers, but of most of the operatives, who had been taught to regard him as an enemy of the industry which gave them employment. "At this period," Mr. Owen writes, "I had no public intercourse with the operatives and working classes in any part of the two islands, not even in the great metropolis. They were strangers to me and to all my views and future intentions. I was at all periods of my progress, from my earliest knowledge and employment of them, their true friend: while their democratic and much mistaken leaders taught them that I desired to make slaves of them in my village of unity and cooperation." When reviled and repudiated by those in whose behalf he labored, Robert Owen continued fighting their battles with ardor undaunted by their misinterpretation of his motives.

A meeting was called of the members of the House of Commons favorable to factory-reform legislation, and Sir Robert Peel was chosen to introduce the measure. It took four years to secure its passage, when the measure came out so mutilated that its provisions brought little relief to those for whose relief it was intended. While this bill was pending, Robert Owen remained in London, and conducted a campaign of education such as England had never witnessed before, and which made his name a household word throughout the kingdom. Thousands of tracts and papers were circulated. Owen bought by the ton copies of newspapers containing his arguments, and on one occasion the London mails were delayed twenty minutes by a deluge of documents posted by him. In 1816 appeared Observations on the Effect of the Factory System. "From certain parliamentary reports," says Robert Dale Owen, "in connection with Sir Robert Peel's factory bill, my father derived data in proof that the machinery employed in Great Britain in cotton-spinning alone, in one branch therefore of one manufacture, superseded at that time the labor of eighty million adults; and he succeeded in proving to the satisfaction of England's ablest statistician (Colquhoun) that if all the branches of the cotton, woolen, flax, and silk manufactures were included, the machine-saving labor in producing English textile fabrics exceeded in those days the work which two hundred millions of operatives could have turned out previous to the year 1760." In 1817 Mr. Owen issued: A Report Addressed to the Committee for the Relief of the Laboring and Manufacturing Poor. In this treatise colonies for the poor were advocated, and the destruction of pauperism by a system of education and manual training was proposed.

It may well be said that Robert Owen secured in the enactment of such legislation the first embodiment of the principle of governmental interference in internal trade relations, a principle which has come to assume large importance in modern legislation. These early laws advocated by Mr. Owen were the first industrial measures designed for the relief of the laboring classes, and established a precedent for all labor legislation since effected in England and America.

About this time Mr. Owen made a public declaration of

religious principles, insistent advocacy of which brought
him, in the language of Sargent, "neglect, hatred, calumny, contempt, and all the evils which follow an excom-
municated man." From this time his popularity as a
reformer began to wane, for the strong religious sentiment
of the English people regarded with apprehension his
sweeping attacks on existing creeds. This declaration was
a strategic mistake, but it revealed the thorough independence of Robert Owen. It lost him the friendship of his
most influential allies, brought him an irresponsible following which injured his cause, and connected his theories in
the popular mind with atheism and anarchy.

Soon after this declaration Mr. Owen visited the educational establishment of M. de Felenberg, at Hoffwyl, Switzerland, whither he had sent his sons for their education.
On this trip he presented a memorial in behalf of the
laboring classes to the crowned heads in convention at
Aix-la-Chapelle. In 1819 he stood for Parliament in Lanark borough. By the combined efforts of labor leaders
and factory-owners he was defeated in his aspirations.
There was nothing of demagogy in his Appeal to the Laboring Classes, issued in 1819, and an opponent who more
loudly swore his fealty to the common people was returned.
Only the working people of a district in which so many
years of Robert Owen's life had been spent in philanthropic
undertakings were to blame for the inability of Mr. Owen
to advocate his principles at the succeeding session of Parliament.

At this time Richard Flower arrived in England, bearing a commission from George Rapp to sell the great Harmonist estate. He found Robert Owen in the disappointment of several of his plans, and suggested "Harmonie"
as an eligible site for putting in practical operation plans
for communistic colonization which Mr. Owen had long
been publicly advocating. "The offer tempted my father,"
writes Robert Dale Owen. "Here was a village ready built,

a territory capable of supporting tens of thousands, in a country where the expression of thought was free, and where the people were unsophisticated. I listened with delight to Mr. Flower's account of a frontier life, and when, one morning, my father asked me, ' Well, Robert, what say you, New Lanark or Harmony?' I answered without hesitation, ' Harmony.' Aside from the romance and novelty, I think one prompting motive was that if our family settled in western America, it would facilitate my marriage with Jessie," a young woman who quickly forgot the younger Owen after his emigration to America. " Mr. Flower could not conceal from us his amazement, saying to me, I remember, ' Does your father really think of giving up a position like this, with every comfort and luxury, and taking his family to the wild life of the far West?' He did not know that my father's one ruling desire was for a vast theater in which to try his plans of social reform." Then, too, the younger Owen tells us, " the success of the Rappites greatly encouraged my father." The preliminaries were arranged with Mr. Flower, and in December, 1824, Mr. Owen came to the United States to complete the purchase of the property afterward officially known as New Harmony. The bargain was closed in the spring of 1825, and Mr. Owen became the owner of an estate consisting of nearly thirty thousand acres of land—three thousand acres under cultivation by the Harmonists, nineteen detached farms, six hundred acres of improved land occupied by tenants, some fine orchards, eighteen acres of bearing vines, and the village of Harmony, with its great church, its brick, frame, and log houses, and its factories, with almost all the machinery. It constituted an admirable site for the great experiment which Robert Owen had decided to inaugurate.

CHAPTER VII

THE NEW MORAL WORLD

" Civilization ! How the term is misapplied ! A state of society based upon ignorance, deranging the faculties of all !

" The affairs of the world carried on by violence and force, through massacres, legal robberies, and devastations, superstitions, bigotry, and selfish mysteries !

" By living a continual life of hypocrisy, and public and private deception !

" By supposing that the most degrading and injurious vices are the highest virtues !

.   .   .   .

" And yet this conduct of gross ignorance and rank insanity is called civilization ! "

THE New Moral World, from which the sentences just quoted are taken, while not published at the time of the New Harmony experiment, was a later compilation of the beliefs held and promulgated by Robert Owen at that time. It embodies the theories upon which the New Harmony communities were founded, and a brief review of its teachings will serve to throw much light upon the history of the New Harmony venture.

" The New Moral World," Mr. Owen declared, " is an organization to rationally educate and employ all, through a new organization of society which will give a new existence to man by surrounding him with superior circumstances only." " New and strange as this statement will appear, even to the most learned and experienced of the present day," the author declares, " let no one rashly pronounce it to be visionary, for it is a system, the result of

59

much reading, observation, and reflection, combined with extensive practical experience and confidential communication with public official characters in various countries, and with leading minds among all classes: a system founded on the eternal laws of nature, and derived from facts and experience only: and it will be found on full examination, by competent minds, to be the least visionary and the most easy of practise of all systems which have been proposed in ancient or modern times to improve the character and to insure the happiness of the human race."

" The religious, moral, political, and commercial arrangements of society have been on a wrong basis since the commencement of history," declared Mr. Owen. The new society which would be possible by the adoption of his principles he prophesied would be a heaven of happiness.

As a basis for his philosophy, Mr. Owen stated what he called " the fundamental laws of human nature." In brief, these were as follows:

Human nature is a compound of animal propensities, intellectual faculties, and moral qualities.

These are united in different proportions in each individual.

The diversity constitutes the difference between individuals.

These elements and proportions are made by a power unknown to the individual and consequently without his consent.

Each individual comes into certain existing circumstances which act upon his original organization, more especially during early life, and by impressing their general character upon him, form his local and national character.

This influence is modified by the original character of the individual; thus character is formed and maintained.

No one decides his time or place of birth, his circumstances, or his training.

Each individual may receive, in early training, either true or false fundamental ideas.

He may be trained to either beneficial or injurious habits, or a mixture of both.

Each person must believe according to the strongest conviction that is made upon his mind, which conviction is not determined by his will.

He must like or dislike, according to his experience.

His feelings and convictions are formed for him by the impression of circumstances upon his original organization. His will is formed by his feelings or convictions, therefore his physical, mental, and moral characters are formed independent of himself.

Impressions which are at first pleasurable become by repetition indifferent, and finally painful. Impressions which succeed each other beyond a certain rapidity are finally dissipated and weakened, and at last destroy enjoyment.

Health, improvement, and happiness depend upon the due cultivation of all physical, intellectual, and moral qualities, upon their being called into action at a proper period of life, and being afterward exercised temperately, according to their strength and capacity.

Bad character results from bad innate tendencies placed in the midst of bad surroundings; a medium character from bad tendencies in good surroundings, good tendencies in unfavorable surroundings, or mixed tendencies in mixed surroundings. A superior character results from a good constitution placed among favorable circumstances, when the laws, institutions, and customs are in accordance with the laws of nature.

From these beliefs regarding human nature, Mr. Owen formed the following " laws ":

I.—Man can not be a subject of merit or demerit.

II.—The feelings and convictions are instincts of human nature.

III.—The individual should always express his feelings without restraint. The will is the mental feeling, and when we speak of the will keeping us from certain action, we simply mean that our mental feeling was stronger than our physical feeling. Nature's laws require that physical, mental, and moral feelings should in all temperance be exercised.

IV.—Personal ambition and vanity will be destroyed by a knowledge of the fact of mental and moral irresponsibility.

V.—The practise means the removal from the world of all inferior circumstances tending to produce bad character.

Happiness depends upon the harmony of physical, mental, and moral proportions. The diversity of mankind is essential to human happiness. The individual who is morally, mentally, or physically weak calls for our compassion, not for our condemnation. Good habits must be given to all, or they can not be given to any. A superior human being, or any one approaching a character deserving the name of rational, has not yet been known among mankind. Before such a being can appear, a great change must occur in the whole proceedings of mankind: their feelings, thoughts, and actions must arise from principles altogether different from the vague and fanciful notions by which the mental part of the character of man has been hitherto formed; the whole external circumstances relative to the production and distribution of wealth, the formation of character, and the government of men must be changed, remodeled, and reunited into a new system. The fundamental errors of the old system have prevented man from becoming rational; the new laws will produce charity, kindness, intelligence, and happiness.

The elements of the science of society, Mr. Owen declared to be as follows:

1. A knowledge of the principles and the application

to practise of the laws of human nature; laws derived from demonstrable facts, and which prove man to be a social being.

2. A knowledge of the principles and practise of the best modes of producing in abundance the most beneficial necessaries and comforts for the support and enjoyment of human life.

The most necessary wealth Mr. Owen declared to be air, water, food, health, clothing, shelter, instruction, amusements, the affection of our associates, and good society. To secure these, there must be a cordial union of mankind. Upon a certain amount of land should be combined skill, labor, capital, and population. These elements should be directed by those who understand the laws of God and principles of society. The greatest loss and waste result from the disunited minds and feelings of mankind. Armies, churches, lawyers, doctors, and exclusive universities are the greatest obstacles to progress. The professions as such should be done away with, and the professional men employed as teachers or rulers of the people under the new principles. There is a great loss from the separation of trades, and the expense of exchange and transportation. Four departments will be instituted in the new social state: (1) of production of wealth; (2) of distribution; (3) of formation of character; (4) of government. These elements should be united in each community. Beautiful surroundings should also characterize each of these new settlements. The greatest saving will result from having the best of all that society requires. These arrangements, with the destruction of the professions, will cause a saving of from fifty to sixty per cent. The departments of production will be made so attractive that labor will be a pleasure which all will desire. As a result of all these arrangements wealth will be put into the hands of the consumer at one-fourth the present cost.

3. A knowledge of the principles and practise of the best methods of distributing wealth.

The middleman Mr. Owen declared to be an expensive luxury. The three classes of these, retailers, wholesalers, and extensive merchants, all strive to get the most out of their materials. There are more establishments than are necessary for handling the goods, and much capital and labor is thus rendered useless. The present system of distribution is a dead weight on society. It is a contrivance " to add to the cost of production, to deteriorate qualities, to employ unnecessary capital, to demoralize the character of those employed, and it trains men to become slaves to their customers and tyrants to their dependents. By keeping separate storehouses in separate establishments on the premises where the material is produced, and from these distributing for daily consumption, ninety-nine per cent of this expense can be saved. Mr. Owen inveighed against " imaginary representations of wealth, such as gold, silver, or paper," and claimed that the monetary systems of England and America were the causes of great distress. He proposed the establishment of " banks of real wealth," with a rather indefinite method of transacting business. The new medium of exchange must have the power of expansion and contraction, as the value of material expanded or contracted.

4. A knowledge of the principles and practises by which to form the new combination of circumstances for training the infant to become the most rational being. The care of the infant has been entrusted to the inferior in mind, manner, and knowledge, and its education has consisted of placing the child within four walls, to sit on a seat and ask no questions. Children should be treated with kindness and judgment.

5. A knowledge of how to govern man most effectively under these new principles. Government must be active to create, watchful and observing to maintain rational laws.

6. To unite these general principles into a rational state of society. Society has been a chaos. The instinct of man is to be happy, but he has learned to think that wealth and happiness are synonymous. There is no necessary connection. Utopian philosophers from Plato to Fourier have failed in their purposes because they taught contradictory principles and practises. " From the contamination, through so many ages, of the errors of theoretical men without practise, and those of practical men without any accurate or extensive knowledge of principle, it will now be difficult, except by practical demonstration, to convince these two classes that by a union of principles derived from unchanging facts, with the experience emanating from extensive practise in accordance with these principles, an intelligent, united, wealthy, virtuous, and happy society may be now formed and made permanent."

Happiness, "the instinct of the universe," Mr. Owen declared to be dependent upon the practise of the principles of The New Moral World. To provide for this general happiness, schools were to be founded for the education of the children, as well as asylums for the afflicted, and to all should be given the opportunity for study, social enjoyment, travel, and the liberty of expressing opinions on all subjects. Women should be accorded the same rights and privileges as men.

A Supreme Power, Robert Owen declared, was the cause of all existence. The practise of religion includes charity, a knowledge of the laws of nature, and efforts to do good for our fellow men. " The practise of the rational religion will consist in promoting, to the utmost of our power, the happiness and well-being of every man, woman, and child, without regard to their sect, class, party, or color, and its worship, in those inexpressible feelings of wonder, admiration, and delight, which, when man is surrounded by superior circumstances only, will naturally arise from the contemplation of the infinity of space, of the eternity of duration, of the order of the universe, and of that Incomprehensible Power by which the atom is moved and the aggregate of nature is governed." Formerly religions have divided man from man and nation from nation; the new religion will bind all men into one great family, based on charity and love. All men should exert themselves to remove evil from society and create good.

Upon these beliefs as a basis, Robert Owen constructed a social scheme for which he seemed to expect universal and immediate acceptance. He declared the United States Constitution to mark the greatest progress of mankind so far made in the direction of liberty. He stated, however, that Adams, Jefferson, Madison, and Monroe had expressed keen disappointment in the result of the Constitution and the character of the American people as developed under it. Thomas Jefferson, Mr. Owen declared, had confessed to him a feeling that society should be reorganized, but had expressed an inability to undertake the work of reformation. The foundation laid by the framers of the Constitution was one of sand, and would yet be dissolved.

Rational government, Mr. Owen declared, will attend solely to the happiness of the governed. There must be liberty of conscience and of speech. Private property must be abandoned as soon as the children of the present generation had been taught in the principles of the new social system. There should be no rewards or punishments except those awarded by nature.

From one to five years of age, the children in Mr. Owen's communities were to be well clothed and fed, and given ample opportunity for exercise; the next five years were to be given to light employment and the continuance of education, which was to be acquired largely by observation, directed by skilled teachers. From ten to twelve years of age they were to assist in the gardens and houses, and from twelve to fifteen, to be given technical training. From fifteen to twenty the education was to be continued, the pupil now assisting in the instruction of the younger children. From twenty to thirty the member was to act as a superintendent in the departments of production and education; from thirty to forty to govern the homes, and from forty to sixty, to assist in the management of the external relations of the communities, or travel abroad, " as suited the will."

The family, Mr. Owen declared, must give way to the scientific association of from five hundred to two thousand people. In these, men, women, and children were to be gathered together " in usual proportions." The various communities were to be united in tens, hundreds, thousands, etc., all assisting one another. Each of these communities was to possess adjacent land sufficient to support its maximum membership. Provisions for " swarming " from these establishments, when they became crowded, were to be made. The communities were to be arranged so as to give each member, so far as practicable, equal advantages with all the rest. Easy communication from colony to colony was provided for by pleasant walks through groves, and other improved methods of travel.

Each community was to be governed in all its home departments by a general council, composed of all members between the ages of thirty and forty. Each department was to be placed under a committee formed of members of the general council chosen by the leader in an order to be determined upon. In its external, or foreign relations, each community was to be governed by its members between the ages of forty and sixty years. There was to be no election to office. All members must act as rational physical and mental beings, or be removed to an asylum.

This, in brief (for The New Moral World fills nearly three hundred closely printed pages), is the panacea presented by Mr. Owen for the cure of social ills. " With this view of society in prospect of easy attainment," said Mr. Owen, " shall the present system, based on falsehood, be

longer supported; a system organized, classified, and arranged in accordance with the fundamental errors on which
society is based—errors producing all manner of inequality,
vices, crimes, and misery, making man an inferior and irrational being, and the earth a pandemonium? Will the
human race longer insanely maintain such a heterogeneous
mass of folly and absurdity, and doom their offspring,
through succeeding generations, to be inferior, irrational
men and women, filled with every injurious notion, and
governed by most ignorant and misery-producing institutions, while excellence, superior external circumstances,
and happiness lie directly before them and easy of attainment? "

CHAPTER VIII

" In 1825 Robert Owen stirred the very life of the nation with his appeals to Kings and Congresses, and his vast experiments at New Harmony. Think of his family of nine hundred members on a farm of thirty thousand acres! A magnificent beginning that thrilled the world."—JNO. HUMPHREY NOYES.

On February 25 and March 7, 1825, Robert Owen delivered addresses in the Hall of the House of Representatives at Washington, before two of the most distinguished audiences ever gathered in the national capital, including almost the entire membership of both houses of Congress, the judges of the Supreme Court, the President and several members of his Cabinet, besides many other men of distinction. To this assemblage Robert Owen explained his plans for the redemption of the human race from the evils of the existing state of society. In connection with these lectures, Mr. Owen exhibited a model of the buildings to be erected, first for the New Harmony community, and afterward for each of the communities to be established. The buildings were to form a hollow square one thousand feet long, including a complete school, academy, and university. Within the squares were the culinary, dining, washing, and similar departments. In the larger buildings which marked the centers of the sides and the corners of the quadrangle were to be lecture-rooms, laboratories, chapel, ball, concert, committee, and conversation rooms. Between these larger buildings were dwelling-rooms occupying the first and second stories. On the third floor were to be departments for the unmarried and the children above two years of age. Each department was to be supplied with gas, water, and all the modern conveniences.

In concluding this memorable address, Mr. Owen declared that he meant to carry these purposes of amelioration into immediate execution, to the full extent of his means. The town of New Harmony, he said, did not present such a combination as his model, and therefore it would present only a temporary purpose for the objects which he had in view. "But it will enable us to form immediately," he declared, " a preliminary society in which to receive the new population, to collect, prepare, and arrange material for erecting several such combinations as the model represents, and of forming several independent, yet united associations, having common property and one common interest. This new establishment will be erected on the high lands of Harmony, from two to four miles from the river and its island, of which the inhabitants will have a beautiful and extensive view, there being several thousands of acres of cultivated land on the rich second bottom lying between the highlands and the river. And here it is, in the heart of the United States, and almost in the center of its unequaled internal navigation, that Power which governs and directs the universe and every action of man has arranged circumstances which were far beyond my control, and permits me to commence a new empire of peace and good-will to men, founded on other principles and leading to other practises than those of present or past, and which principles in due season, and in the allotted time, will lead to that state of virtue, intelligence, enjoyment, and happiness which it has been foretold by the sages of the past would at some time become the lot of the human race.

"I have, however, no wish to lead the way. I am desirous that governments should become masters of the sub-

OWEN'S PROPOSED VILLAGE.

From an old print.

ject, adopt the principles, encourage the practise, and thereby retain the direction of the public mind for their own benefit and the benefit of the people. But as I have not the control of circumstances to insure success in this public course, I must show what private exertions, guided by these new principles, can accomplish at New Harmony, and these new proceedings will begin in April."

Mr. Owen took occasion to deny the report which alleged the unhealthfulness of New Harmony. Many of the Rappites, he said, had died at first, " but last year only two died." The land, he declared, was well drained and cultivated. " I have been asked," said Mr. Owen, " what would be the effect upon the neighborhood and surrounding country where one or more of these societies of union, cooperation, and common property should be established. My conviction is that every interest and inclination of the individual or old system of society would break up and soon terminate; every interest, because the communities would undersell all individual producers, both of agricultural productions and manufactured commodities; every inclination, because it is scarcely to be supposed that any would continue to live under the miserable, anxious, individual system of opposition and counteraction, when they could with ease form themselves into or become members of one of these associations of union, intelligence, and kind feelings.

" ' If,' it has further been asked of me, ' these societies spread by their commercial operations, and the increased advantages and comforts which they offer, to the whole population, what effect will they have upon the government and general prosperity of an extensive empire?' I again reply that a country, however extensive, divided into these arrangements of improved social buildings, gardens, and pleasure-grounds, and these occupied and cultivated by people possessing superior dispositions, will be governed with more ease than it can be with the same number of people scattered over the country, living in common vil-

71

lages, towns, and cities under the individual system. The expense of government will be diminished by as much as the trouble and anxiety, and it is not unlikely that these would be diminished to one-tenth of the present amount. The effect which would be produced on the prosperity of the country would be equally beneficial and important. Any country will be prosperous in proportion to the number and physical and mental superiority of its people."

With the publication of these addresses in 1825 was issued a manifesto announcing that " a new society is about to be formed at Harmony in Indiana." The invitation to membership included all who were in sympathy with the founder in his desire for a new state of society.

The second community at Harmony was instituted under the most auspicious circumstances. The attention of the whole country had been drawn to the project by the addresses of Mr. Owen at Washington and in other American cities. Many of the most distinguished men of the time, both in Europe and America, were giving at least partial approval to the plans of the celebrated English philanthropist. The previous success of the Rappites on the very site of the proposed Utopia furnished an object-lesson in communistic prosperity. There appeared to be no reason why a measure of success even greater should not come to the new community, which seemed to be based on all the good in Harmonist doctrine, with the more disagreeable features eliminated, while it contemplated the practise of theories in local government and education which had proved highly successful at New Lanark. The grade of intelligence in the Harmonist society had been low, and ignorance and superstition had been the most marked characteristics of the membership. The members of the new community would be persons of liberal and progressive ideas, striving toward a high ideal of social life, with superior intelligence and skill. Mr. Owen had demonstrated his business ability as one of the leading cotton manufacturers of England, and was prepared to give substantial backing to his experiment. The hundreds who flocked to New Harmony from every State in the Union, and from every country in the north of Europe, found as the site of the new settlement a princely estate comprising several square miles of fertile land. The extensive industries established by the Rappites seemed to await only the touch of American ingenuity, while the comfortable homes the German communists had built in "Harmonie, the home of love," insured the absence of the privation of early settlement which discouraged many similar communities in later years. The orchards which stood at the edge of the village, and the vineyards that covered the hillsides, were visible promises of plenty during the early spring days of the settlement. The quietly retreating Rappite thousand, too, it was said, had conveyed their golden hoard by bushels from Father Rapp's cellar to the boat which bore them to their new Pennsylvania home. Surely, this was the El Dorado of communistic hopes; surely, as Robert Owen had declared, this was a place providentially set apart for the first great victory of communism.

It was not the hope of even optimistic Robert Owen that a community of equality, based on lofty and liberal principles, could spring full grown into being, as had the Rappite society of religious asceticism in 1805. There must be some years of educational training, of instruction in the principles of the new moral world; the members must be gradually weaned away from "the errors and prejudices which had existed since the time of Adam"—from all the evil ideas and associations of the selfish individual system in which they had been born and reared, before they could, with safety, form themselves into a community such as Robert Owen contemplated. To this end, Mr. Owen enlisted the interest of William Maclure, of Philadelphia, a wealthy scientist who combined excellent ideas on education with peculiar notions in political economy, which, while they did not coincide with Robert Owen's methods of social reconstruction, agreed in the indictment of existing conditions. William Maclure was in many respects a remarkable man, of varied experience, broad views, and a spirit truly philanthropic. In awakening his interest in New Harmony, Mr. Owen certainly procured a promise of educational excellence for his social experiment. Maclure was born in Ayre, Scotland, in 1763. When thirty-three years of age, he came to America with the ambitious intention of making a geological survey of the United States. This purpose he followed with indefatigable energy until the publication of the results of his labors in 1809. In the course of this work he crossed and recrossed the Alleghanies more than fifty times, and tramped on foot through every State and Territory then within the limits of the United States in the search for data. In 1817 he published a revised edition, incorporating the results of further observation. He became justly known, through this herculean pioneer work, as " The Father of American Geology."

Mr. Maclure was the principal founder of the Philadelphia Academy of Natural Sciences, and for twenty-three years, beginning with 1817, he was the president of that organization. To this institution he contributed liberally, transferring to it in later years his library and collections. He was the patron of many American scientific organizations, including the American Geological Society, of which he was president.

Maclure's interest in education was second only to his scientific enthusiasm. He visited Pestalozzi's school in Switzerland, and was the first to introduce the system of the great Swiss educator into the United States. He was one of the earliest champions of the idea of industrial education. He founded an agricultural school near the city of Alicante, Spain, on an estate of ten thousand acres, purchased for this purpose, but an end was put to these plans by a political revolution which resulted in the confiscation of the property. Maclure's friendship for Robert Owen began with a visit to New Lanark, where he was greatly attracted by the plans there in operation for the amelioration of the condition of the working classes.

Mr. Maclure, according to Mr. Owen's subsequent statement, put about one hundred and fifty thousand dollars into the New Harmony experiment, his liability, however, being limited to ten thousand dollars. The avowed intention of Mr. Maclure was to make New Harmony the center of American education through the introduction of the Pestalozzian system of instruction, in which he and Mr. Owen had a common interest. To this end, with the assistance of Mr. Owen, he brought to New Harmony the most distinguished coterie of scientists and educators in America. Among these was Thomas Say, who has been called " The Father of American Zoology." Thomas Say, the son of a medical practitioner in Philadelphia, and a member of the Society of Friends, was born in Philadelphia on July 27, 1787. He was destined by his father to a business life, but failed so signally that he was soon without means. He then became a scientist, having from early life displayed a strong predilection for the study of natural history. He served through the War of 1812 as a volunteer, afterward resuming his scientific studies. Mr. Say was a charter member of the association which founded the Philadelphia Academy of Natural Sciences. Under the auspices of this organization he began the work of cataloguing and describing the American fauna, contributing from time to time the results of his labors to the journal published by the association. In 1817 he was, with William Maclure, a member of a party engaged in investigating the natural history of the Florida peninsula, and in 1818 explored the islands off the coast of Georgia. He became chief zoologist with Long's expedition to the Rocky Mountains in 1819, and in 1823 accompanied this party to the St. Peter's River. After coming to New Harmony, he devoted his time unremittingly to the study and teaching of natural history. He contributed many scientific articles to the New Harmony Disseminator, and contributions from his pen are to be found in the Journal of the Philadelphia Academy of Sciences, Transactions of the American Philosophical Society, Maclurean Lyceum, Nicholson's Encyclopedia, American Journal of Science and Art, and the Western Quarterly Reporter. His scientific papers in all number about one hundred. He edited and arranged almost all of the publications of Prince Charles Lucien Bonaparte written while in America. While at New Harmony his American Entomology, projected in 1816, was completed in three parts. His American Conchology had been carried through six volumes at the time of his death. Copies of these works are to be found in the New Harmony library. They are ornamented by beautiful colored plates, drawn and painted by Mrs. Say, whom, as Miss Lucy Sistare, Mr. Say married at New Harmony. The exquisite engravings, many of them made at New Harmony, were by C. H. Lesueur, L. Lyon, and James Walker. The American Conchology was printed at New Harmony. " He was one of the truest and noblest students of natural science," writes Dr. Schnack. " He was noted for his modesty and reticence—only his intimate friends were aware of his true worth. He has left his impression on every department of natural science that he touched; and his fellow workers after him have given his name to one or more species in every branch of natural history. Thus he will forever remain immortalized through the objects he so much loved and studied." J. S. Kingsley says of Thomas Say, in the Popular Science Monthly : " The number of new species which Say described has probably never been exceeded except in the case of those two exceedingly careless workers, John Edward Gray and Francis Walker, of the British Museum. There is this

in Say's favor which can not be said of the two just mentioned: that his descriptions are almost without exception
easily recognized, and almost every form which he described is now well known. Working as he did almost
without books, and without that traditional knowledge
which obtains among the continental workers, it was unavoidable that he should redescribe forms which were
known before, but owing to the clear insight he possessed,
and the discrimination he exercised in selecting the important features of the form before him, his work has
never caused that confusion which many, in much more
favorable circumstances, have produced."

Charles Alexander Lesueur came from the West Indies
to New Harmony. "He had been engaged," writes Dr.
Schnack, "by the Jardins des Plantes, at Paris, to make
a collection of the various objects of natural history; he
was attached to the unfortunate expedition of La Perouse
and was left on the coast of Australia to examine and
describe the remarkable animals of that continent, otherwise he would have been lost, as all the rest were, by ship-
wreck. He was the first to explore, and publish an account
of the mounds found in Indiana." Lesueur was also the
first to classify the fishes of the Great Lakes. He was an
adept painter, and sketches from his pencil are to be found
in the New Harmony library.

Constantine Samuel Raffinesque was a frequent visitor
to New Harmony during community days, and associated
himself as closely with the experiment there as his nomadic
nature would permit. Dr. Jordan calls Raffinesque "the
first student of our western fishes," and "the very first
teacher of natural history in the West," and devotes to
him an interesting chapter in his Science Sketches. Raffinesque was born in Constantinople in 1784, and in him were
blended French, Turkish, German, and Grecian blood. His
early boyhood was spent at Marseilles, where, he says in
his Autobiography, he became a zoologist and a naturalist.

At the age of twelve he published his first scientific paper. At the outbreak of the French Revolution he was sent, with a brother, to Philadelphia, where he became a merchant's clerk, and devoted his spare time to the study of botany, traveling on foot, in pursuit of his studies, over Virginia and Pennsylvania. In 1805 he went to Sicily, where he spent ten years. There he discovered the medicinal squill, which was the beginning of a profitable business for the natives of the island. In 1810 he published two works on the fishes of Sicily. In 1815 he again sailed for America. Off the harbor of New London the vessel upon which he was a passenger went down, carrying with it Raffinesque's books and scientific collections. Raffinesque drifted westward, making pioneer explorations of the botany of the Ohio River country. After a short time spent at New Harmony, he became professor of natural history and modern languages in Transylvania University, at Lexington, Kentucky. After a stormy experience there, he closed his career as a college professor, for which he was ill fitted. During the course of his travels he visited Audubon, then keeping a small store and studying birds at Henderson, Kentucky. Audubon gives an entertaining description of his queer guest. " His attire," writes Audubon, " struck me as extremely remarkable. A long, loose coat of yellow nankeen, much the worse for the many rubs it had got in its time, hung about him loosely, like a sack. A waistcoat of the same, with enormous pockets and buttoned up to the chin, reached below, over a pair of tight pantaloons, the lower part of which was buttoned down over his ankles. His beard was long, and his long black hair hung loosely over his shoulders. His forehead was broad and prominent, indicating a mind of strong power. His words impressed an assurance of rigid truth; and, as he directed the conversation to the natural sciences, I listened to him with great delight." Returning to Philadelphia, Raffinesque began the publication of The Atlantic Journal and

Friend of Knowledge, Annals of Nature, and other periodicals, of which, as Dr. Jordan remarks, he was not only editor, publisher, and usually sole contributor, but finally sole subscriber also. Says Dr. Jordan: "He became a monomaniac on the subject of new species. He was uncontrolled in this matter by the influence of other writers, that incredulous conservatism as to another's discoveries which furnishes a salutary balance to enthusiastic workers. Before his death so much had he seen, and so little had he compared, that he had described certainly twice as many fishes, and probably nearly twice as many plants and shells, as really existed in the regions over which he traveled. . . . Thus it came about that the name and work of Raffinesque fell into utter neglect. . . . Long before the invention of railroads and steamboats, he had traveled over most of southern Europe and eastern North America. Without money except as he earned it, he had gathered shells and plants and fishes on every shore from the Hellespont to the Wabash." Raffinesque died in abject poverty in Philadelphia in 1840, entirely without the reputation as a scientist which attaches to his name now that zoologists realize the value of his pioneer work.

Dr. Gerard Troost, a Holland geologist, was also one of the group of scientists brought to New Harmony by Mr. Maclure. Troost was a pioneer in the study of western geology, and became a professor in the Nashville University and State geologist of Tennessee after leaving New Harmony. John Chappelsmith, who accompanied Mr. Owen to New Harmony, was a wealthy English artist and engraver. Prof. Joseph Neef, who came to take charge of the educational features of the New Harmony experiment, had come from Pestalozzi's reform school at Iverdun, at the solicitation of Mr. Maclure, to introduce the Pestalozzian system of education into this country. Madame Marie D. Frotageot and Phiquepal d'Arusmont, also Pestalozzian teachers, came with Mr. Maclure's party from Philadelphia, in which city they had been conducting private schools. Professor Neef had conducted two academies on the Pestalozzian system with indifferent success, near Philadelphia. Frances Wright, who became the wife of Phiquepal d'Arusmont, was at New Harmony during the Rappite removal, and accompanied the Harmonists to their new home in Pennsylvania, for the purpose of observation. She was an enthusiastic advocate of the " new principles," the first American advocate of women's rights, and one of the earliest among abolition agitators. The four sons of Robert Owen, Robert Dale, William, David, and Richard, were strong factors in the educational life of New Harmony. All had received their early educational training under private tutors, later entering the manual training and grammar schools founded at New Lanark by their father. All attended the educational institution of Emmanuel Fellenburg at Hoffwyl, Switzerland, David and Richard pursuing a special course in chemistry, and, with Robert, acquiring a knowledge of French and German. David and Richard entered the chemical and physical classes of Dr. Andrew Ure, in the Andersonian Institution at Glasgow, and in November, 1827, left Liverpool to join their father at New Harmony, where they engaged in teaching and conducting chemical experiments with apparatus brought from Glasgow.

Robert Dale Owen was, in his earlier years, an enthusiastic believer in the social theories of his father, and thought with him that three or four hours' work a day, under a system of common property, would support a man. In September, 1825, at the age of twenty-four, he left Liverpool for New York. He landed at New York harbor in November, and set foot on what he called " the Canaan of his hopes." He was accompanied by a Captain McDonald, a young English officer who was an enthusiastic Owenite. They remained at New York for several weeks, and were joined there by the Maclure party of scientists and educators, including, besides those mentioned above, " several cultivated ladies, among them, Miss Sistare, afterward the wife of Thomas Say, and her sisters." Robert Dale Owen is not sure whether William Maclure joined them at New York, or whether he arrived at New Harmony shortly after they reached the place. While in New York, Robert Dale Owen declared his intention to become an American citizen. The trip to New Harmony from Pittsburg was by a keel boat, which has ever since been known as " The Boatload of Knowledge." The party reached New Harmony in the middle of January, 1826, eight months after Robert Owen had formally launched his experiment.

CHAPTER IX

THE PRELIMINARY SOCIETY

" Land of the West, we come to thee,
Far o'er the desert of the sea;
Under thy white-winged canopy,
Land of the West, we fly to thee;
Sick of the Old World's sophistry;
Haste then across the dark, blue sea,
Land of the West, we rush to thee!
Home of the brave : soil of the free,—
Huzza! She rises o'er the sea."

—*Sung by the Owen party on shipboard, en route to New Harmony.*

DURING the spring of 1825, the New Harmony experiment was a subject of general discussion all over the country. The National Intelligencer quoted the Philadelphia papers as saying that "nine hundred inhabitants of that city have expressed a desire to accompany Mr. Owen to New Harmony," although Owen was generally decried by the press as "an unbeliever." New Harmony became the rendezvous of enlightened and progressive people from all over the United States and northern Europe. On the other hand, there came to New Harmony scores of cranks with curious hobbies, many persons impelled by curiosity and many others attracted by the prospect of life without labor. The heterogeneous mass would have afforded Charles Dickens an unlimited supply of character studies, for eccentricity ran riot in a hundred directions. The large majority were freethinkers, attracted by Robert Owen's unorthodox religious views. New Harmony was denominated by Alexander Campbell, "the focus of enlightened

82

CHARLES ALEXANDRE LESUEUR.

atheism." This fact accounted, in no small degree, for the
exodus of scientific men to the place at a time when there
was thought to be irreconcilable disagreement between science and religion. Macdonald says that Owen's proclamation was more successful than he had expected, and that he
was deprived of an opportunity to select the members of
his community by finding the place filled to overflowing
on his arrival.

On April 27, 1825, Robert Owen addressed the community membership, together with many others who had
gathered from the surrounding country to witness the
launching of this strange experiment. The meeting was
held in the old Rappite church, which had been converted
into the "Hall of New Harmony," and dedicated to free
thought and free speech. Amid surroundings so favorable
to the success of his project, Mr. Owen could not be blamed
for speaking optimistically. " I am come to this country,"
he said, " to introduce an entire new state of society; to
change it from an ignorant, selfish system to an enlightened social system which shall gradually unite all interests
into one, and remove all causes for contest between individuals." Reiterating his declaration that happiness, virtue, and the rational being can not be attained under the
individual system, he said that former attempts at social
regeneration had not been made with an accurate knowledge of human nature, but were based on an unnatural and
artificial view of our own nature. Man claims not our
praise and blame, but our compassion, care, attention, and
kindness. The change in system, however, Mr. Owen declared, could not be accomplished at once. New Harmony
is "the half-way house between the old and the new."
The people must for a time admit a certain degree of pecuniary inequality, partly, Mr. Owen explained, because scientists and educators would be brought to the settlement
under inducements. But there would be no social inequalities. He would consider himself no better than the

humblest member. The only distinction in the deference
accorded individuals should be that commanded by age and
experience. While his desire was that the community
should be self-governing, it would be necessary for him to
take the direction of affairs for a time. " Ardently as I
long for the arrival of that period when there shall be no
artificial inequality among the whole human race, yet, as no
other individual has had the same experience as myself in
the practise of the system about to be introduced, I must,
for some time, partially take the lead in its direction, but I
shall rejoice when I can be relieved from this task by the
population of this place becoming such proficients in the
principles and practises of the social system, as to be enabled to carry it on successfully without my aid and assistance." " I now live," said Mr. Owen in closing, " but to
see this system established in the world."

This first address of Robert Owen at New Harmony was
received with enthusiasm. The strong personality of Mr.
Owen impressed itself vividly upon the inhabitants. " He
is an extraordinary man," wrote W. Pelham to his son, W.
C. Pelham, " a wonderful man—such a one, indeed, as the
world has never before seen. His wisdom, his comprehensive mind, his practical knowledge, but above all, his open-
ness, candor, and sincerity, have no parallel in ancient or
modern history."

On May 1, 1825, the " Preliminary Society of New Harmony " was formed and the constitution proposed by Robert Owen on April 27th was adopted. This constitution
is so complete an exposition of the purposes of the Owenite communists, and so fully sets forth the scheme of government devised for " the half-way house between the old
system and the new," that it is worth reproducing in its
entirety. The constitution is preceded by the statement:
" The society is instituted generally to promote the happiness of the world," and continues as follows:

" This Preliminary Society is particularly formed to improve the character and conditions of its own members, and to prepare them to become associates in independent communities, having common property.

" The sole objects of these communities will be to procure for all their members the greatest amount of happiness, to secure it to them, and to transmit it to their children to the latest posterity.

" Persons of all ages and descriptions, exclusive of persons of color, may become members of the Preliminary Society. Persons of color may be received as helpers to the society, if necessary; or it may be found useful to prepare and enable them to become associates in communities in Africa, or in some other country, or in some other part of this country.

" The members of the Preliminary Society are all of the same rank, no artificial inequality being acknowledged; precedence to be given only to age and experience, and to those who may be chosen to offices of trust and utility.

" As the proprietor of the settlement, and founder of the system, has purchased the property, paid for it, and furnished the capital, and has consequently subjected himself to all the risk of the establishment, it is necessary for the formation of the system, and for its security, that he should have the appointment of the committee which is to direct and manage the affairs of the society.

" This committee will conduct all the affairs of the society. It will be, as much as possible, composed of men of experience and integrity, who are competent to carry the system into effect, and to apply impartial justice to all the members of the society.

" The number of the committee will be augmented from time to time, according as the proprietor may secure the assistance of other valuable members.

" At the termination of one year from the establishment of the settlement, which shall be dated from the first day of May, the members of the society shall elect, by ballot, from among themselves, three additional members of the committee. Their election is for the purpose of securing to all the members a full knowledge of the proceedings of the committee, and of the business of the society; but it is delayed for one year, in order to afford time for the formation of the society, and to enable the members to become acquainted with the characters and abilities of those who are proper to be elected.

" It is expected that at the termination of the second year, or between that period and the end of the third year, an association of members may be formed to constitute a community of equality and independence to be governed according to the rules and regulations contained in the printed paper entitled Mr. Owen's Plan for the Permanent Relief of the Working Classes, with such alterations as experience may suggest and the localities of the situation may require.

" The independent community will be established upon property purchased by the associated members.

" The Preliminary Society will continue to receive members preparatory to their removal into other independent communities.

" Every individual, previous to admission as a member, must sign the constitution, which signature shall be regularly witnessed. The members must join the society at their own expense.

" The society shall not be answerable for the debts of any of its members, nor in any manner for their conduct, no partnership whatsoever existing between the members of the Preliminary Society.

" The members shall occupy the dwellings which the committee may provide for them.

" The live stock possessed by members will be taken

and placed to their credit, if wanted for the society, but if not required, it shall not be received.

" All members must provide their own household and kitchen furniture, and their small tools, such as spades, hoes, axes, rakes, etc., and they may bring such provisions as they have already provided.

" All the members shall willingly render their best services for the good of the society, according to their age, experience, and capacity, and if inexperienced in that which is requisite for its welfare, they shall apply themselves diligently to acquire the knowledge of some useful occupation or employment.

" They shall enter the society with a determination to promote its peace, prosperity, and harmony, and never, under any provocation whatever, act unkindly or unjustly toward, nor speak in an unfriendly manner of, any one either in or out of the society.

" Members shall be temperate, regular, and orderly in their whole conduct, and they shall be diligent in their employments, in proportion to their age, capacity, and constitution.

" They shall show a good example, it being a much better instructor than precept.

" They shall watch over, and endeavor to protect, the whole property from every kind of injury.

" The members shall receive such advantages, living, comfort, and education for their children as this society and the present state of New Harmony affords.

" The living shall be upon equal terms for all, with the exceptions hereafter to be mentioned.

" In old age, in sickness, or when an accident occurs, care shall be taken of all parties, medical aid shall be afforded, and every attention shown to them that kindness can suggest.

" Each member shall, within a fixed amount in value, have the free choice of food and clothing; to effect this, a credit (to be hereafter fixed by the committee), will be opened in the store for each family, in proportion to the number of its useful members, also for each single member, but beyond this amount, no one will be permitted to draw on credit. The exceptions to this rule are the following, to wit:

" 1. When the proprietor of the establishment shall deem it necessary for the promotion of the system, and the interest and improvement of the society, to engage scientific and experienced persons to superintend some of the most difficult, useful, or responsible situations, at a fixed salary, then such individuals shall have a credit upon the store in proportion to their income.

" 2. When any peculiar or unforeseen case may arise, a general meeting of all the members shall be called by the committee, who shall state the particulars of the case to the meeting; the members present shall deliberate upon the subject, and give their vote by ballot, and the question shall be decided by the majority.

" Each family and individual member shall have a credit and debit account, in which they will be charged with what they receive, at the prices the Harmonists usually received for the same articles and credits by the value of their services, to be estimated by the committee, assisted by the persons at the head of the departments in which the respective individuals may be employed; the value of their services over their expenditure shall be placed at the end of each year to their credit in the books of the society, but no part of this credit shall be drawn out, except in the productions of the establishment, or in store goods, and with the consent of the committee.

" Members may visit their friends, or travel whenever they please, provided the committee can conveniently supply their places in the departments in which they may be respectively employed.

" To enable the members to travel, they will be supplied

with funds to half the amount placed to their credit, not, however, exceeding one hundred dollars in any one year, unless the distance they have to travel from home exceeds six hundred miles.

" Members may receive their friends to visit them, provided they be answerable that such visitors, during their stay, do not transgress the rules of the society.

" The children will be located in the best possible manner in day-schools, and will board and sleep in their parents' houses. Should any members, however, prefer placing their children in the boarding-school, they must make a particular and individual engagement with the committee; but no members shall be permitted to bind themselves nor their children to the society for a longer period than one week.

" All the members shall enjoy complete liberty of conscience, and be afforded every facility for exercising those practises of religious worship and devotion which they may prefer.

" Should the arrangements formed for the happiness of the members fail to effect their object, any of them, by giving a week's notice, can quit the society, taking with them, in the productions of the establishment, the value of what they brought, which value shall be ascertained and fixed by the committee. The members may also, in the same manner, take out the amount of what appears to their credit in the books of the society, at the end of the year immediately preceding their removal, provided that amount still remain to their credit.

" Any families or members contravening any of the articles of this constitution, or acting in any way improperly, shall be dismissed by the committee from the society and settlement, upon giving them the same notice by which they are at liberty to quit the society.

" Persons who possess capital, and who do not wish to be employed, may partake of the benefits of this society, by paying such sum annually as may be agreed upon between them and the committee, always paying a quarter in advance.

" Persons wishing to invest capital on interest in the funds of the society may do so by making a particular agreement with the committee."

After the adoption of this constitution, Robert Owen addressed the meeting. At the end of the second year, he declared, the members might choose one-half of the committee of control. The next step, which might be taken in the following year, would be the establishment of the perfect community. He recommended that each family consume, so far as possible, " those articles which are the productions of America," so that the society might speedily become independent. He urged that wherever it was possible vegetable gardens be attached to the household premises, and that the dwellings, inside and out, be kept neat and clean. All differences between the members should be settled by arbitration, and all disputes, quarreling, and drunkenness were to be strictly prohibited. It was his desire " to forbid the use of liquors altogether," but he considered " such rigor impracticable for the present." The youth were to be organized into militia companies and drilled for healthful exercise and defense, but children were to be taught that war was contrary to the spirit of the social system.

Though many of the less competent desired to enter at once into communistic association, there were no immediate manifestations of dissatisfaction at the adoption of a temporary semiindividual system. While the power of naming the entire membership of the committee of control was vested in Robert Owen, he contented himself with designating four members, who, with the rest, were elected by the society. Little over a month after the formation of the Preliminary Society, Mr. Owen left New Harmony, *en*

90

route for New Lanark, with the intention of bringing his family to Indiana. He embarked for Liverpool from New York on July 17, 1825, and did not return to New Harmony until the following January. Before leaving, he recommended that the inhabitants meet together three evenings in each week—one for the general discussion of subjects connected with the welfare of the community, another for a concert of vocal and instrumental music, and a third for a public ball. He left a school of one hundred and thirty children, who were educated, clothed, and boarded at the public expense. Mr. Maclure did not remain at New Harmony, but, during the greater part of the lifetime of the experiment, was traveling for his health.

CHAPTER X

"THE HALF-WAY HOUSE"

DURING the absence of Robert Owen in Europe, the New Harmony Gazette, the official organ of the community, was established. Its first issue is dated October 1, 1825, and bears the motto: "If we can not reconcile all opinions, let us endeavor to unite all hearts." The prospectus stated: "In our Gazette, we purpose developing more fully the principles of the social system, that the world, with ourselves, may, by contrast, be convinced that individuality detracts largely from the sum of human happiness." "Although our columns will ever be closed against personal invective," stated the prospectus, "yet they will ever be open to the free expression of opinions, which, however erroneous, may become useful, where reason and truth are left free to combat them." The publication continued through three volumes. Like all its contemporaries of that period, the Gazette devoted little space to what we now denominate local news. Its columns were filled with essays on such subjects as Moral Responsibility and Human Happiness, alternating with selections from Mr. Owen's works, dissertations on agricultural topics, scientific articles, and such general news as might come to the attention of the editor through the medium of exchanges which could not be called recent by the time the river boat or overland carrier had delivered them at New Harmony, which had only a weekly mail service. The more important events at New Harmony are, however, recorded, and from the pages of the Gazette we must draw

the larger part of our information concerning the active
community history.

In one of the first numbers of the Gazette appears an
official View of New Harmony, and a review of the work
accomplished by the society during the first six months
of settlement. " The village," says the Gazette, " is regularly laid out in squares, forming four streets running north
and south, and six running east and west: the whole included in six wards, containing thirty-five brick, forty-five
frame, and one hundred log buildings, occupied for various
purposes. Some of the buildings are spacious and costly,
the principal of which are the town-hall, the mansion-
house, formerly occupied by Mr. Rapp, the public store and
manufactories, the boarding-school, and several large boarding-houses for the accommodation of the members of the
society. Great uniformity of structures is observed in the
dwelling-houses, which have an air of neatness, although
small, and inconvenient for families accustomed to a city
life." Of the town-hall, heretofore described as the Rappite church, the Gazette said: " The whole building has a
grand and imposing appearance. The second stories of
two of the wings are laid off into small rooms, which serve
for music, reading, debating, and other social meetings.
The large lower room is appropriated to deliberative assemblages of the citizens, to balls and concerts, and is lighted
up every evening for the convenience of those who may
choose to pass the time together. The church is a neat
frame building, painted white, the spire of which is furnished with two heavy bells, and is set apart for religious
meetings, and for day and evening schools, to which every
member desirous of elementary instruction has access. The
boarding-school is a convenient, airy, three-story brick
building, ninety feet by sixty-five, and contains accommodations for one hundred and sixty children. The institution is at present under a favorable organization, and the
number of pupils amounts to upward of one hundred."

"Manufactures and trades," continued the Gazette, "are among the leading objects to which associations formed on the cooperative plan should turn their attention, for in no other way can a desirable state of independence be secured. The experience of our predecessors convinced them of this fact, and they have left behind them respectable evidences of their devotion to these two branches of industry. Their principal manufacturing establishment consisted of two spacious buildings, one occupied as a merchandise-mill, and the other filled with machinery for manufacturing cotton and wool, all driven by a steam-engine of sixty horse-power. The weaving, dressing, and dye-houses are built on an extensive and convenient plan, calculated for operations far exceeding the wants of the society. The cloths and flannels hitherto produced at this place have been in high reputation throughout the country. The present society has a no less cheering prospect before them in their capacity of growing to any extent the raw materials of cotton and wool than in their means of prosecuting the manufacture of these articles, equal to the consumption of themselves and their neighbors.

"The mechanical branches possess the requisite facilities for carrying on their respective trades, in workshops and tools, and include an extensive brewery, tan-yard, soap and candle factory, etc., but an accession of skilful hands in nearly all these branches of industry, as well as in some other departments, is still desirable. No fears, however, are entertained that these wants will long remain unsupplied, if an opinion can be formed from the daily applications for admission to membership which the society is and has been under the necessity of rejecting through want of suitable accommodations. In future, or until such accommodations can be provided, no applications can meet with success, except from those who possess a knowledge of the most useful and indispensable arts.

"Our manufacturing and mechanical branches may be

considered in a state of infancy. Notwithstanding the purchase included most things necessary for prosecuting them on a pretty extensive scale, yet we have had no good cause to calculate even on the limited degree of success which has attended them. The commencement of this society may be dated on the first of May last, two months previous to which time our Mr. Owen, with a few exceptions, was an entire stranger to the persons now composing his new association. The transatlantic concerns of our founder left him but little time for completing his arrangements here, and a population of eight hundred persons was, in the short space of three weeks, drawn together, necessarily without much deliberation, or any reference to their professional skill or immediate usefulness. This state of things left us but little to expect from their ability to carry on successfully the multifarious operations necessary for the continuance and comfort of so large a population. Under these and many other unfavorable circumstances, our manufactories have been at work since the middle of June. With the machinery now in hand, our operations in the wool business should turn out one hundred and sixty pounds of yarn per day, but the want of spinners reduces the business. The frilling and dressing departments have, at present, neither regular superintendents nor workmen, consequently they are not prosecuted with effect. The cotton-spinning establishment is equal to producing between three and four hundred pounds of yarn per week, and is under very good direction, but skilful and ready hands are much wanting, which time will furnish from our present population. The dye-house is a spacious brick building, furnished with copper vessels, capable of containing between fifteen hundred and two thousand gallons, and will probably compare in convenience with any in the United States. At present this valuable establishment is doing nothing for want of a skilful person to undertake the direction of it. The manufacture of soap, candles, and glue has hitherto rather exceeded our consumption. A convenient and moderately extensive ropewalk has furnished the store with articles of that trade. The hat-manufactory is under good organization, and has attached to it eight efficient workmen. The boot and shoe department is doing well, seventeen workmen being constantly employed. Besides these, in the employed professions, are thirty-six farmers and field laborers, four tanners, two gardeners, two butchers, two bakers, two distillers, one brewer, one tinner, two watchmakers, four black and white smiths, two turners, one machine-maker, four coopers, three printers, one stocking-weaver, three sawyers, seven tailors, twelve seamstresses and mantua-makers, nine carpenters, four bricklayers, two stonecutters, four wheelwrights, one cabinet-maker and three cloth-weavers. Of the unemployed professions we have three tobacconists and two paper-makers. The pottery is doing nothing for want of hands, and we have at present neither saddlers, harness-makers, leather-dressers, coppersmiths, brush-makers, comb-makers, glaziers, painters, nor bookbinders.

"The merchant-mill, driven by water, at the cut-off (beside the one in the village operated by steam), is a large establishment, having three sets of stones, and complete fixtures for the manufacture of flour, and is capable of turning out sixty barrels in twenty-four hours. One mile from the town is a sawmill capable of furnishing an unlimited quantity of lumber." Evidently both these establishments were still lying idle, as their operation is not mentioned. "A cotton-gin of sixty saws is at this time in active operation, doing a good business for the society as well as for the surrounding country. We have a well-supplied apothecary shop, under the direction of a highly respectable physician, who gives his attendance and dispenses medicine without charge to the citizens.

"The mercantile store is doing an extensive business with the country, while it supplies all the inhabitants with all their necessaries. The tavern, which is large, commodious, and well regulated, is much frequented by strangers, who are attracted to visit us either through curiosity or from a desire to partake of our social amusements."

" In taking a survey of New Harmony," said the Gazette of October 22d, " the mind is struck with a degree of admiration at the appearance, which designates the progress of its late industrious inhabitants, both in the arts of life and in their progress toward a more perfect state of society. Here, the rude log cabin marks their first humble efforts, there the neat frame house bespeaks their improvement in taste and skill; again, their spacious, substantial community houses tell us of their ability to supply an increase of comforts, and the public buildings exhibit a great amount of surplus labor and skill. The two spacious granaries, calculated to lay up stores for the consumption of years, are among the most prominent objects of the place. One is a four-storied frame, one hundred feet by eighty; the other is a vast building of brick and stone, with a tiled roof, and having five floors laid with tile brick. From its strength and appearance, it might have been taken for a fortress rather than a storehouse for grain. The public buildings are calculated to attract the attention of strangers who visit the place, as much from the novelty of design as from the amount of labor and materials consumed in their construction."

The Gazette also stated that the river abounded in fish, " of the description usually found in the western waters. We think our neighborhood is not infected with mischievous animals. Of the panther, the bear, and the fox we have heard nothing. Wolves are said to depredate on our pigs and calves when running in retired forests. Deer are often seen bounding over our fields, and browsing on our corn. Numbers of fawns are offered for sale on our streets during the spring months."

Under date of October 10th, a member of the society

wrote to a friend in Boston: "The society has not been long enough together to acquire any particular character: you can judge yourself that a collection of individuals from all parts of the earth, of all kinds, sects, and denominations, who have hastily rushed together, can have no character as yet, except indeed the absence of one. If this is not strictly true, the exceptions to it are that the people generally show a disposition to do as well as they know how, and to learn to do as much better as they can, which is all that appears to be expected by those who have the burdens to bear." Another letter from a member to an eastern friend, under date of October 30th, stated that "so far, domestic quarrels, disputes between individual members, and religious and political controversies are unknown, at least they are so very infrequent as to be unknown to the writer, probably because we have no opposing interests to generate quarrels; and also because there is no such thing, under the new system, as an insult; every man speaks according to the impression which dictates his words, and all impressions are made upon him by the exercise of faculties over which he has no control."

The Gazette of October 29th contains the following review of the condition of the community affairs:

"Every State in the Union, with the exception of the two most southern, and almost every country in the north of Europe, has contributed to make up our population. We may readily conceive that a population collected from so many different countries, and of different habits and opinions, possessing no common ties of interest or sympathy, could not immediately coalesce nor present to the observer any marked prevailing character.

"In comparing the moral condition of our citizens with the state of the old society, we are struck with the degree of advantage which the former has over the latter; and the mind, accounting for the difference, is involuntarily directed in search of some new principle. Here, social

98

intercourse is not disturbed by conflicting interests, nor the long catalogue of bad feelings generated by them, but every man meets his neighbor with honest confidence.

"This society regards education as public property, . . . and holds that the educating and training of youth should be among the first objects of its solicitude and care. . . . Well-regulated amusements should be no less a part of the business of life than other occupations, but this important object has hitherto been mostly directed by chance: in consequence, immorality and disorder have to a great extent prevailed. . . . This society has made it its especial care to blend amusements with industry and study. Tuesday evenings are appropriated to balls, at which we have an able band of music, and a general attendance of the youthful population: Friday evenings to concerts, at which, in addition to the regular band, such of the children as have musical talent are introduced. On Wednesday evening, public meetings are held, when all subjects relating to the well-being of the society are freely and fully discussed.

"The military of this place consists of one company of infantry, one of artillery, and a corps of riflemen, which together with a company of veterans, and one of riflemen just forming, will amount to two hundred and fifty soldiers; thus, while the people provide for their own protection against the social ills of life, they do not neglect the means of national defense.

"From a review of the circumstances existing at this place, our readers will now perceive that if we have not yet been able to accomplish all the objects contemplated in the formation of this association, so much has, however, been completed, as to convince us of the practicability and assure us of the ultimate success of Mr. Owen's plans for the amelioration of the condition of mankind."

On November 7th occurred the installation of officers of the first secret society in the community—The New

Harmony Philanthropic Lodge of Masons, showing that Mr. Owen's plans did not contemplate the abolition of secret societies. In the Gazette of that date, this announcement is made: " The Regular Meeting of the Female Social Society is postponed until Monday evening." There is no earlier record of a woman's club. The first marriage in the community recorded by the Gazette was that of " Mr. Alfred Salmon to Miss Elizabeth S. Palmer," which took place on October 27th, the ceremony being performed by a minister of the gospel named Meek. In spite of the inauguration of the social system, the New Harmony store was advertising magistrates' blanks.

In an early October issue of the Gazette appeared a communication signed " An Illinois Farmer," in which he declared, " in the most unequivocal manner," that " the principles of Robert Owen, or any society founded upon them, will not and can not succeed. They will at the outset commit suicide on themselves, if steadily adhered to." The editor remonstrated with the correspondent, and assured him of the present and future success of the community. In reply to a further communication the Gazette said editorially: " We would inform the Illinois Farmer, in answer to his second communication on dancing, that we suffer not our amusements to interfere with our regular employments; but, after the fatigue of the day, when we can not see to handle a plow, we consider ourselves at perfect liberty to devote our evenings to intellectual improvement or to any rational recreation."

In an editorial advocating increased rights for women, the Gazette declared: " It is, we believe, contemplated in Mr. Owen's system, by giving our female population as good an education as our males, to qualify them for every situation in life in which, consistently with their organization, they may be placed."

As early as September 19, 1825, the first society formed on Robert Owen's principles, other than that at New Harmony, was in process of organization in Green County, Ohio. This society was called the Yellow Springs community, and a correspondent writes the Gazette hopefully of its progress.

While New Harmony was generally looked upon as a center of infidelity, there were frequent religious services. there. The only reservation made with regard to the use of the church was that two hours on Sunday morning were occupied by a lecture on the social system, " the lecturer confining his remarks to subjects calculated to suppress discord and vice, and studiously avoiding anything that might arouse ill feeling or wound the religious prejudices of his hearers." There was a wide-spread prejudice against the New Harmony schools on account of a belief that atheistic principles were taught. Religious matters, however, were not discussed in the schools, " that being left to the parents or religious instructors." Permission to speak at the church was given to any minister who asked it, " his creed not being asked." Sunday in the community was a day of rest, and to most of the members of the society a day of recreation.

By Christmas of 1825, the population of New Harmony numbered about one thousand. The Gazette published a review of the operations of the society, in which it congratulated the members on their advancement in the direction of unity and harmony, which it declared had been effected by reducing Mr. Owen's principles to practise. " Popular opinion being now decidedly opposed to indolence and vice, the idle member must become industrious, and the vicious become more virtuous, or they can not rest contentedly in the bosom of our community."

Robert Owen had arrived with his party at New York on November 7th, but remained for some time in the East pushing the new propaganda. A Washington paper of December 5th stated: " On Saturday last, Captain McDonald and Stedman Whitwell, friends of Mr. Owen, and deputed by him, waited by appointment upon the President, and presented to him for the use of the general government a model of one of the cities for two thousand people, which Mr. Owen proposes to execute himself, and which he recommends to be universally adopted in society. The model is almost six feet square, and is, therefore, upon a scale sufficiently large to exhibit satisfactorily the various descriptions of buildings and their relative dimensions."

On December 28th, the Gazette said: " From the numerous applications which we have received for membership; from the rapidity with which the liberal principles of the social system are embraced by intelligent and reflecting minds, and from the general disposition, wherever they have been received, toward reducing them to practise, and from the number of social communities springing up in this State, independent of every advantage offered to individual settlers, we have reason to believe that the increase in population will be greater than at any former period; and were it possible to accommodate the applicants with houses, this little town, before the next sitting of the legislature, would have an increase of many times its present population."

CHAPTER XI

THE " PERMANENT COMMUNITY "

The devil at length scrambled out of the hole
Discovered by Symmes at the freezing North Pole:
    He mounted an iceberg, spread his wings for a sail,
    And started for earth with his long, barbed tail.

He heard that a number of people were going
To live on the Wabash with great Mr. Owen:
    He said to himself, " I must now have a care,
    Circumstances require that myself should be there.

" I know that these persons think they are impelled,
And by power of circumstance all men are held,
    And owe no allegiance to heaven or me:
    What a place this for work for the devil will be.

" Since Adam first fell by my powerful hand,
I have wandered for victims through every known land,
    But in all my migrations ne'er hit on a plan
    That would give me the rule so completely o'er man.

" I have set sects to fighting and shedding of blood,
And have whispered to bigots they're all doing good,
    Inquisitions I've founded, made kings my lies swallow,
    But this plan of free living beats all my schemes hollow

" I have tempted poor Job, and have smote him with sores:
I have tried all good men, and caught preachers by scores,
    But never on earth, through my whole course of evil,
    Until now could I say, ' Here's a plan beats the devil.'

" I am satisfied now this will make the coast clear,
For men to all preaching will turn a deaf ear:
    Since it's plain that religion is changed to opinions,
    I must hasten back home, and enlarge my dominions."

The devil then mounted again on the ice,
And dashed through the waves, and got home in a trice,
    And told his fell imps whom he kept at the pole
    Circumstances required they should widen the hole!

—*Poem in opposition to the Owen community in the Philadelphia Gazette,* January, 1826.

103

THE NEW HARMONY MOVEMENT

On January 18, 1826, Robert Owen, with his "boat-load of knowledge," arrived again at New Harmony. He was greeted with great rejoicing by the inhabitants, the children from the boarding-school escorting him from the limits of the village to the tavern. Robert Owen was delighted with the apparent success of the society, and declared that the people had progressed far toward the conditions necessary for the formation of a perfect community. The people generally believed that the arrival of their leader, with his party of "wise men from the East," would rally all retreat and lead on to victory. Under Mr. Owen's practised hand the idle factories would soon be in full operation and all the projected plans of the founder, including the building of his new village of unity and cooperation, would soon be undertaken. The educational feature of the experiment was certain to receive a great impetus from the accession of such a corps of scholars as that which had accompanied Mr. Owen from New York. Mr. Owen was enthusiastic and optimistic, as well as anxious for the immediate trial of his ultimate plans. One week after his arrival, he announced that in consideration of the progress which had been made, the Preliminary Society would be cut off two years before its time, and a community of perfect equality inaugurated. "I think my father must have been as well pleased with the condition of things at New Harmony as I myself was," writes Robert Dale Owen. "At all events . . . he disclosed to me his intention to propose to the Harmonites that they should form themselves into a community of equality, based on the principle of common property. This took me by surprise."

On the 25th of January, 1826, it was resolved in a meeting of the Preliminary Society to organize a Community of Equality from among the members of the society. The meeting resolved itself into a constitutional convention, which was organized by the election of

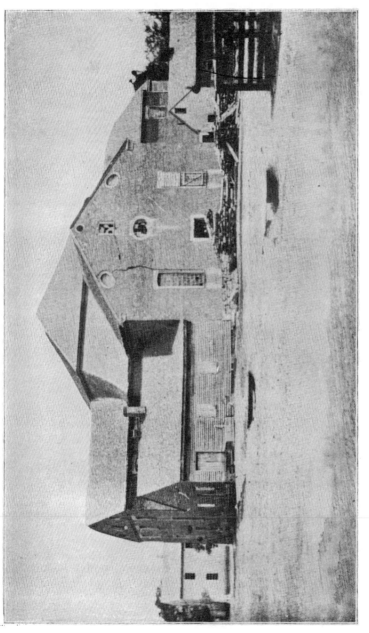

THE RAPPITE CHURCH AND HALL OF HARMONY.

Dr. Philip M. Price as president and Thomas Pears as secretary. A committee of seven was chosen by ballot to frame a draft of the constitution to be submitted at a future meeting of the convention.

The following named persons were chosen: Warner W. Lewis, James O. Wattles, John Whitby, William Owen, Donald McDonald, R. L. Jennings, and Robert Dale Owen. On February 1st this committee made its report, which was vigorously debated through several sessions, several substitute plans being submitted by members of the convention. At the sixth session, the whole subject was submitted to the committee for revision. "The committee again reported at the seventh session," says the Gazette, "and the constitution proposed, after having undergone several alterations and amendments, was at the ninth session of the convention, held on Sunday evening, February 5th, formally adopted."

The constitution was preceded by an interesting and comprehensive declaration of principles. "When a number of the human family associate in principles which do not yet influence the rest of the world," stated the preamble, "a due regard to the opinions of others requires a public declaration of the object of their association, of their principles, and of their intentions." The "Declaration" continued:

"Our object is that of all sentient beings, happiness.

"Our principles are:

"Equality of rights, uninfluenced by sex or condition, in all adults.

"Equality of duties, modified by physical and mental conformation.

"Cooperative union, in the business and amusements of life.

"Community of property.

"Freedom of speech and action.

" Sincerity in all our proceedings.

" Kindness in all our actions.

" Courtesy in all our intercourse.

" Order in all our arrangements.

" Preservation of health.

" Acquisition of knowledge.

" The practise of economy, or of producing and using the best of everything in the most beneficial manner.

" Obedience to the laws of the country in which we live.

" We hold it to be self-evident:

" That man is uniformly actuated by a desire of happiness.

" That no member of the human family is born with rights either of possession or exemption superior to those of his fellows.

" That freedom in the sincere expression of every sentiment and opinion, and in the direction of every action, is the inalienable right of each human being, and can not justly be limited except by his own consent.

" That the preservation of life, in its most perfect state, is the first of all practical considerations.

" And that, as we live in the State of Indiana, submission to its laws and to those of the general government is necessary.

" Experience has taught us:

" That man's character, mental, moral, and physical, is the result of his formation, his location, and of the circumstances within which he exists.

" And that man, at birth, is formed unconsciously to himself, is located without his consent, and circumstanced without his control.

" Therefore, man's character is not of his own formation, and reason teaches us that to a being of such nature, artificial rewards and punishments are equally inapplicable; kindness is the only consistent mode of treatment, and courtesy the only rational species of deportment.

" We have observed, in the affairs of the world, that man is powerful in action, efficient in production, and happy in social life, only as he acts cooperatively and unitedly.

" Cooperative union, therefore, we consider indispensable to the attainment of our object.

" We have remarked that where the greatest results have been produced by cooperative union, order and economy were the principal means of their attainment.

" Experience, therefore, places order and economy among our principles.

" The departure from the principle of man's equal rights, which is exhibited in the arrangement of individual property, we have seen succeeded by competition and opposition, by jealousy and dissension, by extravagance and poverty, by tyranny and slavery.

" Therefore we revert to the principle of community of property.

" Where the will and the power exist, the result produced is proportioned to the knowledge of the agent; and in practise we have found that an increase of intelligence is equally an increase of happiness.

" We seek intelligence, therefore, as we seek happiness itself.

" As the first and most important knowledge, we desire to know ourselves.

" But we search for this knowledge in vain if our fellow creatures do not express to us openly and unreservedly what they feel and think.

" Our knowledge remains imperfect, therefore, without sincerity.

" We have seen misery produced by the great leading principles which prevail over the world; therefore we have not adopted them.

" We have always found truth productive of happiness and error of misery: truth, therefore, leads to our object, and we agree to follow truth only.

" Truth is consistent, and in unison with all facts: error is inconsistent, and opposed to facts.

" Our reason has convinced us of the theoretical truth of our principles—our experience, of their practical utility.

" For these reasons—with this object—and on these principles, we, the undersigned, form ourselves and our children into a society and Community of Equality, for the benefit of ourselves and our children and of the human race, and do agree to the following articles of union and cooperation."

The official name of the community was to be " The New Harmony Community of Equality." " All members of the community shall be considered as one family, and no one shall be held in higher or lower estimation on account of occupation. There shall be similar food, clothing, and education, as near as can be furnished, for all according to their ages; and, as soon as practicable, all shall live in similar houses, and in all respects be accommodated alike. Every member shall render his or her best services for the good of the whole, according to the rules and regulations that may be hereafter adopted by the community. It shall always remain a primary object of the community to give the best physical, moral, and intellectual education to all its members.

" The power of making laws shall be vested in the assembly," consisting of " all the resident members of the community above the age of twenty-one years, one-sixth of whom shall be necessary to constitute a quorum for the transaction of business. The executive power of the community shall be vested in a council, to consist of the secretary, treasurer, and commissary of the community, and four superintendents of departments to be chosen as hereinafter provided. The secretary, treasurer, and commissary shall be elected by the assembly."

" The community shall be divided into six departments: Of agriculture; of manufactures and mechanics; of literature, science, and education; of domestic economy; of general economy; of commerce. These departments shall be divided into occupations. The individuals of each occupation, above sixteen years of age, shall nominate to the assembly for confirmation, their intendent, and the intendents of each occupation, which shall consist of three or more persons, shall nominate the superintendent of their own department; provided, that the commissary shall be superintendent of the department of domestic economy, and the treasurer of the department of commerce; and for the purpose of nominating superintendents the department of commerce shall be united to the department of literature, science, and education, and the department of domestic economy to that of general economy." Where nominations fail of confirmation by the assembly, new nominations must be made. " The secretary, superintendents, and intendents shall hold their offices during the pleasure of the assembly."

It was made the duty of the executive council to make all contracts, to carry into effect all general regulations, and generally to conduct and superintend all the concerns of the community, subject at all times to directions expressed by a majority in the assembly, and communicated in writing by the clerk of the assembly to the secretary.

" The executive council shall also report weekly to the assembly all the proceedings, accounts, receipts, and expenditures of each department and occupation, and their opinion of the character of each intendent, and the intendents' opinion of the daily character of each person attached to their occupation. All the accounts of the community shall be balanced at least once in each week, and the results communicated to the assembly. All the reports of the superintendents and of the secretary, and all the transactions of the assembly, shall be registered and carefully kept for perpetual reference. The assembly shall also register weekly its opinion of the executive council, and the council in like manner its opinions of the proceedings of the assembly.

"No person shall hereafter be admitted a member of this community without the consent of a majority of all the members of the assembly; and no person shall be dismissed from the community but by a vote of two-thirds of all the members of the assembly; and, in neither instance, until the subject shall have been discussed at two successive weekly meetings.

"The real estate of the community shall be held in perpetual trust forever for the use of the community and all its members, for the time being; and every person leaving the community shall forfeit all claim thereto or interest therein, but shall be entitled to receive his or her just proportion of the value of such real estate acquired during the time of his membership, to be estimated and determined as is provided in cases of settlement for the services of members so leaving the community.

"Each member shall have the right of resignation of membership on giving the community one week's notice of his or her intention; and when any member shall so leave the community, or shall be dismissed therefrom, he shall be entitled to receive, in proper products of the community, such compensation for previous services as justice shall require, to be determined by the council, subject to an appeal to the assembly, respect being had to the gains or losses of the community during the time of his membership, as well as to the expenses of the individual and of his or her family for education or otherwise."

The community was not to be responsible for individual debts contracted by members. "No credit shall, on any account, be given or received by the community or its agent or agents except for such property or money as may be advanced by Robert Owen, or William Maclure, or members of the community." Money brought into the community by members shall be returned to them on withdrawal from the society. "Every member shall enjoy the most perfect freedom on all subjects of knowledge and opinion, especially on the subject of religion. Children of deceased members shall continue to enjoy all the privileges of membership. All misunderstandings that may arise between members of the community shall be adjusted within the community.

"As this system is directly opposed to secrecy and exclusion of any kind, every practical facility shall be given to strangers to enable them to become acquainted with the regulations of the community, and to examine the results which these have produced in practise; and an unreserved explanation of the views and proceedings of the community shall be communicated to the government of the country.

"The constitution may be altered or amended by a vote of three-fourths of all the members of the assembly, but not until the subject has been discussed at four successive public meetings to be held in four successive weeks."

This was "liberty, equality, and fraternity in downright earnest," wrote Robert Dale Owen. "It found favor with that heterogeneous collection of radicals, enthusiastic devotees to principle, honest latitudinarians, and lazy theorists, with a sprinkling of unprincipled sharpers thrown in." Services to the community were no longer to be rewarded in proportion to their worth, as under the Preliminary Society, but equal privileges and advantages were assured to every member of the community. "I made no opposition to all this," says Robert Dale Owen. "I had too much of my father's all-believing disposition to anticipate results which any shrewd, cool-headed business man might have predicted. How rapidly they came upon us!"

CHAPTER XII

THE SOCIAL SYSTEM ON TRIAL

AFTER the adoption of the constitution of the Community of Equality, it was resolved that all members of the Preliminary Society signing the constitution within three days could, with their families, become members. Most of the members of the society signed the document, but a few refused to do so. The Gazette failed to state the exact cause of the defection, simply announcing that "a new community in friendly connection with the first is about to be formed on the estate of New Harmony, within a few miles of the town by some respectable families who were members of the Preliminary Society, but from conscientious motives have declined signing the new constitution." Among the members leaving at this time was Captain Donald McDonald, a disciple of Robert Owen, who had sufficient faith in the new principles to follow their author from Scotland to New Harmony. McDonald was one of the founders of the Edinburgh " Practical Society " of six hundred families which formed the nucleus of the famous Orbiston community. He accompanied Robert Owen to Ireland on one occasion when Mr. Owen was investigating the condition of the poor in that country. Evidently McDonald's self-esteem had been wounded in the discussions over the constitution, for he stated in a card published in the Gazette that he had not been accorded " the confidence he had looked for in the community." A further objection of his was that he " did not believe in a written constitution." The defection seems to have occurred, however, almost entirely on religious grounds. The new com-

112

munity, which was called Macluria, included some of the
best members of the Preliminary Society, many of whom
were not in sympathy with the religious latitudinarianism
of Robert Owen. Its constitution was largely modeled
after that of the parent community. A unanimous vote
was required for admission of a member, but any person
voted on could remain one month on trial for each blackball, if the number of these did not exceed twenty-five; a
larger number being cast against the applicant, he might
remain one month for every two blackballs. The legislative body, under the final direction of the assembly, was
called " The Council of the Fathers," which consisted of
the five oldest male members under the age of sixty-five
years. Women were denied the privilege of voting in the
assembly, though accorded in all other matters equal privileges with men. The system of intendents and superintendents contemplated in the constitution of the parent
community was perpetuated in the constitution of Macluria.

About the 15th of February, superintendents were
elected by the parent community as follows:

Agriculture: Dr. William Price.

Manufactures and Mechanics: J. K. Coolidge.

Literature, Science, and Education: Thomas Say.

General Economy: Stedman Whitwell.

Commerce: William Owen.

Secretary: W. W. Lewis.

On February 17th, six new families were admitted, but
matters were already in a state of anarchy. The constitution had failed to work effectively, and the disorder was
so general and so disastrous that on February 19th, two
weeks after the inauguration of the " permanent community," the executive committee unanimously requested
Mr. Owen to assume the directorship of the community
for one year. Practically a dictatorship was established,
although the constitution remained in effect. Mr. Owen

accepted the trust, and a brief period of comparative tranquillity and contentment ensued.

On February 22d, the Gazette stated that since the adoption of the constitution the community had been engaged in organizing the several departments and making such arrangements as were deemed necessary to effect the purposes of association. " Numerous meetings have been held, and various plans suggested to carry into practise the community principles. In a work of such magnitude, combining so many interests and such a variety of feeling, the progress already made affords a sure presage of the harmonious and efficient cooperation of all the members. Most of the community officers have now been elected."

Early in March the second offshooting society was formed, under the name of Feiba Peveli. The name of this community is an evidence that some of the philosophers who came to New Harmony did little else than to evolve fantastic schemes. As a sample of the imaginative productions of one of these oddities—Stedman Whitwell, a London architect and social reformer given to writing verses and planning community palaces on paper—the process by which the name of this community was secured is interesting. Whitwell noted some of the incongruities in American nomenclature, and deplored the repetition which was producing " Washingtons " and " Springfields " in every State in the Union. He proposed to give each locality a distinctive name by expressing in a compound word the latitude and longitude of the place, thus enabling one to locate any community geographically when the name was once known. Letters were proposed as substitutes for the numerals used in expressing latitude and longitude, as follows:

	1	2	3	4	5	6	7	8	9	0
Latitude	a	e	i	o	u	y	ee	ei	ie	ou
Longitude	b	d	f	k	l	m	n	p	r	t

The first part of the town name expressed the latitude, the second the longitude, by a substitution of letters for figures according to the above table. The letter " S " inserted in the latitude name denoted that it was south latitude, its absence that it was north, while " V " indicated west longitude, its absence east longitude. Extensive rules for pronunciation and for overcoming various difficulties were given. According to this system, Feiba Peveli indicated 38.11 N., 81.53 W. Macluria, 38.12 N., 87.52 W., was to be called Ipad Evenle; New Harmony, 38.11 N., 87.55 W., Ipba Veinul; Yellow Springs, Green County, Ohio, the location of an Owenite community, 39.48 N., 83.52 W., Irap Evifle; Valley Forge, near Philadelphia, where there was another branch community, 40.7 N., 75.24 W., Outeon Eveldo; Orbiston, 55.34 N., 4.3 W., Uhio Vouti; New York, Otke Notive; Pittsburg, Otfu Veitoup; Washington, Feili Neivul; London, Lafa Vovutu. The principal argument in favor of the new system presented by the author was that the name of a neighboring Indian chief, " Occoneocoglecococacachecachecodungo," was even worse than some of the effects produced by this "rational system " of nomenclature.

The constitution of Feiba Peveli contained a declaration of principles almost identical with that set forth in the parent constitution, while the plan of government coincided with that adopted by Macluria. The legislative power of the community was vested in its " male members over the age of twenty-one years." The executive duties were vested in the five eldest male members under the age of fifty-five years, " provided three of them shall be good, practical agriculturists." Managers, intendents, and clerks were to be appointed by this council, which in turn was responsible to the assembly. Any person applying for membership receiving no more than five blackballs might reside in the society as a probationary member one month for each blackball received. Arbitration was provided for not only between members of the community, but between Feiba Peveli and any other similar community. " No debt shall be contracted," the constitution declared, " but with Robert Owen and William Maclure, or some society based on similar principles with our own; and no credit shall be given but to some society instituted on similar principles."

" Since our last notice of the proceedings of the community," said the Gazette of March 8, 1826, " circumstances have occurred which have produced much animated and interesting debate. All minds seem now to comprehend the true grounds of future cooperation, and all hearts have united in claiming the benefit of Mr. Owen's experience and knowledge in reducing to practise the principles which form the basis of our association. General satisfaction and individual contentment have taken the place of suspense and uncertainty. Under the sole direction of Mr. Owen the most gratifying anticipations of the future may be indulged in, for knowledge and experience are the only safe guides through the intricacies of the untried system."

Considerable difficulty had arisen from a crowded population, but the formation of new communities began to relieve the congestion. Some inconvenience, the administration declared, must be endured until suitable accommodation could be procured for the members. On March 22d, the Gazette said: " The friends of the new social system will learn with pleasure that we are steadily advancing toward the firm final establishment of the principles of our association. It has been seen and sensibly felt that while we have been discussing the abstract ideas, while we have been in vain trying to reconcile contrary and clashing opinions, we have neglected the practical means within our reach which alone can bind man to his fellow men. In short, we have discovered that our energies have been wasted in fruitless efforts, each one endeavoring to convince others that he alone possessed the power of unlocking

116

the pleasures of social life. This error is happily dispelled. By the indefatigable attention of Mr. Owen, a degree of order, of regularity, of system, has been introduced into every department of business which promises increase and permanency. The town now presents a scene of active and steady industry, the effects of which are visible and palpable. The society is gradually becoming really as well as ostensibly a community of equality based on equal rights and equal duties of all. Our streets no longer present groups of idle talkers, and each one is busily engaged in the occupation he has chosen for his employment. Our public meetings, instead of being the arena of contending orators, have assumed a different character, and are now places of business, where familiar consultations are held, and the most efficient measures are adopted for the comforts of life for all the members. No vain disputes grate upon the ear of patient industry, and all seem strongly impressed with the importance of applying their powers to realize the object of cooperative association. During the past week there has been much done in this way, and there is every reason to believe that progress will not be impeded by idleness, listlessness, and erroneous views of our situation. It would indeed be strange if the experience gained by the greater part of the population during eleven months' schooling, with the aid of Mr. Owen's practical knowledge for the past eight weeks, should be lost upon us." On April 12th, the Gazette declared that "the formation of communities is now pretty generally understood among us, and is entered upon like a matter of ordinary business. The same thing will probably occur throughout the country."

Evidently the administration had begun to realize the impossibility of unifying the interests of any great number of persons associated in a community. The administration organ stated early in April that no more than twenty to thirty persons should form the basis of a community, for if the number be greater, the greater the chance of the members being uncongenial. As far as possible the operations of the society should be very simple and upon an agricultural basis. From this the communities could proceed to mechanical operations at a later date. The community should first make itself useful, and then proceed to the higher development of community life, such as education, etc. "No attempt to combine an unintelligible mass of discordant interests can result favorably unless it be under the direction of a mind, disposition, and talent long exerted in similar combinations."

The pages of the Gazette from this time on continue to reveal the difficulties encountered by the projectors of the social experiment at New Harmony. The numerous suggestions of new plans made by correspondents through the Gazette are evidence of considerable dissatisfaction among the community membership. "A Friendly Spectator" in the Gazette of April 19, 1826, expressed a belief that "the chief good of the community system is that it destroys the love of show and luxury. It also economizes time and enables a man to pay attention to his higher nature." "But," continued the writer, "it appears doubtful to me whether human nature can be brought to such moral perfection as to execute the social system entirely. There must be a controlling motive to urge men to physical exertion. He now has that in the possession of all that his work can give him. In the social system you must make his disposition so virtuous as to make him feel his responsibility. Can you do this?" While a man gains in moral freedom and independence under the new system, this correspondent remarked, he loses in personal liberty. He suggested that extra compensation be given for extra work, but that no one be allowed to spend his money to the loss of society; each person to do a fixed amount of work for his subsistence, and that no one be allowed at table until that assignment of labor had been performed. "You have indolence or the love of ease among you at New Harmony." There should be a uniformity of dress and diet, he declared, but each person should be allowed to choose his occupation; all children under eleven years of age should be busied alone with their education; at eleven the child should perform one-seventh of a day's work; at twelve, two-sevenths, and so on until at seventeen the full amount should be demanded from all.

The administration about this time published some "considerations" for those who desired to unite under the new system, as follows:

(1) It will be necessary to sink individual interests, and (2) to discard all useless and vexatious regulations; (3) persuasion, instead of force, must be employed; (4) there must be no abuse, growling, or loud talking, and (5) no grumbling, carping, or murmuring against the work of other individuals; those who shirk their work are deserving of pity; (6) distinctions in eating and drinking among the members must be discarded; (7) children must be excluded from the dining-room during meals; adult members should not stalk about the dining-hall during meals; (8) the intemperate must never be abused; (9) when individual members are "affected with the disease of laziness" the utmost forbearance will be necessary; (10) criticism should not be resented; (11) cleanliness and regularity must be enforced; (12) "no anger ought to be felt against the female members upon their aversion to the work of cooperation; or when they brawl, quarrel, or indulge in loud talk." The children, however, should be taught better. There is a strong undercurrent of suggestion in all this as to evils evidently existing in the community.

In April the community was disturbed by negotiations said to be going on for the purchase of the estate as private property. An attempt was made to divide the town into several communities. This Mr. Owen resisted, but selected twenty-five men as a nucleus, this body to elect new members, subject to veto by Mr. Owen. Three grades of membership were proposed: full members, probationary members, and persons on trial. "The community was to be under the direction of Mr. Owen, until two-thirds of the members should think fit to govern themselves, provided the time was not less than one year."

In the Gazette of May 17, 1826, appeared a contribution signed "M.," complaining that "industrious members have been compelled to experience the unpleasant sensation of working for others who are either unwilling or unable to do their share of the labor. An effort has been made to bring about a change in this," stated the contributor, "by individual reports of production and making public the number of hours each was occupied in the day, the practise of which was rather invidious, and difficult to be executed impartially; but even if it were possible to get correct returns, it was liable to work injustice, as one workman might do as much in one hour as another might in four." The correspondent suggested that it would be better to divide the members of the community into occupations, or departments, fixing the amount of work to be done by each occupation, and allowing the managers to distribute this amount of work among the individuals of each community. The quality and quantity of the work would be inspected by impartial judges. If it were impossible for the occupations to work together, they might be divided into separate communities, and they might federate into a joint community. "The population must be some time accustomed to the social system to be convinced that those who work with their heads are as productive as those who work with their hands, and it is equally difficult to reconcile a mechanic at one dollar and fifty cents or two dollars a day to putting himself on an equality with the agriculturist at a quarter of a dollar a day." The success of community Number 2, the members of which had been unable to work harmoniously with the original community, but who had progressed admirably since the separation, was pointed to as an indication that the change suggested would be advisable. A division into twenty or thirty societies was therefore suggested " as the best, and perhaps the only way to apportion the labor either justly or accurately, and to reduce the responsibility of payments within the sphere of the previous habits of calculation; education and amusements to remain upon the same footing as before."

In the spring of 1826 the Constitution of the Cooperative Association of Wainborough, Illinois, modeled after the New Harmony plan, was printed in the Gazette. This community was agricultural, and " based upon the principles of union of labor and capital." Food and clothing would be supplied to members of the society. An equal division of the proceeds of the labor and capital of the society should be made annually, after interest charges had been met, including a payment of four per cent on the advances of members contributing capital, ten per cent of the profit to be set apart for the purpose of paying the indebtedness of the society. After fourteen years members of the society should have a claim upon it for the full value of property or money contributed. The direction of the business affairs of the community was placed in the hands of a committee of three.

A correspondent of the Gazette, writing under date of May 24, 1826, suggested names for prospective societies, " as the sanguine friends of the cooperative system believe that in a few years hundreds, and even thousands, may be founded." Among the names offered for consideration were Lovedale, Peace Glen, Everblest, New Duty, Philosophy, Glee, Lovely, Voltaire, Elysium, Olympus, Platonea, Socrates, Utopia, Confucia, and Powhatan.

C. S. Raffinesque, writing from Lexington in April, 1826, to William Maclure, outlined " a plan for cooperative association," and the letter was published in the Gazette. " Money," he said, " is no longer to be a medium of exchange, but stocks, rendered divisible at pleasure *ad libitum* according to the principle of my patent divitial invention. . . . Any number of persons, from five to five thousand, may associate themselves into an organization; they to select trustees of the deposited stocks or sums invested. They shall place a value upon the property merged into the association. The product of material labor will also be received in store and in kind, while mental service done will be estimated according to their need, purposes, or utility to the association. The other forms of income will be received, appraisers to be appointed to determine the exchange value of everything. As soon as any value is deposited, there shall be given to the depositor, not by name, a certificate or certificates of the same upon the principle of the patent divitial invention, divisible into any required amount, and exchangeable into any other required amount, transferable and available by the bearer for their nominal value in dollars and cents. When any profitable value is deposited the certificates will bear four or five per cent interest. . . . These certificates shall be accepted in payment of accounts at the store, for rent or any other purpose. Everything will be exchanged at cost, but a commission of from two to five per cent shall be deducted to meet the general expenses of the society. The profits will be used for the benefit of the sick, the infirm, and other members unable to labor. Instruction and amusement will be provided, to be paid for in deposit tickets. General meetings and mutual intercourse will be provided, and the members shall consider themselves a great family. All books shall be deposited and considered as a public library. Although the mainspring of this scheme is my divitial invention, which I have patented in order to give to it a higher legal claim, it is my intention to allow these societies to use it at such a trifling rate as benevolent institutions, that I hope no selfish views will be ascribed to me on that score."

CHAPTER XIII

THE DUKE OF SAXE-WEIMAR AT NEW HARMONY

NEW HARMONY became an important point on the itinerary of European travelers, as well as a rendezvous of American scientists, early in 1826. Count Bernhard, of Weimar, Saxony, and Eisenach, better known as the Duke of Saxe-Weimar, who made a tour of this country in 1825 and 1826, and recorded his impressions in a published volume, gives a detailed account of what he saw in New Harmony, where he arrived on April 13, 1826. Count Bernhard states that he found Robert Owen and his ideas unpopular in the Eastern States, where he had created an unfavorable impression by publishing a proclamation to the Americans on his arrival at New York, in which he told them that "among many virtues they possessed great faults," among which he alluded to ill-directed propensity to religious feelings, and proposed himself as their reformer in this respect. One public man had told Mr. Owen that he considered his intellect deranged. He had heard favorable opinions of Mr. Owen expressed by those who knew him well, and with these conflicting estimates of the man, he came to New Harmony "with the utmost expectation and curiosity to become acquainted with a man of such extraordinary sentiments. In the tavern," wrote the duke, " I accosted a man, very plainly dressed, about fifty years of age, of rather low stature, who entered into a conversation with me concerning the situation of the place, and the disordered state in which I would find everything where all was newly

established. When I asked the man how long before Mr.
Owen would be there, he announced himself to me, to my
surprise, as Mr. Owen. He expressed pleasure at my visit,
and offered to show me everything and explain whatever
remained without explanation." Mr. Owen outlined his
plans for improving the place, which included the removal
of the cabins and the fences, "so that the whole would
present the appearance of a public park, in which the
houses should be scattered about." Mr. Owen first took his
distinguished guest to the old Rappite church, "the
wooden building provided with a steeple and a clock.
This church was at present occupied by joiners' and shoe-
makers' shops in which the boys were instructed in these
mechanical arts." Count Bernhard then visited the old
Rapp mansion, "now occupied by Mr. Maclure as a residence and office. . . . Mr. Owen, on the contrary,
contented himself with a small apartment in the same
tavern where I lodged."

The duke was introduced to Mr. Owen's two eldest sons
(William and Robert), "pupils of Fellenberg, who is
greatly respected here." . . . "Afterward Mr. Owen
made me acquainted with Mr. Lewis, secretary of the society, from Virginia, and a relative of the great Washington.
He was already pretty well advanced in years, and appeared
to have united himself with the society from liberal principles. Another acquaintance I made was with Mr. Jennings,
of Philadelphia, a young man who was educated as a clergy-
man, and had left the profession to follow this course of
life. He intended, nevertheless, to leave this place and go
back to Philadelphia; many other members have the same
design, and I can hardly believe the society will have a long
duration. Enthusiasm, which soon abandons its subjects,
as well as the itch for novelty, had contributed much to
the formation of this society. In spite of the principles of
equality which they recognized, it taxes the feelings to live
on the same footing with others indiscriminately, and eat

with them at the same table. The society consisted, as I was informed, of about one thousand members; at a distance of about two miles are founded two new communities. Until the common table shall be established, according to the fundamental constitution of the society, the members are placed in four boarding-houses, where they must live very frugally. Some of the most turbulent, with an Irishman who wore a long beard, wished to leave the society immediately to go to Mexico, there to settle themselves, but where their subsistence will be procured with much difficulty.

"In the evening, Mr. Owen took me to a concert in a sort of nondescript building. Most of the members of the society were present." The duke describes a concert by a " surprisingly good " orchestra, and male and female soloists, with several recitations. " Mr. Jennings recited Lord Byron's stanzas on his wife, very good. . . . Between the two parts of the concert, the orchestra played a march; each gentleman gave a lady his arm and a promenade took place, resembling a polonaise, with pretty figures, sometimes in two couples, sometimes in four; two ladies in the middle, the gentlemen separated from the ladies, then again all together. The concert closed with a lively cotillion. I was, on the whole, amused. . . . This general evening amusement takes place several times a week, besides which there is on Tuesday evening a general ball. There is a particular costume adopted for the society. That for the man consists of white pantaloons, buttoned over a boy's jacket, made of light material, without a collar; that of the woman of a coat reaching to the knee, and pantaloons such as little girls wear among us. These dresses are not universally adopted, but they have a good appearance. All the men did not participate in the dance, i. e., the lower classes, but read newspapers which were scattered over the side-tables.

"We went to Rapp's distillery. It will be removed

altogether. Mr. Owen has forbidden distilling, as well as the use of ardent spirits. Notwithstanding this, the Irishmen here find opportunities of getting whisky and fuddling themselves, from the flatboats that stop here.

"The greater number of the young girls whom we chanced to meet at home were found employed in plaiting straw hats. I became acquainted with Madame F., a native of St. Petersburg. She married an American merchant, but had the misfortune to lose her husband three days after marriage, and as she was somewhat eccentric and sentimental, quickly became attached to Mr. Owen's system. She told me, however, in German, that she found herself egregiously deceived, that the highly vaunted equality was not altogether to her taste; that some of the society were too low, and that the table was below all criticism. The good lady appeared to be about to run from one extreme to the other, for she added that in the summer she would go to a Shaker establishment near Vincennes.

"I renewed acquaintance here with Mr. Say, a distinguished naturalist from Philadelphia, to whom I had been introduced there, but unfortunately he had found himself embarrassed in his fortune, and was obliged to come here as a friend of Mr. Maclure. The gentleman appeared quite comical in the costume of the society, with his hands covered with hard lumps and blisters, occasioned by the unusual labor he was obliged to undertake in the garden.

"In the evening I went for a walk in the streets, and met several ladies of the society, who rested from the labors of the day. Madame F. was among them, to whose complaints I had listened. I accompanied the ladies to a dancing assembly which was held in the kitchen of one of the boarding-houses. I observed that this was only an hour of instruction for the unpractised in dancing, and that there was some restraint on account of my presence; from politeness I went away and remained at home the rest of the evening. . . .

" Mr. Owen took me into one of the newly built houses, in which the married members of the society are to live. It consisted of two stories, in each two chambers and two alcoves, with the requisite ventilators. The cellar of the house is to contain a heating apparatus to heat the whole with warm air. Each family will have a chamber and an alcove, which will be sufficient, as the little children will be in the nursery and the larger at school. They will not require kitchens, as all are to eat in common. Unmarried women will live together, as will also unmarried men, in the manner of the Moravian brothers.

" I had a long conversation with Mr. Owen relative to his system and his expectations. He looks forward to nothing else than to remodel the world entirely; to root out all crime; to abolish punishment; to create similar views and similar wants, and in this manner to abolish all dissension and warfare. When his system of education shall be brought into connection with the great progress made in mechanics, which is daily increasing, every man can then, as he thinks, provide his simpler necessaries for himself, and trade will cease entirely. I expressed a doubt of the practicability of this system in Europe, and even in the United States. He was too unalterably convinced of the result to admit the slightest room for doubt. It grieved me to see that Mr. Owen should be so infatuated by his passion for universal improvement as to believe and assert that he is about to reform the whole world, and yet that almost every member of his society with whom I talked, acknowledged that he was deceived in his expectations, and expressed their opinion that Mr. Owen had commenced on too grand a scale, and had admitted too many members without the requisite selection.

" I went with Dr. McNamee to the newly established communities, Number 2, Macluria; the other lately founded, Number 3. Number 2 lies two miles distant from New Harmony, at the entrance to the forest, which will be cleared to make the land fit for cultivation. The settlement, which was established about four weeks ago, consists of nine log houses. The inhabitants number about eighty. They are mostly backwoodsmen with their families, who have separated from community Number 1 in New Harmony because no religion is allowed there, and these people desire to hold their prayer-meetings undisputed. The fields in the neighborhood of this community were, of course, very new. Community Number 3 consisted of English country people, who formed a new association, as the cosmopolitanism of New Harmony did not suit them; they left the colony planted by Mr. Birkbeck at English Prairie, about twenty miles hence on the right bank of the Wabash, after the unfortunate death of that gentleman, and came here. This is a proof that there are two evils that strike at the root of the young societies: one is a sectarian or intolerant spirit; the other natural prejudice.

" In the evening there was a general meeting in the large hall. It opened with music; then one of the members, an English architect of talent, who came to the United States with Mr. Owen, whose confidence he appeared to possess, and was here at the head of the architectural department, read some extracts from the newspapers, upon which Mr. Owen made a very good commentary; for example, upon the extension and improvement of the steam-engine, upon its adaptation to navigation and the advantages resulting therefrom. He lost himself in his theories, however, when he expatiated on an article which related to the experiments which have been made with the Perkins steam-gun. During these lectures I made my observation on the much-vaunted equality, as some tatterdemalions stretched themselves on the platform close by Mr. Owen. The better-educated members kept themselves together, and took no notice of the others. I remarked also that members belonging to the higher classes of society had put on the new costume, and made a party by themselves. After the lecture the band played; each gentleman took a lady and marched with her around the room. Lastly, a cotillion was danced; the ladies were then escorted home, and each retired to his own quarters.

"I went early on the following morning (Sunday) to the assembly-room. The meeting was opened by music. After this, Mr. Owen stated a proposition, in the discussion of which he spoke of the advance made by the society; of the location of another community at Valley Forge, in Pennsylvania, and another in the State of New York. A classification of the members was spoken of afterward. They were to be separated into three classes: first, of such as undertook to be security for the sums due Mr. Owen and Mr. Maclure (that is for the amount paid to Rapp and so expended as a pledge to be redeemed by the society), and who, if desirous to leave the society, must give six months' previous notice; secondly, such as, after a notice of fourteen days, can depart; lastly, those who are received only on trial.

"Afterward I visited Mr. Maclure, and received from him the French papers. Mr. Maclure is old and childless, was never married, and intends, it is reported, to leave his property to the society. Afterward I went with Mr. Owen and some of the ladies of the society for a walk to the cut-off, as it is called, of the Wabash, where this river has formed a new channel and an island, which contains about thirty-five hundred acres of the best land, at present, however, inundated. There is here a substantial grist-mill erected by Mr. Rapp, which is said to contain a very good set of machinery, but we could not reach it on account of the water. . . . In the evening I paid visits to some ladies, and saw the philosophy of a life of equality put to a severe test with one of them. She is named Virginia, from Philadelphia; is very young and pretty; was delicately brought up, and appears to have taken refuge here on account of an unhappy attachment. While she was singing, and playing very well on the piano, she was told that the milking of the cows was her duty, and that they were waiting. Almost in tears, she betook herself to this servile employment, execrating the social system and its so-much-prized equality. After the cows were milked, in doing which the young girl was trod on by one and kicked by another, I joined an aquatic party with the young ladies and some young philosophers in a very good boat upon the inundated meadows along the Wabash. The evening was beautiful, it was moonlight, and the air was very mild; the beautiful Miss Virginia forgot her stable experiences and regaled us with her sweet voice. Somewhat later we collected at house Number 2, appointed for the schoolhouse, where all the young ladies and gentlemen of quality assembled. We amused ourselves during the whole remainder of the evening dancing cotillions and waltzes, and with such animation as rendered it quite lively. New figures had been introduced among the cotillions, among which was one called the New Social System. Several of the ladies made objections to dancing on Sunday; we thought, however, that in this sanctuary of philosophy such prejudice should be entirely discarded, and our arguments, as well as the inclinations of the ladies, gained the victory. . . .

"I was invited to dinner in house Number 4. Some gentlemen had been out hunting and brought home a wild turkey, which must be consumed. The turkey formed the whole dinner. Upon the whole, I can not complain either of an overloaded stomach, or a headache from the wine. The living was frugal in the strictest sense. In the evening I visited Mr. Maclure and Madame Fretageot, living in the same house. She is a Frenchwoman, and formerly kept a boarding-school in Philadelphia, and is called 'Mother' by all the young girls here. The handsomest and most polished of the female world here, Miss Lucy Sistare and Miss Virginia, were under her care. The cows

130

were milked this evening when I came in, and therefore
we could hear their performance on the pianoforte, and
their charming voices, in peace and quiet. Later in the
evening we went to the kitchen of Number 3, where there
was a ball. The young ladies of the better class kept themselves in a corner under Madame Fretageot's protection,
and formed a little aristocratic clique. To prevent all possible partialities, the gentlemen, as well as the ladies, drew
numbers for the cotillions, and thus apportioned them
equitably. Our young ladies turned up their noses at the
democratic dancers who often in this way fell to their lot.
Although, every one was pleased upon the whole, they separated at ten o'clock, as it is necessary to arise early here.
Madame Fretageot and her two pupils I accompanied home,
and spent some time in conversation with Mr. Maclure on
his travels in Europe, which were taken with mineralogical
views. The architect, Mr. Whitwell, showed me the plan
of this establishment. I admired the judicious and economical arrangement for warming and ventilating the
buildings, as well as the kitchens and laundries.

"On the following day I received a visit from one of
the German patriots of the name of Schmidt, who had
entered the society. He had been a first lieutenant in the
Prussian artillery at Erfurt. He appeared to have engaged
in one of the political conspiracies there, and to have deserted. Mr. Owen brought him from England last autumn
as a servant. He was now a member of the society, and had
charge of the cattle. His fine visions of freedom seemed
to be very much lower, for he presented himself to me, and
his father to Mr. Huygens, as servants. Toward evening
Mr. Applegarth arrived. He had presided over the school
in New Lanark, and was to organize one here when practicable. . . . In the evening there was a ball in the
large assembly-room. . . . There was a particular
place marked off for the children to dance in, in the center
of the hall, where they could gambol about without run-

ning between the legs of the grown persons. . . . **We** took a walk to community Number 3. The work on the houses had made little progress; we found but one workman there, and he was sleeping quite at his ease. . . .

"After we returned to Madame Fretageot's, Mr. Owen showed me some interesting objects of his invention. One of them consisted of cubes of different sizes, representing the different classes of the British population in the year 1811, and showed what a powerful burden rested on the laboring classes, and how desirable an equal division of property would be in that kingdom. The other was a plate, according to which, as Mr. Owen asserted, each child could be shown his own capabilities, and upon which, after a mature self-examination, he can discover what progress he had made. The plate has this superscription: 'Scale of Human Faculties and Qualities at Birth.' It has ten scales with the following titles, from the left to the right: Self-attachment; Affections; Judgment; Imagination; Memory; Reflection; Perception; Excitability; Courage; Strength. Each scale is divided into one hundred parts, which are marked from five to five. A slide that can be moved up and down shows the measure of the qualities, therein specified, which each one possesses, or believes himself to possess.

"Mr. Owen considers it an absurdity to promise neverending love on marriage. For this reason he has introduced the civil contract of marriage, after the manner of the Quakers, and declares that the bond of matrimony is in no way indissoluble. The children, indeed, cause no impediment in case of a separation, for they belong to the community from their second year, and are all brought up together. . . .

"I passed the evening with the amiable Mr. Maclure and Madame Fretageot, and became acquainted through them with a French artist, Mr. Lesueur, who calls himself an uncle of Miss Virginia; also a Dutch physician

132

from Herzogenbusch, Dr. Troost, a naturalist. Both are members of the community, and had just arrived from a pedestrian tour to Illinois and the southern part of Missouri, where they have examined the iron and particularly the lead mine works. Mr. Lesueur has besides discovered several species of fish, as yet undescribed. Mr. Lesueur accompanied the naturalist Perouse as draftsman in his tour to New South Wales under Captain Baudin, and possessed all the illuminated designs of the animals which were discovered for the first time upon this voyage, upon vellum. I count myself fortunate to have seen them. He showed me also the sketches he made while on his last pedestrian tour, as well as those during the voyage of several of the members to Mount Vernon, down the Ohio from Pittsburg. On this voyage the members of the society had many difficulties to contend with, and were often compelled to cut a path for the boat through the ice. He had come to Philadelphia from France in 1815, and had since devoted himself to the arts and sciences."

CHAPTER XIV

TWO VIEWS OF NEW HARMONY

No American autobiography surpasses in literary charm Robert Dale Owen's Threading My Way—a collection of reminiscent sketches written in Mr. Owen's characteristically clear, strong style. As Mr. John Holliday remarks: " In their frankness of statement and fulness of detail about personal matters, they remind one of Rousseau's Confessions, though lacking the apparent vanity of the Frenchman." The younger Owen's account of life at New Harmony during the community period is interesting, though disappointingly brief, for the subject was always distasteful to him. " When I reached Harmony early in 1826," he says, " these general ideas (of the possibility of the amelioration of the condition of mankind) prevailed in my mind uninterrupted by the sober second-thought which an after-life brought with it. I looked at everything with eyes of enthusiasm; and, for a time, the life there was wonderfully pleasant and hopeful to me. This, I think, is the common experience of intelligent and well-disposed persons who have joined the Brook Farm or other reputable community. There is a great charm in the good fellowship, and in the absence of conventionalism which characterizes such association.

" There was something especially taking, to me, at least, in the absolute freedom from all trammels, alike in the expression of opinion, in dress, and in social intercourse, which I found there. The evening gatherings, too, de-

134

lighted me; the weekly meetings for the discussion of our principles, in which I took part at once. The weekly concert, with an excellent leader, Josiah Warren, and a performance of music, instrumental and vocal, much beyond what I had expected in the backwoods; last, but not least, the weekly ball, where I found crowds of young people, bright and genial, if not especially cultivated, and as passionately fond of dancing as in those days I myself was.

"The accommodations seemed to me indeed of the rudest, and the fare of the simplest; but I cared no more for that than young folks usually care who desert pleasant homes to spend a summer month or two under canvas— their tents on the beach, perhaps, with boats and fishing-tackle at command, or pitched in some sylvan retreat, where youth and maiden roam the forest all day, returning at nightfall to merry talk, improvised music, or an impromptu dance on the greensward.

"I shrank from no work that was assigned to me, and sometimes, to the surprise of my associates, volunteered when a hard or disagreeable job came up, as the pulling down of the dilapidated cabins throughout the village. But after a time, finding that others could manage as much at common labor in one day as I could in two or three, and being invited to take general charge of the school and to aid in editing the weekly paper, I settled down to what I confess were more congenial pursuits than wielding the ax or holding the plow-handles.

"I had previously tried one day sowing wheat by hand, and held out until evening, but my right arm was comparatively useless for forty-eight hours thereafter. Another day, when certain of the young girls, who were baking bread for one of the large boarding-houses, lacked an additional hand, I offered to help them; and when the results of my labors came to the table, it was suggested that one of the loaves be voted to me as a gift for my diligence, the rather as by a little manipulation, such as apothecaries use in making pills, it might save me the trouble of making bullets the next time I went out rifle-shooting. . . .

"On the whole, my life at Harmony for many months was happy and satisfying. To this the simple relation existing between youth and maiden there much contributed. We called each other by our Christian names only; spoke and acted as brothers and sisters might; often strolled out by moonlight in groups, sometimes in pairs; yet withal, no scandal or other harm came of it, either then or later, unless we are to reckon as such a few unsuited and improvident matches that turned out poorly, as hasty love-matches will. What might have happened to myself amid such favorable surroundings, if my heart had not been pre-occupied, I can not tell. I met almost daily, handsome, interesting, and warm-hearted girls; bright, merry, and unsophisticated; charming partners at ball or picnic; one especially, who afterward married a son of Oliver Evans, the celebrated inventor and machinist, to whom, I believe, we owe the high-pressure engine.

"Naturally enough, under the circumstances, I was not haunted by doubts as to the success of the social experiment in which we were engaged. The inhabitants seemed to me friendly and well disposed. There was much originality of character.

"One example occurs to me—an old man named Green-wood, father of Miles Greenwood, known afterward to the citizens of Cincinnati as chief of their fire department, and still later as proprietor of the largest foundry and machine-shops then in the West.' We had, during the summer of 1826, several terrific thunder-storms, such as I had never before witnessed. The steeple of our hall was shattered, and it was during one of these storms, when the whole heavens seemed illuminated and the rain was falling in torrents, that I saw old Greenwood, thoroughly drenched and carrying straight upright, as a soldier carries a musket, a slender iron rod, ten or twelve feet long. He was walking

136

in the middle of the street, passing with slow step the house in which I was, and, as I afterward learned, paraded every street in the village in the same deliberate manner. Next day I met him and asked him for an explanation. 'Ah! well, my young friend,' said he, 'I am very old; I am not well; I suffer much, and I thought it might be a good chance to slip off, and be laid quietly away in the corner of the orchard.'

"'You hoped to be struck by lightning?'

"'You see, I don't like to kill myself; it seems like taking matters out of God's hands; but I thought He might send me a spare bolt when I put myself in the way. If He had only seen fit to do it, I'd have been at rest this very minute, all my pains gone, no more trouble to any one, and no more burden to myself.'"

Early in the spring of 1826, there came to New Harmony a curious character named Paul Brown. In 1827 he published a pamphlet entitled Twelve Months in New Harmony, in which he recounted his experiences as a member of the community. Brown states that when he came from his home in one of the Eastern States to visit relatives in Tennessee, he found the New Harmony experiment a common topic of conversation among people there, and he determined to visit the place at once. Paving the way by forwarding a huge letter to Mr. Owen, he proceeded to the settlement, arriving there on April 2d. He learned on his journey, he says, that the original constitution had been set aside, and that the people were being compelled to sign contracts to pay for property at an appraised valuation.

"It was anything but a tranquil neighborhood," writes Brown. "The impression I took from what I could gather was that this stipulation about appraisal not having been made to the people until after they had signed the constitution, the disturbance first arose from some of them being backward about taking such a yoke upon themselves, which generally had not been expected; whereupon an ad-

137

vantage was immediately taken thereof by some aspiring, aristocratical spirits to make a division of the town into several societies, as, one of the school, one of the tavern, etc., another of the mechanics, and another of the farmers; the school and tavern societies offering to take upon themselves the greater part of the debt; exchanges to exist between these different bodies politic by what they called 'labor for labor.' This was overruled by Mr. Owen, who refused to contract with them upon such a plan, and declared he knew no parties in New Harmony and would countenance but one homogeneous union in that place. He afterward shifted his ground, and said that in one society they could not exist, and suggested the formation of three. In this he could not prevail."

"Owen," Paul Brown declares, "then selected a nucleus of twenty-five men as the beginning of a new association. All agreed to sign contracts with Owen and Maclure for the real and personal property 'as appraised by somebody.' Three grades of membership were established: conditional, probationary, and members on trial. All the affairs of the society were submitted to the direction of Owen, unless within twelve months two-thirds of the members should decide to rule themselves. By this very act of requiring money for the estate purchased by the community, Owen proved himself to be a trading man, and not a philanthropist; proved himself incapacitated to found a real commonwealth; proved that it could not have been the sole object and pursuit of his life to bring such a thing into existence; proved himself to be lacking of integrity, magnanimity, and all those sublime principles essentially requisite to form a character competent to introduce into life an example of the state of society in the true order of human perfection, of a sort which he had recommended."

This carping critic grants that freedom of speech and of the press were accorded by the New Harmony administration, but he took great offense at "the keeping of books." "The dancing and the instrumental music," he added, "engrossed more of energy than the more important considerations of community welfare. There must be a regular ball and a regular concert once a week." He says that there were restless spirits constantly urging some new experiment. Owen, he states, recommended a motion, to be made before all the people, to decide whether they should be divided into four societies, each signing its own contract for such a part of the property as it should purchase, trading to be carried on among them by means of representative paper money. Robert Owen submitted two propositions, one to have one community divided into occupations, and one to institute four distinct communities. The last proposition was adopted.

Linked with Brown's cynical atheism was a puritanical spirit which railed against the social diversions of which the Harmonists were so fond. "The instituting of such amusements as public balls, promenades, and music," he says, "seemed to be propitious to interest the young and enamor them of the place. But the constant succession of this sort of thing clearly induced volatility and aversion to serious duties." Brown also objected to the industrial school founded by William Maclure, on the ground that young persons thus taught trades or parts of trades "became dependent on others for their support thereby." He also claimed that Mr. Owen, according to the new plan of contract with four societies, would receive for half of the estate twenty thousand dollars more than he paid for the whole, a statement that had no foundation in fact, as Mr. Owen gave exceedingly favorable terms to the societies proposing settlement on the estate.

"Mr. Owen," says Brown, "seems to have constantly inculcated upon these people, from the beginning, lessons of thrift and knacks of gaining and saving money; yet profusions of musical instruments were provided, and great quantities of candles burned at their balls." A great part of the time, he declared, the people were stinted in their allowances of tea, butter, milk, etc. " Mr. Owen constantly boarded at the tavern, where luxurious regale was copiously provided to sell to traveling men of the world and loungers. Here he drank coffee and tea while a multitude of laboring people who were quartered in the large boarding-houses, being circumscribed in their rations, were very much in the habit of drinking rye coffee, or rye mixed with store coffee." Other visitors to the community during this period agree that Mr. Owen was content with the simplest fare, and Mr. Owen, in a lecture at Philadelphia, stated that he lived on an expenditure of six cents a day while the experiment was in progress—eating but two meals each day, one at 7 A. M. and one at 5 P. M.

Brown speaks of the neglect and confusion which characterized the conduct of community enterprises. " The gardens were neglected, and though several skilled gardeners lived in the community, much ground lay fallow which might have made handsome gardens. The people, instead of employing their thoughts to execute their work well, were musing on plans of new arrangements in the system of government of the society." The reporting of the number of hours of labor, " and the keeping of debit and credit, was a constant weight upon those who would work from principle. Some of the ground was called private ground. Everything was at sixes and sevens. The place was full of clamor, disaffection, and calumny. Complaints were often made that some houses got a greater supply of provisions than others."

So Brown continues with his catalogue of grievances. He was not the only member of the community who was ready to discredit the motives of the unselfish Robert Owen, and to contribute to the growth of " clamor, disaffection, and calumny."

140

CHAPTER XV

Ah, soon will come the glorious day,
   Inscribed on Mercy's brow,
When truth shall rend the veil away
   That blinds the nations now.

When earth no more in anxious fear
   And misery shall sigh;
And pain shall cease, and every tear
   Be wiped from every eye.

The race of man shall wisdom learn,
   And error cease to reign:
The charms of innocence return,
   And all be new again.

The fount of life shall then be quaffed
   In peace by all that come;
And every wind that blows shall waft
   Some wandering mortal home.

                    —Owenite Poem, 1826.

ROBERT OWEN'S retrospect of the first year's proceedings of the "permanent community," delivered at New Harmony Hall on May 9, 1826, is another evidence of hopefulness which continued in him after doubt and despair had seized many of his followers. The happiest side of everything was turned to the world. His expectations, he declared, had been far surpassed. He had not hoped that the town would be full in less than two or three years, but it had been crowded in half that time. "Leaving home in the fall of 1824, I made arrangements to return in the spring of 1825. After completing the purchase of this property in April, and founding the Preliminary Society in May, I was compelled to set out on my journey to Europe in June. I left the new settlement in the charge of a committee chosen by a majority of the adult population, and I did not suppose that during my absence they could do more than receive the people as they came in.

"As soon, however, as the formation of the Preliminary Society was announced, people came flocking from all quarters into the colony to offer themselves for membership in such numbers that the dwelling-houses were filled in two months, and the press for admission was such that it became necessary to insert advertisements in the newspapers of the surrounding States to prevent others coming who could not be accepted for want of accommodations. On my arrival in January last, I found every room occupied."

The affairs of the society, he declared, had been managed much better than he had expected they would be. "About a thousand individuals of all characters and dispositions had come together from far and near. Their manners and tastes were as various as the varying circumstances under which their character had been formed. Many of the children were extremely wild, rude, and uncultivated, and strangers who came to see what was going forward could perceive only a babel-like confusion. They came and wondered and went away disappointed."

"In one short year," Mr. Owen stated, "this mass of confusion, and in many cases of bad and irregular habits, has been formed into a community of mutual cooperation and equality, now proceeding rapidly toward a state of regular organization. Out of it two communities have been formed and located in this neighborhood." The members of the first community, Macluria, "have built themselves temporary comfortable cabins, and they have cultivated more land than will be necessary to supply their wants, and the young persons are spinning and weaving more cloth than will be necessary to clothe them. With the exception of two refractory members, the community seems to comprehend the new principles." These refractory members, Mr. Owen declared, would probably withdraw.

Feiba Peveli had a large and well-cultivated garden, said Mr. Owen, and an extensive and well-kept farm. This community had good prospects of paying off a part of the debt on their property this year. Macluria had about one hundred and twenty members; Feiba Peveli sixty or seventy. Applications had been made for the formation of other communities, and as soon as houses could be located for them, they would be admitted.

There was hardly a State in the Union, Mr. Owen declared, where this subject did not attract considerable attention, "and in many of them we have communities proceeding under these principles, notably in New York, Kentucky, Pennsylvania, Ohio, Indiana, and Illinois. Some, we know, are in operation in each of those States. In England and Scotland also, the cause has made great progress, the Orbiston community having had notable success."

"Perhaps," said the hopeful philosopher in closing, "no system of equal magnitude, involving such extensive changes in the conduct of human affairs, ever made progress in any degree approaching to it in so short a time. Hereafter, no one who comes and visits Macluria or Feiba Peveli will doubt the practicability of this scheme." "But," said Mr. Owen, "the great experiment in New Harmony is still going on to ascertain whether a large, heterogeneous mass of persons, collected by chance, can be amalgamated into one community and induced to acquire the genuine feelings of kindness and benevolence which belong solely to the principles on which the new social system is founded, and which no other principles can produce.

The friends of the new social system may rejoice and be exceeding glad, for they may be assured that deliverance from poverty, ignorance, and the oppression of riches is at hand."

The conditions under which Feiba Peveli and Macluria secured their land, conditions which were later accepted by other communities, comprehended the following provisions:

1. That they should always remain communities of equality and cooperation in rights and property, and should not be divided into individual shares or separate interests.

2. That any surplus property their industry might acquire must not be divided, but used to found similar communities.

3. That there should be no whisky, or other distilled liquors, made in the communities.

This was advanced ground on the liquor question, at a time when it was not so seriously considered as at present, and Robert Owen was already enforcing strict prohibition at New Harmony. Mr. Owen, about this time, suggested the formation of occupational communities, that is, associations of mechanics engaged in similar trades, farmers, etc. There was evidently some friction between those who labored in the fields and factories, and those who desired to derive a living from their professional training or knowledge of trade.

On May 17th, the Gazette said that there were already ten communities and several societies in operation on the New Harmony plan. In this issue of the community organ is also found an account of the formation of a cooperative association on the Owen plan at Wainborough, Illinois, and of the " Franklin community," located on the Hudson, sixty miles above New York City, this society adopting *in toto* one of the numerous New Harmony constitutions. In the latter part of May, advertisements of mercantile business in the town began to appear in the Gazette. We also

learn from the Gazette that on May 26th, Paul Brown
delivered a lecture in opposition to the management of the
community.   He spoke vehemently against card-playing,
and also complained of the " horse-laughing " of the children, which disturbed his thoughts and " rendered life
unendurable."

The dissenters at New Harmony were by this time becoming bold enough to attack Mr. Owen's philosophy. A
complainant deluged the Gazette with questions which
called for an answer from Mr. Owen. He wished to know
what is to be the stimulus to superior industry? how money
is to be rendered useless in The New Moral World? why
the people of the community can not see the model of the
proposed community building, as shown at Washington?
in Mr. Owen's plan for such a building what is the superiority of the hollow square over parallel sides at a convenient distance apart, or over a hollow triangle, pentagon,
or hexagon? how, in the erection of the new building, will
the unevenness of the ground be avoided? etc., etc. Such
questions dealt rather roughly with Mr. Owen's fanciful
details, and his answer was that these minor arrangements
were not an essential part of the great plan. On May 28th,
Mr. Owen reminded the people that a community can not
exist without a true community spirit. Two weeks later,
a member of the society complained through the Gazette
that the thousand members of the society had come to New
Harmony at an expense of twenty thousand dollars to find
that communism was not being practised. Emulation,
declared another correspondent, must be admitted into the
community in order to make it a success, and lawyers and
capitalists ought not be spoken of as outlaws, but their
friendship should be cultivated. Members who steal or
destroy the property of others, this correspondent insisted,
ought to be expelled, as well as those who drink intoxicating
liquors. "This, of course, has never happened at New
Harmony," declared the cautious contributor. The Gazette

had declared on May 24th, that " the system of prevention destroys drunkenness in New Harmony."

On July 4, 1826, the fiftieth anniversary of the signing of the Declaration of Independence, Robert Owen made the effort which he seemed to consider the chief event in history since the signing of the American Declaration, in delivering what he called " The Declaration of Mental Independence." " I now declare to you and to the world," he began, " that man up to this hour has been in all parts of the earth a slave to a trinity of the most monstrous evils that could be combined to inflict mental and physical evil upon the whole race. I refer to private or individual property, absurd and irrational systems of religion, and marriage founded upon individual property, combined with some of these irrational systems of religion." Then followed a reiteration of principles as set forth in The New Moral World. With undaunted optimism he declared, in closing: " Our principles will spread from community to community, from State to State, from continent to continent, until this system and these principles shall overshadow the whole earth, shedding fragrance and abundance, intelligence and happiness upon all the sons of men." This declaration, Mr. Owen said upon this occasion, he considered the most important event in his life. The Gazette was thereafter dated in the " first " and " second " years of " mental independence."

Early in July, Sunday meetings for instruction in the new principles were instituted. At these sessions Robert Owen presided, and led in the discussions. Accounts of these meetings are given in the community paper, and we learn that Mr. Owen's addresses were often followed by spirited debates among the members. Although many of the members, Mr. Owen declared on July 30th, had not seen their way clear and had fainted by the way, still he had witnessed a uniform progress from the old system to the new. " From present appearances, in twelve

146

months we will be able to contend against the world."
Six months ago he would not have imagined that the progress since made could have been effected in years.

"Suppose," said an interrogator at one meeting, "one-
third of the population should pledge themselves to go
the whole way with you (into communistic association),
would you be willing to go the whole way? Would you
be willing to make common stock of your property?"
"Yes," Mr. Owen answered, "I am ready and will join you
whenever there shall be a sufficient number who follow
and understand the principles, and who will honestly carry
them into effect."

On July 30, 1826, the New Harmony Agricultural
and Pastoral Society adopted a constitution modeled after
those previously adopted by New Harmony communistic
associations. The membership, limited to thirty families,
was less exclusive than that of former societies, a two-
thirds vote being sufficient to admit an applicant. Members leaving the society previous to the payment of the
debt to Robert Owen must relinquish all share in
the property. The last clause of the constitution pledged
the society to "furnish its quota of soldiers, statesmen, and
politicians."

The fact that the administration organ gave few particulars of the progress of the communities during the
summer of 1826 is evidence that there was little to report
that was favorable to the prospects of the New Harmony
experiment. We only know that numerous expedients were
tried to better the condition of the communities, and that
all ultimately failed. The summer was full of projects,
auspiciously begun and disastrously ended.

For lack of a better authority, we must fall back on
Paul Brown. The mechanics, he states, entered into in-
denture with Owen for lands and houses aggregating in
value twenty-three thousand dollars, agreeing to pay five
per cent interest on this amount, and the property not

to be deeded to them until the last instalment on the principal had been paid. The " School Society " made a contract for nine hundred acres of land, and the best of the buildings, leasing these for ten thousand years, and agreeing to pay forty-nine thousand dollars therefor. The " Pastoral Society " had a similar contract for a large tract of land. There was great jealousy against the educational society, the commoners deeming it an aristocracy. There were many changes from society to society, and the communities devoted much time and energy to wrangling with one another. Brown says : " The claim to some crops being unsettled between two societies, a large patch of cabbages went to ruin from neglect. . . . Everything was at sixes and sevens at the very time when everything ought to have been in complete order and the people tending busily to saving the products."

Brown found no attraction even in the social diversions which enlivened the place. " The people of the town," he says, " continued strangers to each other, in spite of all their meetings, their balls, their frequent occasions of congregating in the hall, and all their pretense of cooperation. From the first time I set my foot within this little town of one-half mile square, I think there is not one, within the range of my observations during my traveling in other towns of the United States, where the same number of persons, living together within such a compass for so many months, and daily and hourly passing and repassing each other, were so perfectly strangers, and void of all personal intimacy with each other's feelings, views, situations, and, very generally, names."

At a meeting held on August 20th, Robert Owen said : " Believe me, that if you and your children will only regularly meet here three evenings in the week, and give your attention to the subject, one year will not have passed before the minds of all will have become generally well informed. We ought to at once lay the foundation of this general

A TYPICAL RAPPITE HOUSE.

Residence of Thomas Say, "The Father of American Zoology."

knowledge." On motion it was agreed that Monday, Wednesday, and Friday evenings should be given to this purpose. These meetings were continued, with decreasing attendance, for only a few weeks. On August 27th, Mr. Owen stated "that the last week had been well employed in commencing the education of the children belonging to the manufacturing, mechanical, and pastoral societies." While Mr. Owen was delivering an excellent course of lectures on early education, Paul Brown does not think that the children were progressing far in the straight and narrow way. The mechanics became confused in the intricate machinery created by their constitution, and relieved themselves by abolishing their numerous offices, and creating in their stead a trinity of dictators, which they blasphemously called God the Father, God the Son, and God the Holy Ghost. The farmers became offended by some proceeding of the educational society, and decided to remove their children from school, paying their tuition up to that time. The mechanics, who seemed to be greater revolutionists than the farmers, became involved in another quarrel, and also withdrew their children, but refused to pay anything for the instruction they had already received.

Brown says that gardens and fields were almost entirely neglected. Large holes were made in the fences "by brutes and boys." These openings into cultivated enclosures grew wider and wider, until "swine ranged at pleasure throughout, then cows, and next horses." A pilfering spirit, he says, pervaded the place. "Two dames of House Number 4, where abode the pastorals and shepherds, had a battle with their fists." The children, Brown declares, ran morally mad. To crown it all, the Gazette refused to publish some essays written by Paul Brown himself. The Gazette does not agree with Brown in its accounts of community conditions, but stated about this time that, "from a neglect of the principles of the system, some very well-meaning individuals are committing mistakes which deprive them of the enjoyment of a happy state of mind. They blame individuals upon conjecture; they become angry at these individuals, and do and say things which they afterward deeply regret."

At length the refractory farmers and mechanics agreed to allow Mr. Owen to have charge of the schooling of their children, and a school was set up in the shoe-factory, with Mr. Owen as principal. Following this there seems to have ensued a period of temporary hopefulness and community convalescence.

At the Sunday meeting for instruction on August 23d, Robert Owen quoted from a book entitled The Three Wise Men of Gotham, which held the Owenites up to ridicule. He stated that the book was embellished with a picture of three wise men sailing in a bowl, with the motto accompanying it:

"Three wise men of Gotham put out to sea in a bowl:
If the bowl had been stronger, my tale had been longer."

The book, Mr. Owen stated, was divided into three parts, the first intended to give a ludicrous history of a pupil of the new system; the second to show the absurdities, uncertainties, and consequent evils of law under the individual system; the third was a satire on frivolity. The first chapter treated of a man machine who was supposed to tell his own story. Mr. Owen read some pages which treated of the employment of young children in the factories of Great Britain, and accused Mr. Owen of cupidity and a desire to make money by the labor of his followers.

On September 17, 1826, a general meeting of the societies and the population of New Harmony was held at the hall. A message from Robert Owen was submitted, proposing a plan for " the amelioration of the society, to improve the condition of the people, and make them more contented." Mr. Owen offered to join any number of per-

sons, the present existing communities being abolished, in
the formation of a new general community, to be called
" The New Harmony Community Number 1." The agreement stipulated that the real and personal property held
by members, and located in the United States, should be
made common stock, except what might be sufficient to pay
the just debts of members, and their wearing apparel,
household furniture, and whatever they might feel disposed
to set apart for the support of absent relatives who were
not members of the community. The government of this
new community, Mr. Owen proposed, should be invested in
himself and four directors to be appointed by him. This
administration should continue for five years, at the end
of which time the majority might decide as to the future
government of the community. The members were to obli-
gate themselves to " use their best endeavors by temperate,
economical, and prudent habits to contribute to the interest
of all and the happiness of each."

The existing communities did not at once concur in this
plan. The members of the educational society denounced
it as a despotism. On October 24th, Macluria had removed
three of its directors and its agent. Soon after it split in
two, on account, it is said, of a religious controversy, and
returned the community property to Mr. Owen, who merged
it into the estate of the new community Number 1.
Ninety-six members were secured for this association in
a few days. The educational society opposed the plan
so vigorously that, according to Paul Brown, its supplies
were cut off for a few days.

The formation of the new community seems to have
created a better state of affairs for a time, while Mr.
Owen's instruction of the children was accomplishing
much good. The Gazette of October 11th declared : " For
several weeks past, the steady progress in good habits and
substantial improvement among the younger part of the
population has been obvious to every one. They have com-

menced a system of instruction which at once fixed their attention, and changed their whole conduct. They are most punctual in their attendance upon the lectures, and take an extraordinary interest in them; and in the same proportion that these good feelings and higher views have arisen, they have abandoned their wild and irrational mode of conduct; they are now seldom heard to swear or seen engaged in quarrels, as was their common conduct at their first coming. Their industry keeps pace with their other improvements, and their parents generally express the greatest satisfaction in the change effected in their children. The parents also have made a considerable advance in temperance and industry. There are but two or three among the whole population who are seen occasionally to trespass against the former virtue, and such is the general feeling of disapprobation in consequence that it is evident to every one that they must speedily change this deplorable habit, or leave the society.

" The most eccentric and violent characters, who were unprepared to give up their eccentricities, having left the society, all have agreed to commence the social system upon its true foundation of common property, good feeling, and true conduct. The community unanimously agreed that Mr. Owen should take the direction of its formation until it was so far advanced that the members should be instructed in the practise of the whole as well as in the principles. The declaration of mental independence having cleared away the greater part of the errors which previously prevailed in the minds of many, and removed all doubts from the strong minded in regard to Mr. Owen's real views and ultimate objects, mutual confidence has been established. The town is so full that several await the completion of some houses which are yet in progress. The applications for membership have also largely increased lately. There can be little doubt, therefore, that as soon as the public mind shall be calmed after the first surprise of such an attack as was the Declaration of Mental Independence, as soon as the productive classes shall have time and opportunity to discover how grievously they are injured by the old system in every part of the world, and more especially when they reflect upon the fate of the producers of all wealth in Great Britain, they will bestir themselves everywhere, and adopt principles and arrangements by which they will securely enjoy the full benefit of their mental and physical exertions."

On November 8th, the Gazette declared that at the beginning of the experiment some intemperate, thievish, aristocratic, violent, eccentric, ill-tempered, vain, and scheming persons came to the community. " Some of the most defective characters have left the community, however, as well as some who would have made good members had they persevered. It would be an act of very great injustice to the community and the public, to say that the community character has yet been attained by us; all parties as yet have scarcely become known to each other, and we are but partially acquainted with the materials around us. Some progress has, however, been made. Drunkenness has been diminished until it is now scarcely known. Industry has become steady and regular among all classes, with a few exceptions. The children are gradually losing the wild and thoughtless habits which they once possessed, and are beginning to acquire those of attention and refinement.

" The principal thing to be contended with is the character formed by a new country. Families have been here collected without any relation to each others' views and peculiarities. Many of these persons, after their arrival, have been deprived of more or less of their property, and a general system of trading speculation exists among them, each one trying to get the best of the other. Confidence can not, therefore, exist among them, and there is an unreasonable spirit of suspicion prevalent. Inexperience in community enterprises is another great obstacle, and education alone can overcome these difficulties."

On November 29th, the Gazette announced that arrangements had been perfected for educating all the children of the community in one family. It says, further: " Some of the population entertain the opinion that a few of the members are not so careful and industrious as they ought to be, and it is probable that there may be some truth in these surmises. Nothing, however, is so damaging as a suspicious spirit.

" Another cause of dissatisfaction among the members of the educational society arose from a misconception among them as to the best line of separation between their lands and those of the other societies. They thought some other line, giving them more land in a particular direction inconvenient to their neighbors, was necessary for them; a little reflection, however, will convince them of their error, there being more land than is requisite for ten other communities, and whenever they are prepared to require more for cultivation, it can be obtained without difficulty. It deserves not a moment's reflection whether one society has a little more or a little less for the present, providing a line shall be adopted which will prevent them from interfering with each other's principles, objects, and arrangements. Shortly each member of all these societies will discover that they have but one and the same interest. These little matters, creating some temporary difference of feeling, being once adjusted, the rapidity of our progress will be much accelerated."

At a meeting of the society on November 11, 1826, Robert Owen said: " We meet particularly for the purpose of taking a survey of the last half-year's proceedings, and the progress the community has made toward the attainment of the great object which has brought me across the Atlantic, and which has induced you to collect yourselves together at this place. Many are ridiculing the project, but the members should not heed in the slightest what the world has said or may say relative to our discussions here. It knows no more of this subject, which is new in the annals of the human race, than a man born blind knows of colors," Mr. Owen proceeded to state, after reading the first chapter of a new work on the " social system," which had been done preparatory to the introduction of the new state of society. He commenced with the purchase of the estate, and the collection of persons desirous of trying the experiment. He mentioned the establishment of the Gazette " for the promulgation of true principles." These results, he said, were accomplished during the first year. During the succeeding six months, the Declaration of Mental Independence had been made, the publication of which he regarded as laying the foundations of the new social system " on a rock immovable through future ages." Then the association was formed into a community of common property. " In the next place, an experiment has been made which proves how easily the whole community may be reeducated into one family, or true community. The community has discovered by experience the utility of delegating the direction of this organization to some of the members until the majority of them acquire the knowledge of the best mode of acting in general measures, or upon an extensive combination. It had further ascertained the qualities, character, or virtues which are necessary to be acquired by all members of a community of common property, equality and justice, and without which no community can be successful. . . . A long discussion followed," states the Gazette.

CHAPTER XVI

COMMUNITY DISINTEGRATION

"In my own behalf I rejoice that I could once think better of the world probably than it deserved. It is a mistake into which men seldom fall twice in a lifetime, or, if so, the rarer and higher the nature that can thus magnanimously press onward. . . . Whatever else I may repent of, therefore, let it be reckoned neither among my sins nor follies that I once had faith and force enough to form generous hopes of the world's destiny."—NATHANIEL HAWTHORNE in *The Blithedale Romance.*

"BESIDES those who came to New Harmony with good intentions," said the late Colonel Richard Owen, in a letter to John H. Holliday, "there were a good many who came thinking to make money by getting lands and houses into their hands on pretense of being strong advocates of socialism. Some of them were very unscrupulous in the means employed, notably William Taylor, who afterward was in the Ohio penitentiary, I think, for forgery; Amos Clark, who moved to Texas, and some others whose relatives are still living—hence I do not mention their names."

Chief among these dishonest speculators was the William Taylor referred to in this letter. Gaining the confidence of Mr. Owen, he induced him to sell him fifteen hundred acres of land. It is said that the contract read "with all thereon," and that Taylor moved all the agricultural implements and live stock he could find on other parts of the estate upon his tract the night before the day upon which the contract went into effect. Taylor established a distillery, contrary to the wishes of Mr. Owen, and in every way possible made trouble for the management of the community enterprise.

156

Near the close of the year 1826, many of the members of the community were being expelled for incapacity. Paul Brown says of the sale of land to Taylor: "This maneuver swept away the last cobweb of fairy dreams of a common stock and community." A funeral of the social system was projected by some of the New Harmonites. A coffin was procured and properly labeled, and arrangements were made for an imposing procession; but the night before the day set for the funeral the building in which the coffin was concealed was broken into and all the paraphernalia destroyed, so that the project was abandoned, and the system was allowed to die in its own way. "Owen's practises about this time," says Brown, "tended to inspire cupidity, and his preaching tended to inspire apathy and licentiousness." Without doubt Mr. Owen was now attempting to extricate himself from the financial embarrassment which overhung the experiment, for he doubtless realized that the end of the scheme was near.

"Moreover," complains Brown, "the individual sufferings from the privations and embarrassments arising out of the continual shifting of arrangements, as well as by the circumscription of subsistence, deadened the wonted sympathy of many ingenuous souls. Money was in higher repute than in any other town, and became almost an object of worship. The sexes fought like cats and dogs about individual marriages; there was no politeness between the single persons of the two sexes, but a dark, sullen, cold, suspicious temper, and a most intolerable, miserly allusion to individual property as the standard of worth. The single men of the town were generally obliged to make their own beds, carry their clothes to wash and recover them when they could, as much as if they had belonged to an army. Every one was for himself, as the saying is."

The pretense of communism was kept up by the admin-

157

istration, perhaps with the hope that something would turn up to change the trend of affairs. The Sunday meetings for instruction, which had for some time been discontinued on account of a lack of heating accommodations at the hall, were resumed. About this time two more communities were formed on the New Harmony estate— Number 3, within a half mile of New Harmony, and Number 4. Delegates arrived during the latter part of January, bringing tidings of the Blue Springs community, near Bloomington, Indiana. They reported it to be in a prosperous condition.

About this time the Gazette declared in an editorial: "We have not ourselves for some weeks expressed an opinion as to the progress of the community, both on account of the difficulty of getting a correct statement, and then again because the state of the public mind in a young and heterogeneous society like this varies easily and rapidly, producing a corresponding impulse and revulsion. If a community is to grow together and harmoniously, its members must meet frequently, a thing that has not been done here lately on account of the heating of the hall. Nine-tenths of the advantages of community life are lost in the absence of meetings for social intercourse."

"In March," Brown says, "a plan was made by some to ascend the Ohio River, and form a community near Cincinnati." The granary, public eating-house, cook-house, meeting-house, and sitting-rooms were deserted and the remaining members of the society took their meals at the boarding-school. On March 21st, eighty persons left New Harmony by boat. A greater part of the town was now resolved into town lots, and signboards began to go up everywhere. "A sort of wax figure and puppet show was opened up at one end of the boarding-house, and everything was getting into the old style."

The New Harmony Gazette of March 28, 1827, in an editorial written by Robert Dale Owen and William

Owen, acknowledged the defeat of the experiment in the town itself, although faith was still affirmed in the principles involved in the general plan, and confidence in the future success of other communities located on the estate. " Robert Owen, in his first address, did not designate New Harmony even as the site of the future community, but only as a half-way house. We think that this was the wisest plan, and it was well that the Preliminary Society should have continued two years.

" Robert Owen, after his return from England, nine months after the formation of the Preliminary Society, thought that further delay would be inadvisable, and, unfitted as the town was by its variety of people and unique occupations for the purposes of community life, heterogeneous as was the character of its numerous inhabitants, and little as they knew of each other, he thought they might be formed, with a few exceptions, into a self-governing community. A vote of the society determined that no exceptions should be made, and the members of the Preliminary Society resolved themselves into a community.

" We have yet to learn that the character of a person educated among the surroundings of the old world, can be entirely changed. The experiment, to ascertain at once whether a mixed and unassorted population could successfully govern their own affairs as a community, was a bold and hazardous attempt, and, we think, a premature one.

" Our own opinion is that Robert Owen ascribed too little influence to the early antisocial circumstances that had surrounded many of the quickly collected inhabitants of New Harmony before their arrival here, and too much to the circumstances which experience might enable them to create around themselves in future. He sought to abridge the period of human suffering by an immediate and decisive step, and the plan was boldly conceived; the failure would only afford proof that the conception in this particular case was not as practical as it was benevolent, inasmuch as the mass of the individuals at New Harmony were not prepared for so advanced a measure.

"Whether the project was executed in the best and most prudent manner, it is not for us to judge. We are too inexperienced in its practise to hazard a judgment on the prudence of the various individuals who directed its execution, and the one opinion we can express with confidence is of the perseverance with which Robert Owen prosecuted it at great pecuniary loss to himself. One form of government was first adopted, and when that appeared unsuited to the actual state of the members another was tried in its place, until it appeared that the whole population, numerous as they were, were too various in their feelings, too dissimilar in their habits, to unite and govern themselves harmoniously as one community, and they separated, therefore, into three, each remaining perfectly independent of Robert Owen. But these societies were again incautious in their admission of members, and it soon became evident that their size was too unwieldy for their practical knowledge. Two of them abandoned their separate independence, and requested Robert Owen, with the assistance of four trustees, to take the general superintendence of affairs, which were getting into some confusion. Only the third society, called the educational, continued, under the auspices of William Maclure, and still continues its original and separate form.

"Thus was another attempt made to unite into a community of common property and equal rights, but it soon became too apparent to the trustees in whom the management was vested that the establishment did not pay its own expenses. Therefore some decisive changes became necessary to arrest this continued loss of property, thus, by rendering the society successful in a pecuniary way, to secure its independence of foreign assistance.

"The deficiency in production appeared immediately attributable in part to carelessness of many members as

160

regarded the community property; in part to their want of interest in the experiment itself—the only true incitement to community industry—and the discordant variety of habits among them. The circle was so large, and the operations it embraced so various and extensive, that the confidence of minds untrained in the correct principles, and able to see but a small part of the whole, who had witnessed, too, the various previous changes, was shaken. Their care and their exertions diminished with their confidence in themselves, and the natural consequences ensued.

" A remedy presented itself in the voluntary association, out of the population of New Harmony, of those individuals together who had confidence in one another's intentions, and mutual enjoyment in one another's society. Land and assistance for the first year were offered to those who chose to unite in this plan, and the consequence was the formation of another community on the New Harmony lands.

" And we regret that for those who remained in town the only effectual and immediate remedy appeared to be in circumscribing each other's interests and responsibility. As the circle was too large for their present habits and experiences, smaller circles were described within it. The community was subdivided into occupations, each of which became responsible for its operations alone.

" And this is the present situation in New Harmony. Each occupation supports itself, paying weekly a small percentage toward the general expenses of the town. Each regulates its own affairs, determining its own internal regulations and distributing its produce.

" New Harmony, therefore, is not now a community; but, as was originally intended, a central village, out of and around which communities have formed, and may continue to form themselves, and with the inhabitants of which these communities may exchange their products thus obtained for those manufactured articles which the limited operations incidental to the incipient colonies do not enable them to produce themselves.

" Let us not, then, be misunderstood, for it is important that our friends should know the exact position on which we stand, more particularly those who may wish to join us here. It is not in the town itself, but on the lands of Harmony, that the community system is in progressive operation.

" About a year ago, and soon after the formation of the community in this town, a number of families, separating from the principal body, located themselves on the lands at about a mile eastward from the town and founded the community of Feiba Peveli, or Number 3. It has progressed successfully, and we believe that its members are now convinced by present experience of the benefits of the social system.

" In addition to community Number 4, whose lands lie south of the town, we have now to notice the commencement of another community, whose formation preceded the separation into occupations. The land of this community is situated about two miles distant from the town, on both sides of the Princeton road.

" The communities commenced on a small scale, intending to increase their membership gradually. They will afford an example of how easy it is to begin a cooperative community in a simple manner, with little capital, provided industry and good feeling exist among the members. Their progress will not probably be sudden and astonishing, but it will be constant.

" Another society, Macluria, or Number 2, which separated from the principal community about the same time that Number 3 was formed, and continued its operations for about a year, succeeded perfectly from an economical point of view. Their original motive for secession was, in part, we believe, a religious one, and we have been told that their subsequent dissolution was attributable to a

162

similar cause. Their lands have been taken by a party of German settlers, to the number of about fifteen families, who have already disposed of their property and will arrive here probably next month to commence a community of mutual labor and common property."

While Robert Owen was making his preparations to depart for Europe, the trouble which had long been brewing between him and Mr. Maclure—a natural result of the association of two leaders of such marked individuality—developed into an open quarrel, and the closing year of the communistic experiments witnessed a dispute over individual property between the joint projectors of the new social and educational system. Under date of April 30th the following was posted in public places:

NOTICE.

Notice is hereby given to all whom it may concern, forewarning them not to trust Robert Owen on my account, as I am determined not to pay any debts of his, or in any way be responsible for any transaction he may have done or may attempt to do in my name.

WILLIAM MACLURE.

Within a few hours the town store contained the following retaliatory

NOTICE.

Having just now seen the very extraordinary advertisement put upon some of the houses in this place, and signed by William Maclure, it becomes necessary in my own defense to inform the public that the partnership between William Maclure and myself is in full force, and that I shall pay any contract made either by William Maclure or myself on the partnership account.

ROBERT OWEN.

Next day, Paul Brown declares, Maclure prosecuted Owen for the recovery of forty thousand dollars, with a view of making him give a deed in fee simple for the property Maclure had bought, or refunding such amount of money. Owen retaliated by getting out a writ against Maclure for ninety thousand dollars. A compromise, Brown says, was finally effected, and Owen gave to Maclure a deed in fee simple for his share of the property.

Robert Owen made the following statement in regard to the trouble: The friends of Mr. Maclure proposed that Mr. Owen and Mr. Maclure each put one hundred and fifty thousand dollars into the experiment just to be tried at New Harmony, and Mr. Owen consented. Mr. Maclure's liability, at his request, was limited to ten thousand dollars. Mr. Maclure went on to New Harmony to establish the Pestalozzian system. He failed to do it with any degree of swiftness, and Mr. Owen and the population itself became impatient. Mr. Maclure thought he could do better with part of the property under his control, and requested that a portion be set apart for him. Mr. Owen did not want such a division, not wishing the town hall to be separated from the community population, and so would not consent. Rapp had been paid one hundred thousand dollars by Owen, and notes had been made for forty thousand more. Rapp came after twenty thousand dollars when it was due, and wanted twenty thousand dollars that was due a year later. Owen paid the first twenty thousand dollars. Maclure refused to pay a cent toward this unless Owen would give him an unrestricted deed to the property which he had sold under restrictions. Maclure finally paid Rapp, and after getting the bonds in his possession he had Owen arrested and posted a notice disclaiming any intention to pay any of Owen's obligation. A board of arbitration decided Maclure to be five thousand dollars in Owen's debt. Mr. Owen had, he supposed, irritated Mr. Maclure, for he had inaugurated a

164

separate system of education in New Harmony, independent of Mr. Maclure's.

A. J. Macdonald, who spent some time at New Harmony, long enough after the trouble had subsided to make possible an impartial judgment of the controversy, says that the trouble " was most likely attributable to the fact that Owen commenced a system of education under the direction of Mr. Dorsey, differing from that of Maclure. Mr. Maclure had advanced only a small portion of the purchase money for the Rappite property, and after the formation of Macluria refused to pay any more without receiving from Mr. Owen a deed for the property he held. This Mr. Owen refused, unless the restriction relative to the property being used forever for community purposes was allowed to remain. The difficulty was, however, made up, and Mr. Maclure afterward paid forty thousand dollars and a balance of five thousand."

CHAPTER XVII

ROBERT OWEN'S FAREWELL ADDRESSES

"Mr. Owen's generosity and sincerity will survive all the sneers which have been cast upon them. His reward for his losses has been the consciousness of spending his time and means in doing good! Those who have shared his bounties or caught some of the sympathy elicited through his influence and diffused among those who desired to practise his benevolence, will look back as long as they live to the brief space when, amidst surrounding conflictions, they tasted a particle of true happiness on earth!"—MACDONALD.

ON Sunday, May 26, 1827, Robert Owen delivered at New Harmony Hall a "farewell address to the citizens of New Harmony and the members of the neighboring communities."

"A second year," he said, "has just expired since the experiment was commenced in this place to supersede the individual by the cooperative system of union and equality, under the form of a Preliminary Society.

"It is known to you that the persons who composed this society were entire strangers to each other; that some had come from every State in the Union, and some from almost every kingdom in Europe; that the society was instituted to enable these persons to become acquainted with each other, so that those who were capable of acting faithfully and cordially together might afterward form a community upon the social system; that after the Preliminary Society was constituted and the members had elected a committee to govern themselves, I went to Europe and returned again in about nine months; that soon after

166

my return it was proposed that a community of common property and equality should be formed from among the members of the Preliminary Society, and many of you know that it was my intention that the society should at first consist of those only who had acquired confidence in each other's qualifications for such a state of society, and it is also known to many who are present that this intention was frustrated by a motion being made at one of the public meetings that all the members of the Preliminary Society should be admitted members of the community. This motion was too popular to be resisted by those who did not otherwise expect to become members. From that period the most intelligent among the population foresaw that this measure would retard the formation of one large, united community in this town of Harmony; there were too many opposing habits and feelings to permit such a mass, without more instruction in the system, to act as one cordially together.

" This singularly constituted mass, however, contained materials out of which, by patience and perseverance, several communities might be ultimately formed; and all my subsequent measures were directed to accomplish this object.

" Although many here at that time were unprepared to be members of the community of common property and equality, yet there was much good feeling among the population generally. And if the schools had been in operation upon the very superior plan upon which I had been led to expect they would be, so as to convince parents, by ocular demonstration, of the benefits which their children would immediately derive from the system, it would have been, I think, practicable, even with such materials, with the patience and perseverance which would have been applied to the subject, to have succeeded in amalgamating the whole into a community.

" As these difficulties regarding the education of our

children were to be overcome, as well as many others to which this gave rise, I waited patiently for such change of circumstances as would enable me to make progress toward my object. With deep interest I attended to the various changes which the different parties desired to make, and I always met their wishes as far as circumstances would permit. I did so because I had not yet attained sufficient knowledge of the persons or of the country to act with my customary decision.

" These changes gave me a more speedy insight into the character of the population, and enabled me to obtain a better knowledge of those who were in some degree prepared for the social system. They also elicited knowledge of the means by which future communities might be most easily and safely formed; and to me this was invaluable experience, to be hereafter applied for the benefit of the inhabitants of this country and of Great Britain.

" Among those who first came here were many with whom none could be found to unite in communities. These persons became a great obstacle in the progress of our proceedings. It was necessary for the safety, comfort, and happiness of those who remained, and for the success of the system itself, that they should remove. Difficulty arose from the expense of their removal, and from the necessity of informing them that they were not such members as would be admitted into the communities. If I paid for the removal of one family, all would expect to be assisted in a like manner, an expenditure my funds would not admit of, after the large sums which had been previously expended in the experiment; and no one would like to be informed that none could be found who would admit them to become members of their community. This, however, was a difficulty which it was absolutely necessary, for the sake of all, should be overcome.

" That every one might have a fair and equal chance, I proposed to supply land in proportion to numbers, on

the estate of Harmony, to all who would associate, even
in small numbers, to commence a community, and that
they should be aided in food and implements of hus-
bandry to the extent that our means would afford, and this
was a public offer, made equally to all, and those who came
here with a view of forming communities accepted it, and
are now industriously occupied in preparing crops for this
season.

" Those persons who would not, or could not, so connect
themselves, were informed that they must leave Harmony
or support themselves by their own industry, or until they
could find persons of good character who would join them
in forming a community.

" This measure, unpleasant as it was to my feelings,
became unavoidable to prevent the entire loss of the property which had been appropriated to carry on the experiment; and by this course of proceedings, those persons who
were in a condition to promote the social system, were
relieved from the permanent support of those individuals
who were daily diminishing the fund which had been devoted for the more general beneficial purposes.

" Under these circumstances, many families, as you
know, left New Harmony, with their feelings more or less
hurt, and, in proportion to the knowledge and love of the
principles really possessed by each of them, are no doubt
active in their statements for or against my proceedings
and for or against the social system.

" This period, the most unpleasant and trying of any
which I have had to pass through—for my object in coming here was to benefit all, and, if possible, to injure none—
has, happily, passed. The social system is now firmly
established; the natural and easy means of forming communities have been developed by your past experience.
Already eight independent communities have been formed
upon the New Harmony estate, exclusive of Mr. Maclure's
educational society and of the town of New Harmony,

which has naturally become the place for the reception of strangers who have the desire to join some of the existing communities, or of forming others.

"New Harmony is now, therefore, literally surrounded by independent communities, and applications are made almost daily by persons, who come from far and near, to be permitted to establish themselves in a similar manner. The essential difference between our first and the present proceedings is this: at the commencement, strangers to each others' characters, principles, habits, views, and sentiments were associated together to acquire a knowledge of each other and to learn the practise of the social system; now, those only associate in communities who were previously well acquainted with each other, and possess similar habits, sentiments, and feelings, and who have made some advance in obtaining a knowledge of the principles and practises prerequisite to be known by those who become members of communities of equality and common property. Experience has proved that between these two modes of proceeding the difference is great indeed.

"Since those persons have removed from New Harmony who from one cause or another were disposed to leave us, the remainder of the population are, you perceive, gradually taking those situations best suited to their inclinations and former habits, and in some instances the occupations have formed among themselves a kind of preparatory society and are doing well. The lands of the communities around us have been put into a good state of cultivation, and are well fenced; there is, as you see, at this time, every appearance of abundance of fruit, all kinds of food and materials for clothing, and no want of industry to preserve the former and to manufacture the latter. Upward of thirty cabins have lately been erected upon the lands of communities Numbers 2, 3, and 4, and yet not a spare room can be obtained for any who come to us.

" The town and immediate vicinity of New Harmony have been, as you perceive, greatly improved lately, and other important improvements are in progress. No site for a number of communities in close union together can be found finer than that which surrounds us; its natural situation and the variety of its productions exceeds anything I have ever seen in Europe or America; the rich land, intermixed with islands, woods, rivers, and hills in a beautiful proportion to each other, presents, from our high ground, a prospect which highly gratifies every intelligent stranger. It is true, misconceptions of our proceedings and of our present state have gone forth to the great grief of those who were looking forward with an intense interest to an amelioration of the classes from the measures which were to commence here; but these reports have been beneficial. They have prevented us from being overwhelmed with numbers.

" These operations have been going on so successfully that perhaps no pleasure has been more pure than that which I have enjoyed for some time past in my daily visits to some of these establishments, where, by the industry of the persons engaged, I see the sure foundations laid of independence for themselves and for their children's children through many generations. From the new order of influences arising around them they must become a superior race—intelligent, virtuous, and happy; beings whose chief occupation, after a few years of temperance and industry, will be to distribute to others the means of becoming as independent, prudent, happy, and useful as themselves.

" I had also made my arrangements to settle, before my departure from Europe, every outstanding account against myself and those concerned with me in this establishment and experiment, that no obstacle should remain after my departure to impede the progress and success of the young colonies; and, looking back through the two years just expired, I could not but feel an almost inexpressible delight and inward satisfaction from reflecting upon the obstacles which had been overcome, and from viewing in the mind's eye the cheering prospects which are before us.

" While preparing for my journey to Europe, and just as I was going to set out, an event occurred which arose, as I must believe, from some extraordinary misconception in the minds of our well-meaning friends, which, fortunately, has delayed me some days among you. These misconceptions are, I believe, now completely removed, and I have had, by this delay, the pleasure of receiving and of becoming acquainted with some highly respectable families from the South, who have traveled several hundred miles on purpose to live some time among you, and to make themselves familiar with the new system."

On May 27th Mr. Owen delivered an address, full of parting counsel, to " the ten social colonies of equality and common property on the New Harmony estate,"— the two additional communities being colonies of Germans, one from Pennsylvania, and one from Germany, as we learn from the Gazette of May 23d. " With the right understanding of the principles upon which your change from the old to the new has been made," he said in part, " you will attain your object. Without that understanding you can not succeed. You should have honesty of purpose; devotion to the success of each and all communities; confidence in one another and submission to majority rule; well-regulated industry and wise economy; to make provision for the schools should be an object of first importance. . . . Industry, economy, beauty, order, and good feeling are silently and gradually growing up around you, and the right spirit of the great system, not derived from enthusiasm or imagination, but from a real knowledge of your own nature and of your true interest, is gaining ground among you, and can not fail soon to become general. . . . New Harmony can not be numbered among the colonies of the social system, but there is progress, and the day is not far distant when it will join the ranks of the faithful. . . .

"With regard to the schools, it is my desire that all your children should be educated in the best manner and at the least expense to you. I should like to add, without any expense to you; this would be the proceeding most gratifying to my feelings that could now occur; but having expended a large capital in putting you into your present independent condition; having paid for the whole of the real and personal property that I purchased since I came to this country, and having discharged every other debt, I do not yet know whether my remaining income will enable me, with the prudence that is necessary in my situation, to undertake to clothe, feed, and educate all your children without cost, or with such aid from your surplus produce as you can spare without inconvenience. Relying, however, upon the faithful stewardship of the parties in whose hands the remaining property which I possess here has been entrusted, I shall appropriate three thousand dollars this year toward defraying the expenses of this all-important subject, the general direction of which I leave to Mr. Dorsey, late treasurer of Miami University, in whose steadfastness, integrity, ability, and disinterested devotion to the cause I have full confidence. . . .

"When I return I hope to find you progressing in harmony together."

On June 1, 1827, Mr. Owen left New Harmony for England, stopping *en route* to New York in several cities to deliver lectures on the social system, and to paint hopeful pictures of conditions at New Harmony.

CHAPTER XVIII

ROBERT OWEN had met the Waterloo of his communistic schemes, but he retired from a field of hopeless defeat as if he had been the Wellington, rather than the Napoleon, of the contest. It soon became evident that the enthusiastic spirit of Robert Owen, with the funds at his command, had alone kept the population so long together in the semblance of communistic association. With the commander-in-chief gone the little army broke into disastrous retreat before the self-assertive forces of individualism. The last evidence of the existence of any of the communistic societies is a report of a Harvest Home celebration by Feiba Peveli on July 26, 1827, when "fifty persons sat down to an excellent supper laid out on the lawn near their village; the utmost order prevailed, and appropriate songs and toasts added to the hilarity of the evening." One by one these societies became disorganized by dissension, and when Robert Owen returned to New Harmony, on April 1, 1828, his optimism failed in the face of a complete collapse of the "social system," though his confession of defeat was a grudging one.

"I had hoped," he said, in an address delivered at New Harmony Hall on April 13, 1828, "that fifty years of political liberty had prepared the American people to govern themselves advantageously. I supplied land, houses, and the use of capital, and I tried, each in their own way, the different parties who collected here; and experience proved that the attempt was premature, to unite

174

a number of strangers not previously educated for the purpose. I afterward tried what could be done by those who associated through their own choice and in small numbers; to those I gave leases of large tracts of good land for ten thousand years for a nominal rent, and upon moral conditions only; and these I did expect would have made progress during my absence; and now upon my return I find that the habits of the individual system were so powerful that these leases have been, with a few exceptions, applied for individual purposes and individual gain, and in consequence they must return again into my hands.

"This proves that families, trained in the individual system, have not acquired those moral characteristics of forbearance and charity necessary for confidence and harmony; and communities, to be successful, must consist of persons devoid of prejudice, and possessed of moral feelings in unison with the laws of human nature.

"Monopolies have been established in certain departments without my indorsement; it was not my intention to have a petty store and whisky shop here.

"I can only feel regret, instead of anger," said Mr. Owen, in closing. "My intention now is to form such arrangements on the estate as will enable those who desire to promote the practise of the social system, to live in separate families on the individual system and yet to unite their general labor; or to exchange labor for labor on the most beneficial terms for all; all to do both or neither as their feelings or apparent interest may influence them; while the children shall be educated with a view to the establishment of the social system in the future. . . . I will not be discouraged by any obstacle, but will persevere to the end."

Some of the leases offered by Robert Owen to small communistic societies in 1827, were taken by sincere and industrious workers; others were obtained by speculators, who cared nothing for Owen or his schemes. To those

who had acted in good faith, Mr. Owen finally sold, at a
low figure, the lands they occupied. Through the speculators he lost a large amount of personal property. His
expenditures in the purchase and maintenance of the property, with his losses by adventurers, aggregated two hundred thousand dollars—his entire fortune at the beginning
of the experiment amounting to but fifty thousand dollars
more. Had the community system proved practicable, his
intention was to deed this land in trust to the associations
without exacting any payment whatever. What was left
of his fortune he soon expended in the furtherance of
similar social schemes. As some one has said: " He seems
to have felt it a point of honor, so long as he had means
left, to avert reproach from the cause of cooperation by
paying debts left standing at the close of unsuccessful
experiments, whenever these had been conducted in good
faith." In later years he conveyed the residue of the New
Harmony estate to his four sons, only requiring of them
that they execute a deed of trust for thirty thousand dollars' worth of land, which yielded an annuity of fifteen
hundred dollars. This was his sole source of support for
many years.

It is impossible to trace the processes by which the
property of the various communities passed into individual
hands. Dr. Schnack says that Messrs. John Cooper, James
Elliot, James Maidlow, Jonathan Stocker, and others continued community Number 3 under the original lease for
several years, but that at the dissolution of the organization the property was bought and divided by Messrs.
Cooper, Maidlow, and Elliot. The lease of community
Number 2 finally came into the hands of Jacob Schnee, the
postmaster at New Harmony during community days, and
later was merged in a purchase by W. C. Pelham. Other
individuals undertook the management of the several factories, but with little success, so that the buildings were
finally diverted to other purposes than that of manufactur-

176

ing. So many of the communists remained in New Harmony and its immediate vicinity, that Dr. Schnack, with
the assistance of several old residents, compiled in 1890
the following list of New Harmony family names which
still survive the community period: Beal, Birkbeck (descendants of Morris Birkbeck, of the English colony in
Edwards County, who was drowned in Fox River while returning to Albion, Illinois, from a visit to the community), Bolton, Brown, Cooper, Cox, Dransfield, Duclos,
Evans, Fauntleroy, Fretageot, Gex, Grant, Hugo, Johnson,
Lichtenberger, Bennett, West, Lyons, Mumford, Murphy,
Neef, Owen, Parvin, Pelham, Robson, Sampson, Schnee,
Snelling, Soper, Twigg, Warren, and Wheatcroft.

A. J. Macdonald, in his unpublished manuscript on
American Communities, gives the data contained in the
following table concerning the communistic societies, exclusive of those located on the New Harmony estate, which
had their origin in the Owenite movement:

Name.	Place.	Capital.	Debt.	Duration.
Blue Spring ...	Monroe Co., Ind.			One year.
Cooperative Society......	Valley Forge, Pa.			
Coxsackie	New York.	Small.	Large.	Between 1 and 2 yrs.
Forrestville....	Indiana.	325 acres of land.		1 year.
Franklin	New York.			
Haverstraw (80 members)....	New York.	120 acres of land.	$12,000.	5 months.
Kendal (200 members)....	Ohio.	200 acres of land.		2 years.
Nashoba.......	Tennessee.	2,000 acres of land.		3 years.
Yellow Springs (100 families).	Ohio.			

The total number of communities was nineteen; of which twelve were situated in Indiana, three in New York, two in Ohio, one in Pennsylvania, and one in Tennessee. It is certain that this list is not complete. In southwestern Indiana, especially, the communistic fever was prevalent during the years through which the New Harmony experiment continued and many neighborhoods were affected by it. In some cases branches of families united in communistic association for brief periods. By 1830 not an association was left to continue the movement so auspiciously inaugurated by Robert Owen five years before.

Explanations of the failure of the Owenite communities have been as numerous as commentarians upon them. The most comprehensive estimate of the causes leading to failure is that of Macdonald, who spent eighteen months at New Harmony in 1853–54, twenty-five years after the last vestige of communistic association disappeared from the estate. His remarks are interesting. " I was cautioned," he said, " not to speak on socialism, as the subject was unpopular. The advice was good—socialism was unpopular, and with good reason. The people had been wearied and disappointed, had been filled full of theories until they were nauseated, and had made such miserable attempts at practise that they seemed ashamed of what they had been doing. An enthusiastic socialist would soon be ' cooled down,' because the people would see his ignorance.

" During a residence of nearly eighteen months in New Harmony, I endeavored to ascertain some particulars regarding the failure of the community. It was a difficult endeavor, for as Mr. Warren truly said: ' If you ask a dozen individuals, you will get a dozen different causes.' The cause Mr. W—— assigned was ' error in the principles,' and for many years he has endeavored to prove the error by introducing his plan of ' equitable commerce.'

" From Mr. C—— I heard the story, as he ended it, by

178

saying, that with all the troubles and vexations of that important period it was the happiest time of his life. Mr. A—— said that many persons came there and lived as long as they could get supplies for nothing. Many things were obtained from the public store which were lost or wasted. Mr. B—— said that there were some noble characters there, with names that have since stood high in the localities to which they belonged, who set examples of industry and self-denial worthy of a great cause. I could mention some of them that I have known in my travels. Mr. C—— said that Mr. Owen forbade the use of spirituous liquors in the town; yet it was obtained from the distillery in a variety of cunning ways. Persons went at night and deposited bottles, mugs, and cans, and returned at certain periods and found them filled.

"I was one day at the tan-yard, and Squire B—— and some others were standing talking around the store. During the conversation Squire B—— asked if he had ever told them how he had served 'old Owen' in 'community time.' He then informed us that he came from Illinois to New Harmony, and that a man in Illinois was 'owing him,' and asked him to take a barrel of whisky for the debt. As he could not well get the money, he took the whisky. When he came to New Harmony he did not know where to put it, but finally hid it in his cellar. Not long after this Mr. Owen found that the people still got whisky from some quarter, he could not tell where, though he did his best to find out. At last he suspected Squire B——, and accordingly came right into his shop and accused him of it; on which Squire B—— had to 'own up' that it was he who had retailed the whisky, saying he had to take it for a debt, and what was he to do to get rid of it. Mr. Owen turned 'round and in his simple manner said, 'Ah! I see you do not understand the principles.' This story was finished with a good hearty laugh at 'old Owen.' I could not laugh, but felt that such men as Squire B—— did *not*

179

understand the principles, and no wonder there are failures, when such men as he frustrate benevolent designs.

" Mr. Owen has often said that the New Harmony experiment failed because the members did not understand the principles. It may be so—facts speak for themselves, and every individual must be free, as he is, to find out, each his different cause. All agree that a battle was fought, that there was some gain, and some loss, but though many years have now passed away it still remains for time to prove whether the battle was for the good or evil of mankind.

" The reader will no doubt, think with me, that the history of the New Harmony community, so far as I have been able to collect it, is but a mass of confusion; so many theories were tried, and so many failures took place, that, like a ball of entangled thread, it is difficult to unravel. If he glances at Mr. Owen's principles, he will see what Mr. Owen wished to practise, and if he understands the materials with which this practise was to be made, he will see how impossible it was to produce the desired results.

" Mr. Owen said he wanted ' honesty of purpose,' but he got dishonesty; he wanted temperance, and, instead, he was continually troubled with intemperance; indeed, this appears to have been one of the greatest troubles with which he had to contend in those times. . . . He wanted industry, but he found idleness; he wanted carefulness, and found waste; he wanted cleanliness, and found dirt; he wanted ' desire for knowledge,' but he found apathy. He wanted the principles of the formation of character understood, but he found them misunderstood. He wanted these good qualities combined in one and all the individuals of the community, but he could not find them self-sacrificing and enduring enough to prepare and educate their children to possess these qualities. Thus it was proved that his principles were either entirely erroneous

180

in practise or much in advance of the age in which he promulgated them.

"He seems to have forgotten that if 'one and all the thousand persons assembled there possessed all the qualities which he wished them to possess, there would be no necessity for his vain exertions to form a community, because there would of necessity be 'brotherly love,' charity, industry, and plenty, and all their actions would be governed by nature and reason. We want no more than this, and if this is the material to form communities of, and we can not find it, we can not form communities. And if we can not find parents who are ready and willing to educate their children to give them qualities for a 'community life,' then when shall we have 'communities of united effort'?

"There is no doubt in my mind that the absence of Robert Owen was one of the great causes of the failure of the community, for he was naturally looked up to as the head, and his influence might have kept people together, at any rate to effect something similar to what had been effected at New Lanark. But with a people free as these were from a set religious creed, and consisting as they did of all nations and opinions, it is doubtful if, even Mr. Owen had continued there all the time, he could have kept them together. No comparison can be made between that population and the Shakers or Rappites, who are each of one religious faith. . . .

"Wm. Sampson, of Cincinnati, was at New Harmony from the beginning to the end of the community. He went there on the boat which took the last of the Rappites away. He says the cause of failure was a rogue named Taylor, who insinuated himself into Mr. Owen's favor, and afterward swindled and deceived him in a variety of ways; among other things establishing a distillery contrary to Mr. Owen's wishes or principles, and injurious to the community. Owen thought it would be ten or twelve years

181

before the community would fill up, but no sooner had the Rappites left than the place was taken possession of by strangers from all parts, when Owen was absent in Europe and the place was under the management of a committee. When Owen returned and found the condition of things, he deemed it necessary to make an alteration, and notices were published in all parts telling people not to come there, as there was no accommodation for them, yet still they came, until Owen was compelled to have all the log cabins razed.

"Taylor and Fauntleroy were Owen's associates. When Owen found out Taylor's rascality he resolved to abandon the partnership with him, which Taylor would only agree to do upon Owen's giving him a large tract of land upon which he proposed to form a community of his own. . . . Instead of forming a community, he built a distillery, and set up a tan-yard in opposition to Mr. Owen's.

"In the Free Enquirer, of June 10, 1829, there is an article by Robert Dale Owen on New Lanark and New Harmony, in which, after comparing the two places and showing the difference between them, he makes the following remarks relative to the experiment at New Harmony: 'There was not disinterested industry; there was not mutual confidence; there was not practical experience; there was not unison of action because there was not unanimity of counsel. These were the points of difference and dissension—the rocks on which the social hulk struck and was wrecked.'

"In The New Moral World of October 12, 1839, there is an article on New Harmony in which it is asserted that Mr. Owen was induced to purchase that place on the understanding that the population then resident there, the Rappites, would remain until he had gradually introduced other persons to acquire from them the systematic and orderly habits, as well as practical knowledge which they had gained by many years of practise. But through the removal of Rapp and his followers Mr. Owen was left with all the property on his hands, and he was compelled of necessity to get persons to come there to prevent things from going to ruin. It shows the unsuitableness of the persons who went there, and how they failed in their attempts, and proves the sincerity of Mr. Owen in the terms upon which he granted them land, viz.—the perpetual lease of the lands so long as the principles of the new system were carried into practise. They failed to do this, and the estate reverted to Mr. Owen."

Josiah Warren in his Practical Details of Equitable Commerce, says: "Let us bear in mind that during the great experiments in New Harmony everything went on delightfully except pecuniary affairs. We should no doubt have succeeded, but for property considerations. But then the experiment would never have been commenced except for property considerations. It was to annihilate social antagonisms by a system of common property that we undertook the experiment at all."

John Pratt, a Positivist, as quoted by Noyes, said: "Like most men of the last generation Robert Owen looked upon society as a manufactured product, not an organism endowed with imperishable vitality and growth. . . . The internal affinities of Owen's Commune were too weak to resist the attractions of the outer world."

Horace Greeley and Charles A. Dana attributed the failure principally to the lack of a religious basis upon which all successful communities had been founded— Owen having been the first to attempt the establishment of a non-religious community. Greeley said that a great obstacle encountered in such experiments was "the class of people attracted—the conceited, the crotchety, and the selfish"; while Dana concluded: "Destroy selfhood, and you destroy all motive to exertion."

Sargent, one of Owen's biographers, thinks there should have been some religious bond among the members

183

to insure success. Paul Brown, in his Twelve Months at New Harmony, questioned the sincerity of Robert Owen himself, while E. H. Hamilton, as quoted by Noyes, says that Owen " required other people to be what he was not himself; he himself was unreceptive as a thinker." Noyes thinks that drink had much to do with the failure, in spite of prohibitory enactments. Noyes quotes some of his associates as saying:

L. R. Leonard: " He found democrats harder to manage than the servile workmen of Scotland."

G. W. Hamilton: " The Owenites were too independent."

F. W. Smith: " He did not have enough deputies."

C. W. Burt: " Communism must be ruled either by law or grace. He abolished law and did not employ grace."

George Jacob Holyoke, in his History of Cooperation, says that " the cranks killed the colony," which was composed, " for the most part, of the selfish, the headstrong, the pugnacious, the unappreciated, the played-out, the idle, and the good-for-nothing generally, who, discovering themselves out of place, and at a discount in the world as it is, rashly conclude that they are exactly fitted for the world as it ought to be. . . . Nevertheless, the men of good sense reigned at first, and prevailed intermittently throughout. . . . The absence of Mr. Owen during the years when personal inspiration and training were most important were causes quite sufficient to account for the fluctuations and the final effacement of New Harmony."

Noyes gives us the explanation offered by the members of four of the branch communities, as follows:

Yellow Springs: " Self-love was a spirit that could not be exorcised."

Nashoba: " The projectors acknowledge that such a system can not succeed unless the members composing it are superior beings."

184

Haverstraw community: " There was a lack of men and women of skilful industry, sober and honest, with a knowledge of themselves and a disposition to command and to be commanded."

Coxsackie community: " Too many persons engaged in law-making and talking, who did not work at any useful employment."

Robert Dale Owen, writing many years after the conclusion of the New Harmony venture, says, in speaking of the Gazette editorial before quoted as an obituary of the New Harmony and Macluria communities: " In enumerating the causes leading to the failure of the experiment, the Gazette . . . omits the one most potent factor. All cooperative schemes which provide equal remuneration to the skilled and industrious and the ignorant and idle, must work their own downfall, for by this unjust plan of remuneration they must of necessity eliminate the valuable members—who find their services reaped by the indigent—and retain only the improvident, unskilled, and vicious members. . . . Robert Owen distinguished the great principle, but, like so many other devisers, missed the working details of his scheme. If these, when stated, seem to be so near the surface that common sagacity ought to have detected them, let us bear in mind how wise men stumbled over the simple puzzle of Columbus; failing to balance the egg on one end till a touch from the great navigator's hand solved the petty mystery."

CHAPTER XIX

WOMAN AT NEW HARMONY

" Woman : May the experiment being tried in New Harmony of the same intellectual cultivation of the sexes, prove that woman's capabilities are equal to those of men."—*Toast responded to at the Semi-Centennial celebration at Marietta, Ohio, July 4, 1826.*

THE last century was a great iconoclast. Errors overthrown, fallacies exploded, superstitions vanquished, and broken idols lie strewn along its pathway. In its humanity the century shamed its predecessors. There was no social condition which it did not ameliorate and no social class which it did not lift and better. The nineteenth century did more for womankind than for any other social group. To woman it threw wide open the doors of its schools and universities. For her it wrote welcome above the threshold of every vocation for which she has shown herself to be adapted and in which she has made herself proficient. It broke down the idolatry by which men had perpetuated the errors of the Common Law and relieved woman of its cruelties by legislative enactment. It protected her from the drunkenness and brutality of unworthy husbands and bestowed upon her every right, save that of suffrage, formerly enjoyed by the sterner sex alone. The twentieth century found woman a legal slave and sent her into the twentieth century man's legal as well as his social equal.

Much of the battle for equal rights of women centered around the demand for equal political rights. The group of agitators in the forefront of the woman-suffrage movement attacked every abuse and every injustice from which their sisterhood suffered. Public sentiment yielded to every demand save the one for which they labored most zealously, but bequeathed its solution to posterity. In the history of woman suffrage published by those three able leaders in the movement, Elizabeth Cady Stanton, Susan B. Anthony, and Matilda Joslyn Gage, the following are given as the chief of the immediate causes that led to the demand for the equal political rights of women in this country:

(1) " The able lectures of Frances Wright on political, religious, and social questions. Ernestine L. Rose, following in her wake, equally liberal in her religious opinions and equally well informed on the science of government, helped to deepen and perpetuate the impression Frances Wright had made on the minds of unprejudiced hearers." Frances Wright was a member of The New Moral World, a devotee of its communistic theories and the coadjutor of the Owens. She saw practised there a many-phased emancipation of woman ere she contended for it before the lyceum of the nation. Ernestine Rose, who came from England to settle in the State of New York after the failure of the great experiment on the Wabash, was a follower of Robert Owen.

(2) " The discussion in several of the State legislatures on the property rights of married women. These were heralded by the press with comments grave and gay, became the topic of general interest around many fashionable dinner-tables and at many humble firesides. In this way all phases of the question were touched upon, involving the relations of the sexes, and gradually widening to all human interests—political, religious, civil, and social. The press and pulpit became suddenly vigilant in making out woman's sphere while woman herself seemed equally vigilant in her efforts to step outside the prescribed limits." Robert Dale Owen stood foremost among legislators in

187

championing the rights of woman. At New Harmony had been advocated and practised most if not all the innovations in the legal status of women which he in later years wrote into the laws of his own State. The advanced notions concerning the equality of the sexes which The New Moral World proclaimed attracted the attention of the entire country at the time, led to much vigorous discussion of woman's true sphere and rights, and doubtless paved the way for the reforms of later years.

(3) "Above all other causes of the woman-suffrage movement was the antislavery struggle in this country. The early abolitionists numbered in their ranks some of the most splendid specimens of womanhood in physical appearance, in culture, refinement, and knowledge of polite life." Their eloquence thrilled the country. The question of their right to speak, vote, and serve on committees in antislavery organizations precipitated to the fullest a fierce discussion of woman's political rights. In abolitionist conventions women learned to debate and transact business affairs. Broad discussions of justice, liberty, and equality taught them the lesson of freedom for themselves. Equality before the law for the negro suggested the justice of a similar equality for them. Suffrage bestowed upon the liberated bondsman afforded an unanswerable argument in favor of political rights for the gentler sex.

The New Moral World opposed slavery with bitterness. Frances Wright denounced it from the rostrum and sought to abolish it by colonization. Robert Dale Owen fought it vigorously for almost forty years, became one of the most conspicuous of the antislavery orators and played no small part in the overthrow of the institution.

The New Moral World revolutionized the condition of woman within its boundaries and hoped through the example which it set to effect a similar revolution everywhere. The philosophy of Robert Owen contemplated equal privileges for the sexes. The educational institutions at New

FRANCES WRIGHT.

Harmony were coeducational from the beginning—a pioneer venture which attracted wide attention and comment. In the original community, women were given an equal voice with men in legislation. In several of the later communities women were given a vote in legislative assemblages and in others the right to participate in debate. In all cases the widows of deceased members of The New Moral World succeeded to the rights and privileges which their husbands had enjoyed. The Common Law wrested all property from the hands of a married woman and bestowed its management and enjoyment upon her husband. By abolishing the institution of private property, Owen's system annulled so far as the Commune was concerned the greatest injustice which that law had for centuries inflicted upon womankind.

The broad philanthropy of Owen and Maclure knew no distinctions of color or sex. They sought in the enterprise on the Wabash "the happiness and well-being of every man, woman, and child, without regard to their sect, class, party, or color." The principle of human equality was a cardinal one with them. But they were more consistent in its application than the government which wrote the Declaration and tolerated slavery. There was no escaping the logic of their reasoning. If woman was man's equal, then there was not a social, a property or a political right which he enjoyed, to which she was not justly and equally entitled.

Perhaps the chief cause for the advanced position of the Commune upon woman's rights lay in the chivalric regard for women that characterized the Owens, both father and son. In his day, the charge was widely made and believed that the elder Owen stood sponsor for free love. It still lingers as a popular impression which never had foundation in fact. The private character of Robert Owen was exceptionally pure and his family life was happy. Robert Dale Owen relates that his mother declared to him

189

upon a number of occasions that his father was all that her heart could desire him to be.

Like father, like son, was never more truthfully illustrated than by the elder and younger Owen. Seldom have parent and offspring held as many common interests or stood for as many common principles. There are few finer tributes to woman in the language than the one offered by Robert Dale Owen during the progress of the debates concerning the property rights of married women in the last Indiana Constitutional Convention.

"I owe to woman, as wife, as friend, all the best, the happiest,—yes, and the purest hours of my life. Sir, no man of sense or modesty unnecessarily obtrudes upon the public personalities that regard himself and his private thoughts and actions. But yet grossly assailed as my conduct and principles have been upon this floor, it may not be unfitting that I should say here, that to a good father, to an excellent mother, I owe it that my youth was preserved from habits of excess, from associations of profligacy. . . . I have no associations connected with the name of woman save those of esteem and respectful affection. I owe to her sex a debt of gratitude that can never be paid though my days were extended to the term of life assigned to the ancient patriarchs and though all those days were spent in her service and were devoted to the vindication of her rights."

Robert Owen's desire to ameliorate the condition of woman led him into a radical and much discussed attitude on the institution of marriage. But it is certain that he looked upon his attack on the existing form of marriage as a step in the direction of a higher morality and a wider justice. One of the severest indictments that he urges against the existing state of society was that in it a natural marriage was almost impossible. He hastened to explain that he meant by natural marriage "a marriage where a union is formed under those institutions which provide for all parties an equal education, under which they are enabled to acquire an accurate knowledge of themselves and of human nature; wherein no other motive shall influence the affections but intimate sympathy and unaffected congeniality, founded on a real knowledge of each other by both parties; where the imagination has been carefully excluded and where the judgment has been guide and director."

The charge that Robert Owen stood sponsor for free love is preposterous. To him, both in practise and precept, the marriage of one man and one woman was one of the most sacred institutions that has blessed the race. No community practised a higher morality than did New Harmony under his *régime* and nowhere was the marriage relation held in greater esteem or more happily and faithfully observed than at New Harmony during community days. Owen did object to the form of marriage then observed, because, he declared, " It obligates the contracting parties to do what they may not be able to perform and because it marks a disposition to enslave one-half of our fellow creatures." While he devised a new ceremony by which the people of the community regarded themselves as equally bound, yet in compliance with custom and the laws of the State the new ceremony was observed not as a substitute for but an addition to the old.

The New Harmony Gazette gives an interesting account of a double marriage ceremony performed under the auspices of the community on the first Sunday in April, 1826. At a regular meeting of the society in New Harmony Hall, Rev. John Burkitt joined in marriage " Philip M. Price, late of Philadelphia, to Matilda Greenbree, late of Washington City, and Robert Robson, late of Washington City, to Eliza E. Parvin, late of Princeton, Indiana."

" In compliance with a resolution passed at a previous meeting of the community," says the Gazette, " the four parties, previous to the performance of the marriage ceremony, entered a protest against the usual form of marriage in the following manner: Each couple standing up in the meeting, and taking each other by the hand, severally repeated: ' I, A. B., do agree to take this man (woman) to be my husband (wife), and I declare that I submit to any other ceremony upon this occasion only in conformity with the laws of the State.' They then went through with the marriage ceremony in usual form."

The elder Owen's solicitude for the welfare of the women of the community was characteristic. When at one of the Sunday meetings during the summer of 1826 it was agreed that the society should meet on three evenings each week for instruction, the point was raised that "the females would hardly have time to get done with supper to meet there so early and so often." "Mr. Owen said," an account of the meeting states, "that he had been endeavoring to ascertain the cause why so much difficulty is experienced by the females of this community in the performance of their domestic duties." Female labor, he declared, ought to be lighter under the community than under the individual system. Perhaps the women spent too much time talking, he suggested. "By coming to these meetings for instruction they might perhaps get rid of the desire and the occasion for so much useless talk."

The further suggestion was made at this meeting that "there existed great jealousy among the females of this place; that some were afraid of doing more than their share of the work, and some were afraid of doing anything at all." Mr. Owen responded that "education begun at the age of three years would eradicate these evil passions from the coming generation."

In the New Harmony library is still to be seen the desk over which Frances Wright delivered lectures in which woman suffrage was first advocated, and some of the first arguments in favor of the abolition of slavery and the granting of suffrage to the negroes were advanced.

Frances Wright was one of the most interesting figures in the brilliant coterie of eccentric reformers which gathered about Robert Owen at the announcement of his New Harmony plans. With her sister Camilla she was left an orphan at an early age, and these girls of large fortune and gentle birth were confided to the care of Jeremy Bentham, who at one time was associated in business with Robert Owen.

" He had them educated according to his own peculiar crotchets," says one writer, " and very eccentric women he made of them; they fitted into no social map, no domestic form. Frances had a strong masculine mind and character, and took to the manly rearing Bentham gave her." " She was thoroughly versed in the literature of the day," says Robert Dale Owen, " was well informed on general topics, and spoke French and Italian fluently. She had traveled and resided for years in Europe, was an intimate friend of General Lafayette, had made the acquaintance of many leading reformers, Hungarian, Polish, and others, and was a thorough republican; indeed, an advocate of universal suffrage without regard to color or sex. . . . Refined in her manner and language, she was a radical alike in politics, morals, and religion. She had a strong, logical mind, a courageous independence of thought, and a zealous wish to benefit her fellow creatures; but the mind had not been submitted to early discipline, the courage was not tempered with prudence, the philanthropy had too little of common sense to give it practical form and efficiency. Her enthusiasm, eager but fitful, lacked the guiding check of sound judgment. Her abilities as an author and lecturer were of a high order, but an inordinate estimate of her own mental powers, and obstinate adherence to opinions once adopted, detracted seriously from the influence which her talents and eloquence might have exerted. A redeeming point was, that to carry out her convictions she was ready to make great sacrifices, personal and pecuniary.

She and a young sister, a lady alike amiable and estimable, had always lived and journeyed together, were independent in their circumstances, and were devotedly attached to each other.

"She had various personal advantages—a tall, commanding figure, somewhat slender and graceful, though the shoulders were a little bit too high; a face the outline of which in profile, though delicately chiseled, was masculine rather than feminine, like that of an Antinous, or perhaps more nearly typifying a Mercury; the forehead broad, but not high; the short chestnut hair curling naturally all over a classic head; the large blue eyes not soft, but clear and earnest. When I first met her, at Harmony, in the summer of 1826, some of the peculiarities of character above set forth had not developed themselves. She was then known in England and here only as the author of a small book entitled, A Few Days in Athens, published and favorably received in London, and of a volume of travels in the United States, in which she spoke in laudatory tone of our institutions and of our people."

Frances Wright first appeared at New Harmony after the purchase of the estate by Mr. Owen, but before the removal of the Rappites, whom she accompanied to Pennsylvania, and there studied their methods of settlement. She spent some time at New Harmony after the founding of the Preliminary Society, and in the summer of 1825 issued a prospectus announcing plans for founding a community in which not only the industrial problem but the slave question was to be solved.

She purchased two thousand acres of woodland situated on both sides of Wolf River thirteen miles above Memphis. With fifteen negroes purchased of neighboring slaveholders, she began her experiment in the autumn of 1825, giving the name "Nashoba" to her colony. Her idea was to elevate the negro by education, and to found a community system which, by spreading, would eventually result in the abolition of slavery; but there was to be in each community a coterie of " good and great men and women of all countries," as Noyes says, " who might there sympathize with each other in their love and labor for humanity. She invited congenial minds from every quarter of the globe to unite with her in the search for truth and the pursuit of rational happiness." Half of the earnings of each negro was to be set apart to purchase his emancipation, if necessary. Each community was to be managed by the whites.

" The theory was benevolent," says Noyes, " but practically the institution must have been a two-story commonwealth, something like the old Grecian states which founded liberty on Helotism. It might be defined as a Brook Farm plus a negro basis, thus obviating the difficulty encountered in that experiment, which Hawthorne designates, namely, that the amateurs who took part in that picnic, ' did not like to serve as chambermaids to the cows.' "

Early in the history of this experiment, failing health compelled Frances Wright to make a trip to Europe. During her absence matters became sadly tangled, and on her return in December she made over the estate to a board of trustees composed of General Lafayette, William Maclure, Robert Owen, Cadwallader Colden, Richeson Whitby, Robert Jennings, Robert Dale Owen, George Flower, Camilla Wright, and James Richardson, " to be held by them, their associates, and their successors in perpetual trust for the benefit of the negro race." By two other deeds she gave to these trustees the negro slaves on the estate, and all her personal property.

In an appeal to the public issued at this time she declared that no difference in education or other advantages would be made between white and colored children. Conditions did not greatly improve under the management of the trustees, and in March, 1828, they published a com-

munication in the Nashoba Gazette in which the failure of
the cooperative feature of the scheme was practically admitted, and it was proposed that each white member of
the community pay into the treasury one hundred dollars
annually for board; "each one must also build himself a
small brick house with a piazza, according to a regular plan,
and upon a spot of ground selected for the purpose near
the center of the lands." Frances Wright, Richeson Whitby, Camilla Wright Whitby, and Robert Dale Owen signed
this communication as resident trustees.

Soon after this the community was abandoned, and in
the following June Frances Wright moved to New Harmony, where, in conjunction with William Owen, she
edited the New Harmony Gazette, which became the New
Harmony and Nashoba Gazette, or Free Enquirer.

During community days Frances Wright gathered
about her at New Harmony a coterie of kindred spirits and
founded an organization of women for study and discussion. This organization succeeded what was known as the
Woman's Social Society, established during the continuance
of the Preliminary Society in 1826. In turn the society
founded by Frances Wright, after it had lapsed for over
twenty-five years, was succeeded on September 20, 1859,
by the Minerva Society, a woman's literary club, founded
by Mrs. Constance Fauntleroy Runcie, a granddaughter
of Robert Owen. This club was the first woman's club in
the United States, in the present sense of that term. The
Minerva Society antedated the Boston Women's Club and
Sorosis of New York by nine years. "It was," Mrs.
Runcie writes, "a complete, fully officered club. The club
procedure adopted by this organization has since been followed by all clubs as to the main idea."

Shortly after the downfall of Owen's social order, the
New Harmony Gazette, with the title of Free Enquirer,
was removed to New York and for several years ably edited
by Frances Wright and Robert Dale Owen. These gifted

iconoclasts attacked every social and political abuse, but none more vigorously than the unjust provisions of the Common Law respecting the rights of married women. From the metropolis, Frances Wright soon began a whirlwind lecturing tour of the country. One of her favorite themes was the equality of the sexes. Her brilliancy and radicalism attracted wide-spread attention. Her eloquent plea for equal rights for the gentler sex and her fierce denunciation of the existing legal status of woman sowed the seeds of a later agitation that wrested from the reluctant hands of the dominant sex every legal right for which she had contended save that of suffrage.

Misunderstood and vilified by her contemporaries, Frances Wright has come into a tardy recognition of the valuable pioneer service which she rendered in behalf of the legal emancipation of womankind.

John Humphrey Noyes, in his History of American Socialisms, says: "This woman, little known to the present generation, was really the spiritual helpmate and better half of the Owens, in the socialistic revival of 1826. Our impression is, not only that she was the leading woman in the communistic movement of that period, but that she had a very important agency in starting two other movements that had far greater success and are at this moment in popular favor, viz.: antislavery and woman's rights. If justice were done, we are confident her name would figure high with those of Lundy, Garrison, and John Brown on the one hand, and those of Abby Kelly, Lucy Stone, and Anna Dickinson on the other. She was indeed the pioneer of strong-minded women."

In the tenth National Woman's Rights Convention, Ernestine L. Rose, herself a pioneer in the advocacy of woman's rights, paid this just tribute to the founder of the agitation:

"Frances Wright was the first woman in this country who spoke on the equality of the sexes. She had indeed a hard task before her. The elements were entirely unprepared. She had to break up the time-hardened soil of conservatism, and her reward was sure—the same reward that is always bestowed upon those who are in the vanguard of any great movement. She was subjected to public odium, slander, and persecution. But these were not the only things that she received. Oh, she had her reward! —that reward of which no enemies could deprive her, which no slanders could make less precious—the eternal reward of knowing that she had done her duty; the reward springing from the consciousness of right, of endeavoring to benefit unborn generations. How delightful to see the molding of the minds around you, the infusing of your thoughts and aspirations into others, until one by one they stand by your side, without knowing how they came there! That reward she had. It has been her glory, it is the glory of her memory; and the time will come when society will have outgrown its old prejudices, and stepped with one foot, at least, upon the elevated platform on which she took her position. But owing to the fact that the elements were unprepared, she naturally could not succeed to any great extent."

At a celebration of the twentieth anniversary of the National Woman Suffrage Association, held in Apollo Hall in New York City on the 19th day of October, 1870, Paulina W. Davis, who had called the first National Convention twenty years before, was unanimously chosen to preside. On taking the chair, Mrs. Davis gave a *résumé* of the Woman's Rights Movement, in the course of which she gave this testimony to the purity of life and the unselfishness of the labors of Frances Wright in behalf of a world-wide sisterhood:

" To this heroic woman, who left ease, elegance, a high social circle of rich culture, and with true self-abnegation gave her life, in the country of her adoption, to the teaching of her highest idea of truth, it is fitting that we pay

a tribute of just, though late, respect. Her writings are
of the purest and noblest character, and whatever there
is of error in them is easily thrown aside. The spider
sucks poison from the same flower from which the bee
gathers honey; let us therefore ask if the evil be not in
ourselves before we condemn others. Pharisaism, then as
now, was ready to stone the prophet of freedom. She bore
the calumny, reproach, and persecution to which she was
subjected for the truth, as calmly as Socrates. Looking
down from the serene heights of her philosophy she pitied
and endured the scoffs and jeers of the multitude, and
fearlessly continued to utter her rebukes against oppression, ignorance, and bigotry. Women joined in the hue
and cry against her, little thinking that men were building
the gallows and making them the executioners. Women
have crucified in all ages the redeemers of their own sex,
and men mock them with the fact. It is time now that
we trample beneath our feet this ignoble public sentiment
which men have made for us; and if others are to be
crucified before we can be redeemed, let men do the cruel,
cowardly work; but let us learn to hedge womanhood round
with generous, protecting love and care. Then men will
learn, as they should, that this system of traducing
women is no longer to be used as a means for their subjugation. Let us learn to demand that all men who come
into our presence be as pure as they claim that women
should be. Let the test be applied which Christ gave, that
if any is without sin in word, or deed, or thought, he shall
' cast the first stone.' "

Robert Owen's advanced views regarding the equality
of the sexes did not receive immediate acceptance, but in
after years they deeply influenced American legislation
through the labors of his distinguished son, Robert Dale
Owen. Both the elder and the younger Owen were pre-
eminently reformers and humanitarians. While still a
young man Robert Dale Owen visited Lafayette at his

home in Lagrange, France. In one of their conversations, Lafayette said: "My young friend, you will probably some day be one of the lawmakers in your adopted country. If you ever become a member of a legislative body, bear this in mind: That utter seclusion from one's fellow creatures for years is a refinement of cruelty which no human being has a right to inflict on another, no matter what the provocation. Vote against all attempts to introduce into the criminal code of your State, as penalty for any offense, solitary confinement, at all events for more than a few months. Prolonged beyond that time, it is torture, and not reformatory punishment!" "I told him," says Owen, "I should surely conform to his advice, and when, seven or eight years later, I served in the Indiana legislature, I kept my promise."

Out of all the service which in his illustrious career as editor and legislator he rendered to the cause of humanity, none was more efficient and certainly none attracted more attention than the determined battle which for over a quarter of a century he waged in behalf of woman's rights. Though he believed in woman suffrage, yet, feeling intuitively that the time was not ripe for its attainment, he devoted his efforts to the legal emancipation of married women from other and more crying injustice.

Till the late '40s the Common Law provisions respecting the property rights of married women obtained in every State save Louisiana. These provisions wrested from married women all property rights. If an unmarried woman through gift or inheritance came into possession of property, real or personal, she forfeited all claim to it and all right to its management and control when she married. It then at once became the property of her husband, and if he died leaving no children it passed to his nearest kin, leaving the widow with but a dower in real estate and a small share in the personal property.

Bitter was the indictment which in the columns of

the Free Enquirer, Owen, out of a deep-seated love of justice and fair play, brought against the oppression which the Common Law inflicted upon woman.

" How, but from the monopoly of legal authority and the consequent partiality of legal rights, shall we account for the fact that at this day of comparative civilization the person and the property of a married woman belong to her matrimonial master, as in the case of any other slave? She can inherit nothing, receive nothing, earn nothing, which her husband can not, at any time, legally wrest from her. All her rights are swallowed up in his. She loses, as it were, her individual existence. She may be—thanks to occasional and gratuitous generosity she sometimes is— kindly and even rationally treated; but she has no right to demand—I will not say kindness—but even the most common justice or humanity. A man may not beat his wife too unmercifully, nor is he allowed to kill her. Short of this he can scarcely transgress the law, so far as she is concerned. When we find justice and affection among those who are commanded by law to love each other— and whatever the satirist may say, these are now and then to be found, if we are but patient and persevering enough in our search after them—when, I say, we find such sentiments as these among married persons, let us recollect that they exist *in despite* of the unjust and partial laws that tend to exclude and destroy them."

Robert Dale Owen both practised and advocated the inviolate sacredness of the marriage relation. Like his distinguished father, however, he objected to the usual form of marriage ceremony. A romantic courtship terminated in the marriage of the younger Owen and Mary Robinson in the city of New York on the 12th day of April, 1832. The ceremony was simple and unique. The contracting parties signed a written document, witnessed by the attending justice of the peace and the immediate family, concluding as follows:

" Of the unjust rights which in virtue of this ceremony an iniquitous law tacitly gives me over the person and property of another, I can not legally, but I can morally divest myself. And I hereby distinctly and emphatically declare that I consider myself, and earnestly desire to be considered by others, as utterly divested, now and during the rest of my life, of any such rights, the barbarous relics of a feudal, despotic system, soon destined, in the onward course of improvement, to be wholly swept away; and the existence of which is a tacit insult to the good sense and good feeling of this comparatively civilized age."

To make the parallel complete between his own and his father's position with reference to the relation that should exist between the sexes, Robert Dale Owen did not escape the same charge of being an advocate of free love that had been urged against the unblemished public and private life of the elder Owen. Its best refutation is the description which his talented daughter gives of the happiness and purity of the family life that grew out of the younger Owen's strange compact. In the History of Woman Suffrage (vol. i, pages 293–306), Rosamond Dale Owen writes:

" After a wedding tour in Europe, the young couple, returning to America, settled in New Harmony, Indiana, a small Western village, where their father, Robert Owen, had been making experiments in community life.

" It was a strange, new world into which these two young creatures were entering. The husband had passed his youth in a well-ordered, wealthy English household; the wife had passed the greater part of her girlhood in Virginia, among slaves. They were now thrown upon the crudities of Western life, and encountered those daily wearing trials which strain the marriage tie to the utmost, even though it be based upon principles of justice. But there was a reserve of energy and endurance in this delicately reared pair; they felt themselves to be pioneers in every sense of the word, and the animus which sustains many a struggling soul seeking to turn a principle into a living reality, sustained these two.

". . . While my father was exerting his energies for the welfare of the nation, my mother was giving her life to her children. Sons and daughters were welcomed into the Owen homestead, and the wide halls and great rooms of the rambling country house rang with the voices of children. Three of these little ones slipped back to Heaven before the portals had closed. The stricken parents, with blinded eyes, met only the rayless emptiness of unbelief. May God help the mother, fainting beneath a bereavement greater than she can bear, who cries for help and finds none; who stretches her empty arms upward in an agony of appeal and is answered by the hollow echo of her own cry; may God help her, for she is beyond the help of man. Other children came to fill the vacant places, other voices filled the air, but the hearts of father and mother were not filled until years later, when a sweet faith thrilled the hopeless blank. . . . Well do I remember the cheer of this our home. Simple were its duties, simple indeed its pleasures. Well do I remember the busy troop of boys and girls, with the busy mother at their head, directing their exuberant energy with a rare administrative ability. Besides her own children, four of whom reached maturity, she took during her life seven other young people under her protection, so that the great old-fashioned house was always filled to overflowing with fresh young life. . . .

"When her children were grown, and the task she had undertaken years before had been well done, our mother turned her attention for a time to public work. She gave much thought to the Woman Question, especially that portion of it pertaining to woman's work, and addressed one or two meetings in New York on this subject. Miss Anthony recently said to me: 'Miss Owen, you do not know how great an impression your mother made upon

203

us—a woman who had lived nearly her whole life in a small Western village, absorbed in petty cares, and yet who could stand before us with a calm dignity, telling us searching truths in simple and strong words.' The only lecture I heard my mother deliver was in the church of our village. Her subject was the rearing of children. A calm light rested on her silver hair and broad brow; her manner was the earnest manner of a woman who has looked into the heart of life. Blessed is the daughter to whom it is given to reverence a mother as I reverenced mine that night. A quiet, but deep attention was given to her words, for the fathers and mothers who were listening to her knew that she was speaking on a subject to which she had given long years of careful thought and faithful endeavor. . . .

"The name of Mary Owen was not written upon the brains of men, but it is graven upon the hearts of these her children; so long as they live, the blessed memory of that home shall abide with them, a home wherein all that was sweet, and strong, and true was nurtured by a wise hand, was sunned into blossoming by a loving heart.

"A benediction rests upon the brow of him who has given his best work to help this world onward, even though it be but a hair's breadth; but the mother who has given herself to her children through long years of an unwritten self-abnegation, who has thrilled every fiber of their beings with faith in God and hope in man, a faith and a hope which no canker-worm of worldly experience can ever eat away, she shall be crowned with a sainted halo."

The election in 1836 of the younger Owen as a member of the Indiana legislature, in which he served two consecutive terms, gave that earnest champion of woman's rights a long cherished opportunity to write some of his advanced theories, concerning the legal relation of the sexes, into statutes. In the twenty-second session (1837–'38) he sought to have a bill passed giving married women separate property rights. His effort met with overwhelming defeat. In the same year, Judge Hertell, the pioneer champion of woman's rights in New York, endeavored to have the legislature of that commonwealth take the same action. His attempt suffered the same fate as that of his Western contemporary. Owen renewed the battle in the twenty-third session but without avail. In the twenty-second session he did succeed in abolishing the Common-Law dower by which the widow received only a tenancy or life interest in one-third of her deceased husband's real estate. His statute conferred upon her the absolute ownership of one-third of all of her husband's property.

Elected a member of the second Constitutional Convention of 1850, Mr. Owen renewed the battle for the overthrow of the barbarities of the Common Law with respect to married women, that he had inaugurated in the earlier years. Early in the convention, as chairman of the committee on rights and privileges, he proposed that this provision be incorporated into the bill of rights of the New Constitution:

" Women hereafter married in this State shall have the right to acquire and possess property to their sole use and disposal; and laws shall be passed securing to them under equitable conditions all property, real and personal, whether owned by them before marriage or acquired by them afterward by purchase, gift, devise, or descent; and also providing for the wife's separate property."

This proposition was fiercely opposed on the floor of the convention. With the earnestness and bitterness usually born of sane convictions, these ultraconservative members of the dominant sex resisted Owen's manly attempt to render a simple and tardy justice to woman, with declarations of this type:

" I am of opinion that to adopt the proposition of the gentleman from Posey (Mr. Owen) will not ameliorate the condition of married women."

" I can not see the propriety of establishing for women a distinct and separate interest, the consideration of which would, of necessity, withdraw their attention from that sacred duty which nature has, in its wisdom, assigned to their peculiar care. I think the law which unites in one common bond the pecuniary interests of husband and wife should remain. The sacred ordinance of marriage, and the relations growing out of it, should not be disturbed. The Common Law does seem to me to afford sufficient protection."

" If the law is changed, I believe that a most essential injury would result to the endearing relations of married life. Controversies would arise, husbands and wives would become armed against each other, to the utter destruction of true felicity in married life."

" To adopt it would be to throw a whole population morally and politically into confusion. Is it necessary to explode a volcano under the foundation of the family union? "

" I object to the gentleman's proposition, because it is in contravention of one of the great fundamental principles of the Christian religion. The Common Law only embodies the divine law."

" Give to the wife a separate interest in law, and all those high motives to restrain the husband from wrong-doing will be, in a great degree, removed."

" I firmly believe that it would diminish, if it did not totally annihilate, woman's influence."

" Woman's power comes through a self-sacrificing spirit, ready to offer up all her hopes upon the shrine of her husband's wishes."

" Sir, we have got along for eighteen hundred years, and shall we change now? Our fathers have for many generations maintained the principle of the Common Law in this regard for some good and weighty reasons."

" The immortal Jefferson, writing in reference to the

then state of society in France, and the debauched condition thereof, attributes the whole to the effects of the civil law, then in force in France, permitting the wife to hold, acquire, and own property separate and distinct from the husband."

" It is not because I love justice less, but woman more, that I oppose this section."

" This doctrine of separate estate will stifle all the finer feelings, blast the brightest, fairest, happiest hopes of the human family and go in direct contravention of that law which bears the everlasting impress of the Almighty hand. Sir, I consider such a scheme not only as wild, but as wicked, if not in its intentions, at least in its results."

Nor did the opponents of the proposed constitutional provision neglect to rain down misrepresentation and abuse upon the devoted head of its author. Every visionary idea for which the Owens had stood, those well-meant, but unhappy experiments on the Wabash, their peculiar views respecting the marriage ceremony, and their avowed lack of orthodoxy were pictured and denounced before the convention. These attacks the younger Owen met with a courtesy and yet with a courage and skill in debate which disarmed the assaults of his enemies and won for all time the respect of the country for the foremost legislative champion with whom the American woman has thus far been blessed.

Though defeated in the Constitutional Convention, Mr. Owen, as a member of the first legislature under the new instrument of government, renewed the fight for the property rights of women. The following is a summary of the features which he contributed to the Indiana law:

(a) He procured for women the right to own and control their separate property during marriage.

(b) He procured for married women the right to their own earnings.

(c) He abolished the simple dower of the Common

Law and procured for widows the absolute ownership of one-third of the deceased husband's property. Owen accomplished this in 1838. The session of 1841 overthrew the reform. He reestablished it in 1852.

(d) He modified the divorce laws of the State so as to enable a married woman to secure relief from habitual drunkenness and cruelty.

For his persistent and finally successful efforts to reform unjust laws, the women of Indiana, or a comparatively small number of them, in 1851, presented him with a handsome silver pitcher, inscribed, " Presented to the Hon. Robert Dale Owen by the women of Indiana, in acknowledgment of his true and noble advocacy of their independent rights to property, in the Constitutional Convention of Indiana." The presentation took place before a large audience in the hall of the House on the evening of May 28, 1851.

The women of this country owe to Robert Dale Owen a debt of gratitude which they can discharge in no better way than by a tardy respect for his memory. And nearly a half century after Robert Dale Owen wrote into the statute law of his adopted State the modern conception of the legal rights of women, we find the women's clubs of Indiana cooperating in a movement to place the bust of their great emancipator in the rotunda of the Indiana State capitol, almost on the site of the structure within which he carried on his victorious battle in their behalf.

CHAPTER XX

THE EDUCATIONAL EXPERIMENT

" Awake! ye sons of light and joy,
    And scout the Demon of the schools :
The fiend that scowls but to decoy,
    To pamper zealots : frighten fools :
To blind the judgment : crib the soul.
       Wake up! And let your actions tell
       That you with Peace and Virtue dwell.

" Away with studied form and phrase,
    Away with cant, and bigot zeal,
Let Truth's unclouded beacon blaze,
    From Nature's kindness learn to feel :
      From Nature's kindness learn to give
      Your hands, your hearts, to all that live.
      Wake up! 'Tis deeds alone can tell
      That you with Peace and Virtue dwell."

—Poem dedicated to the children of the New Harmony Boarding-School, New Harmony Gazette, October 8, 1825.

" An age of hatred, strife and woe
    Has long in terror reigned.
Its numerous victims are laid low,
    The world in blood is stained,
      But now the time is coming fast
      When strife shall be forever past.

CHORUS

" The day of peace begins to dawn,
    Huzza! Huzza! Huzza!
Dark Error's might will soon be gone,
    Huzza! Huzza! Huzza!
Poor mortals long have been astray,
But Knowledge now will lead the way,
    Huzza! Huzza! Huzza!

" Now Vice and Crime no more shall stalk
  Unseen in open day,
To cross our silent, peaceful walk
  Through life's enchanting way :
    Old Ignorance with hoary head
    Must seek his everlasting bed.

" Each warrior now may sheath his blade
  And toil in vain no more,
To seek fair Virtue's genial shade,
  For now all wars are o'er.
    The battle's done, the day is won,
    The victory's gained by Truth alone."
      —*Song written for the children of New Harmony.*

" MAN does not form his own character but it is made
for him." This is the motto which Robert Owen caused to
be inscribed upon the title-page of every issue of the New
Harmony Gazette, a publication which was at once the
official organ of the Communities and the medium through
which Owen and those associated with him exploited their
peculiar social, educational, and religious ideas. By this
Owen meant to declare in the language of psychology that,
though heredity, will, and environment are the forces
which mold the characters of men, the greatest of these is
environment. It does not lie within the scope and purpose of this chapter to discuss the truth of Owen's belief.
To do so would be to reopen an ancient battle of the
psychologists in which the victor is yet to be named. But,
in order to understand the various schemes which the
founder of New Harmony projected for the betterment of
society in general and of the working class in particular,
it is necessary to remember that he always believed that
men were the creatures of their surroundings—that they
were in a sense but the clay which the Great Potter presses
against the plastic wheel of circumstance.

There is a sense too in which environment is to-day
recognized as a greater factor in the shaping of human

210

NEW HARMONY DURING THE OWEN OCCUPATION.

From an old print.

character than in the days when Owen wrought. We have come to recognize what Owen saw, though his age did not, that the much vaunted human will itself, if not largely the result of the many-sided circumstances which have touched it, can be and is being skilfully trained in the schools, a training which one must of necessity denominate as environment.

There are two great agencies which the social reformer may invoke in his efforts to regenerate society. These are environment and religion. Acquiring at the very outset of his remarkable efforts for the betterment of his fellows a deep-set hatred for the clergy and the church, Owen deliberately divorced his social schemes from the aid of the Christian religion and pinned his faith to environment, which to him was the only medium whereby the character of the individual could be bettered and a Golden Age be consummated.

Out of his belief in the all potency of environment as a reforming agency came his doctrine that it is vitally important that human beings be surrounded with circumstances favorable to their development. " How may we make men and society better? " The most unselfish social reformer since the days of Savonarola would answer, " By making their environment better." The story of Robert Owen's career as philanthropist and reformer is the story of one man's earnest efforts, some wise and some unwise, to surround human beings with more favorable conditions, within which, if Owen's theory be true at least, they must of necessity become better men and better women.

To him there were at least four phases of the environment surrounding the subjects of his philanthropy from time to time. These phases were their home environment, their social environment, their industrial environment and their educational environment.

It was home environment he sought to better when he taught the people of New Lanark cleanly habits and enforced in the houses of the employees of his cotton-mills a rigorous sanitation. It was only in order that the deplorable industrial conditions under which the English factory-hand labored might be made such as should give him at least a chance to become a man, that Owen began that wonderful sixteen years of agitation of the labor problem which culminated in the quickening of the conscience of the British public, in the enactment of child-labor laws, in increased wages for the productive classes, in parliamentary regulations of factory sanitation, in the inauguration and firm establishment of the idea that government has a right, in the interest of common justice and the general welfare, to interfere in internal trade and with industrial relations.

Swept from his usual safe moorings as a practical business man by his strong belief that under ideal surroundings a perfect race might be developed, the hero of New Lanark sought to establish at New Harmony an ideal social environment within which, unhampered by the artificial atmosphere with which our social system has enveloped us, man, living close to nature, might work out a better character and attain a more perfect manhood.

So it was when Robert Owen sought to change the educational surroundings of the children of his beneficence. So far as his connection with schools was concerned, they were only a phase of his struggle to create a better environment for the development of character among the working people who were the object of his care. In his days no schools opened their doors to the children of the poor. Forced into the factory at a tender age, denied even the rudiments of an education and surrounded at home by squalor and vice, these unfortunates grew into a distorted and debased maturity. To Owen, the school was a weapon for social regeneration to be used as a device by which these children of the great Fourth Estate might be surrounded by a refining atmosphere during their tender and formative years. He was not an educator in the sense in which we use the term to-day. He was not a teacher and did not attempt to act as one. Unlike the schools which Pestalozzi established, his schools were not experiments made for the purpose of testing and proving the efficiency of preconceived educational theories nor attempts to exploit any pet methods and devices of teaching. They were machinery for social and moral regeneration.

Let it be remembered that primarily, Robert Owen was a social and a moral rather than an educational reformer. And yet we shall see that his search for social and moral reform through the avenue of the schools led him into educational innovations, which justify us in placing his name high in the list of great educational thinkers.

THE SCHOOL AT NEW LANARK

Sixteen years after assuming charge of the mills at New Lanark, Robert Owen made his first experiment in education as a means of social reform by founding a school for the benefit of the children of that dreary factory town. From An Outline of the System of Education at New Lanark, written by Robert Dale Owen during the existence of the school and dedicated to his distinguished father, we learn that the training was given in special quarters erected for that purpose; that these quarters were made much more attractive for the children of the factory-hands than those of many of the most prominent boarding-schools of Dickens' day; that a large play-room, the first which the history of pedagogy has recorded, was attached to the school; and that the enrolment exceeded seven hundred.

Of this number, one hundred children between the ages of two and five years were taught in what, for want of a better name, was termed the infants' school; and six hundred over five years of age in a higher or advanced school.

These six hundred pupils of the higher school were divided into two sections of three hundred each. The first section, consisting of children between the ages of five and ten years, constituted a day-school; and the second section, consisting of the children over ten years of age, who worked in the factory during the day, constituted a night-school. Both the infant school and the higher school were in session each day of the week save Sunday from 7.30 to 9.30 A. M., from 10 to 12 A. M., and from 3 to 5 P. M.; while the night session of the higher school began at 7 and closed at 9.30 P. M.

Of the two schools, which were really two departments of a single school held under a common roof, the infant school received the greater portion of Owen's enthusiasm and attention. It was not only the feature of the educational work projected by him at New Lanark which attracted more attention and drew more distinguished visitors there than did all the other innovations which he introduced into town and factory, but it is also that feature which, perhaps more than any other educational experiment he attempted in his long career as a reformer, best entitles him to be classed as a pioneer and thinker in the educational field.

For the infant schools of that isolated Scottish factory town were the first of their kind, and to Robert Owen rather than to Froebel must be given the credit for the discovery and practical application of the idea that there is a type of educational training beneficial to both intellect and moral fiber, which can be successfully given by the schools to children under the tender age of five years. Strip from the kindergarten as we know it to-day the gifts and the games, the devices and the educational ideas with which the name of Froebel will ever be associated, and look upon it as a garden for the training of children, and we may say without fear of giving offense that Robert Owen was the founder of the first kindergarten. The infant school at New Lanark was inaugurated in the year 1816. It was not until twenty-one years later (1837) that Froebel opened his first kindergarten, or " Garden of Children," in the village of Blankenburg.

This little village is not more than fifty miles distant from the town of Hofwyl, where M. De Fellenberg conducted a school whose training was based upon the educational ideas of Pestalozzi and to which Robert Owen sent his sons for an education. Here, in 1819, eighteen years before Froebel established his garden for children at Blankenburg, came Robert Owen to investigate Pestalozzi's ideas and methods of teaching. For three years previous to this time, Robert Owen had been carrying on a school at New Lanark. We know but little concerning the instruction in it during this period, for his educational work at New Lanark had not as yet attracted public attention. We do know that, visiting Hofwyl, with a kindling enthusiasm for educational reform, he received there both information and added enthusiasm.

There can be no doubt that Owen was greatly influenced in his educational thought by his visit to Hofwyl and his contact with the educational principles laid down by Pestalozzi. Owen and Pestalozzi were kindred spirits. Both, like Abou-ben-Adhem of old, loved their fellow men; both sought to raise the laboring class out of a degraded state; both had an abiding faith in the potential uplifting of the common people; both believed that education was a necessary means by which that uplifting was to be consummated. To the question, how may the peasantry be raised out of its degraded state, Pestalozzi had one answer, and only one. This was, *by education.* More a man of affairs and a deeper student of the whole sweep of the social problem than Pestalozzi, Owen sought the aid of every phase of man's environment, yet recognized and appealed to education as the most effective of all weapons in the struggle for permanent social betterment.

When he returned from Hofwyl, whatever may have been his previous views, Robert Owen transplanted to British soil Pestalozzi's enthusiasm for education and many of his cardinal educational principles, of which he made immediate application in his school at New Lanark, then in its third year. If he had done nothing else, Owen would be entitled to notice in pedagogical circles as a carrier of good seed. Though not an educational theorist, he had instinctively applied much of the Pestalozzian creed in his school before his visit to Switzerland. After his return, the school was modeled almost entirely upon the educational principles which he held in common with the great Swiss schoolmaster. We shall see that this is particularly true of the higher school.

THE INFANT SCHOOL

The infant school, however, was a distinct departure in educational thought and procedure in many respects. Its one hundred children were given in charge of a simple-hearted, almost illiterate fellow named Buchanan, who, though cursed by a shrewish wife, loved little children, and was when free from her domination tender and skilful in their moral training. Little attempt was made to impart serious knowledge whether in or out of books. The children were gradually and incidentally taught the nature and uses of common things by familiar conversation and little stories, when the children's curiosity either on the playground or in the schoolroom led them to ask questions.

" Infants above one year attended school under special care." Play and stories were the medium through which the heart and mind of the child were besieged and led ; and games, sometimes within the attractive schoolroom and sometimes, when the weather permitted, out on the green, constituted the major part of the curriculum. Buchanan was really the first kindergartner and Owen's school the anticipation of Froebel's later attempt. Aside from the theory and the system which the Prussian pedagogue introduced into the infant school there is little if anything of pedagogical value in the modern kindergarten which is not to be found at New Lanark. Let us see if this can not be readily demonstrated.

(1) Like all the kindergartens or infant schools which follow it, the purpose of Owen's infant school was to influence the character of children at a tender and formative age. This was Froebel's purpose in inaugurating his kindergarten. " In his conference with teachers Froebel found that the schools suffered from the state of raw material in them. Till the then school age was reached the children were entirely neglected. Froebel's conception of harmonious development naturally led him to attach much importance to the earliest years."

Twenty-one years earlier we find Robert Owen founding his infant school to meet the same difficulty. Like Froebel's school, it was an afterthought. In his description of the higher school at New Lanark, Robert Owen complained that the work was handicapped by the habits which the children had formed before the opening of school-life. How keenly every modern school-teacher can sympathize with this complaint! To meet it the infant school was established by means of which it was hoped that children transplanted at a tender age into an atmosphere of love and refinement might be dominated in their habits by the influence of the schoolroom and not by that of their rude homes. How like this is our modern practise of placing kindergartens in the slums of the large cities!

Like Froebel, and many years in advance of Froebel, Robert Owen saw that " each age has a completeness of its own. First the blade, then the ear, then the full corn in the ear. The perfection of the later stage can be attained only through the perfection of the earlier. If the infant is what he should be as an infant and the child as a child, he will become what he should be as a boy just as naturally as new shoots spring from the healthy plant. Every stage then must be cared for and tended in such a way that it may attain its own perfection."

(2) Like all the true kindergartens which follow it, the aim of the infant school at New Lanark was not to impart serious knowledge whether in or out of books, but to fix habits and shape character. To the master of New Lanark, the formation of character was the chief end of all educational efforts not only in the infant school, but also in the higher school, where the imparting of serious knowledge was made a secondary though important consideration. Almost half a century before Dickens attacked the " cramming system " of the English boarding-schools, a system which throttled the development of character as well as intellect, Robert Owen said: " It must be evident to common observers that children may be taught to read, write, account, and sew and may yet acquire the worst habits and have their minds rendered irrational for life. . . . Reading and writing are merely instruments by which ideas either true or false may be imparted, and when given to children are of little comparative value unless the children are also taught how to make a proper use of them."

Of his infant school it could be said even more truthfully than of Pestalozzi's school at Stanz, more truthfully than of any other school preceding Froebel's: " The thing was not that they should know what they did not know, but that they should behave as they did not behave. If they could be made conscious that they were loved and cared for, their hearts would open and give back love and respect in return."

The elimination of all serious knowledge, the absence of the teaching of all facts as such, is the feature of Owen's school which stamps it as a pioneer in a new field. Overenthusiastic admirers of Pestalozzi have maintained that he operated an infant school on the Continent before the New Lanark school came to be. But the records of the schools at Neuhof and at Stanz, which were the only educational experiments in which Pestalozzi preceded Owen, reveal, according to the declarations of Pestalozzi himself, that the children of both schools were of a variety of ages, the oldest being not more than fifteen and the youngest not less than five years old. Neither was, in the sense in which the term was used at New Lanark, an " infants' " school. Nor did Pestalozzi ever conduct a school of any type in which the acquirement of serious knowledge, the teaching of facts as such was not made an important though a subordinate aim of the training bestowed. This more than the difference in the ages of the children is the distinguishing mark between the infant school at New Lanark and all previous educational attempts upon the Continent.

The difference between Owen's infant school and its contemporaries is the difference between the mission of the modern kindergarten and the mission which this utilitarian age is seeking to thrust upon it. An impatient thirst for the glittering prizes of this industrial epoch has taken hold upon the prospective college student. He is asking that some arrangement be made so that he with his sheepskin may step into the arena of business or professional life at an earlier age. There are not wanting signs to indicate that in the interests of this earlier graduation the domination from the top may next demand that the kindergarten shall serve chiefly as a preparatory school for the primary unit. Then the kindergarten must decide whether, like the other units of the system, it will bow its neck to the yoke or whether, ignoring the call from above, it will continue to solely seek the moral development of all childhood rather than the higher educational interests of the few who are destined for college walls.

The claim has been made repeatedly and the dictum accepted without controversy that Froebel's kindergarten at Blankenburg was the first infant school that did not attempt to teach any serious knowledge, the first to make games a means of training the character of children. This dictum merely overlooks Owen's attempt. It is true that after Pestalozzi's repeated failures as a school manager, numerous " infant schools " arose on the Continent; that these sought to apply Pestalozzian educational principles; and that, like all of the attempts made by him whose efforts they imitated, these infant schools made the teaching of elementary knowledge the nucleus of their training. But these differ as much from the infant school at New Lanark as they do from the kindergarten at Blankenburg, whose forerunner they were.

Sargent, in The Social Philosophy of Robert Owen, says, " The Infant School System was an inevitable consequence of Owen's doctrine as to the vital importance of surrounding human beings with circumstances favorable to their development. It has been said that the plan was previously carried out on the Continent. That may be true. It has also been said that the experiment was suggested in a conversation between Owen and a lady. Both statements may be true, and yet Owen's claim to the invention remains unimpeached. Owen's glory is not that he sent for a Swiss instructor, nor that he went about craving the advice and aid of any one, but that he threw his own energy into the work, and with the feeble instruments at his command commenced and completed his long projected task."

In a speech delivered at a memorial exercise in Kensal Green Cemetery on the 21st of April, 1871, T. H. Huxley, the great English scientist, said:

" I think that every one, who is compelled to look as closely into the problem of popular education, must be led to Owen's conclusion that the infant school is, so to speak, the key of that position; and that Robert Owen discovered this great fact and had the courage and patience to work out his theory into a practical reality is his claim, if he had no other, to the enduring gratitude of the people."

(3) Just as in all other infant schools and kindergartens worthy the name, love was the dominating factor in Owen's school. In the face of ridicule, Owen retains as the head of his infant school a teacher who is both illiterate and without professional training because "he does not know how to teach what is found in books, but he does know Nature and loves children, and by that love will bring Nature and the children together." With Owen as with Pestalozzi and Froebel, "the essential principle of education is not teaching. It is love. The child loves and believes before it thinks and acts."

(4) In the New Lanark school the "benevolent superintendence" which Pestalozzi and Froebel practised characterized the teaching. This was an educational idea which Owen received at the feet of Pestalozzi. His great faith in the ultimate uplift of the common people made him a steadfast believer in the innate possibilities of childhood—in its large capacity for physical, intellectual, and moral development. Powers are hereditary, but it is the duty of the schoolroom environment to assist to the fullest extent in calling them forth. There is a natural method by which these powers unfold. The natural method is as certain, if we could but discover it, in the development of moral and intellectual powers as in that of physical powers.

Bacon taught that we command Nature only by obeying her. Nature is in the schoolroom with the teacher eager to assist in the developing process. Let the teacher beware lest in his blind following of a system or in his devotion to a false educational creed, or in his anxiety to cram childish minds with the letter that killeth, he interfere with that development which Nature at his elbow seeks to bring about. Let him rather practise that benevolent superintendence which remembers that "the purpose of teaching is to bring ever more out of man rather than to put more and more into him "; which perceives that the purpose of instruction is not to teach but to develop; which follows Nature and not a system; which leads the mind of the child and yet follows it with trusting footsteps; and which vaunteth not itself but stands in the presence of Nature, the handmaiden, with uncovered head.

To the criticism that the teacher of the infant school at New Lanark merely played with the children, let it be urged that though he would not have understood the term "benevolent superintendence," yet with Owen's encouragement he practised it almost a quarter of a century before Froebel made it one of the chief features of his kindergarten. For the simple pedagogue of New Lanark gave his charges, through play, that which Nature asked for them at their stage of growth, and drew out of them through its physical exercise, spontaneity, quickness of thought and action, happiness, and love.

What part ought benevolent superintendence to play in the schoolroom to-day? In 1889 Charles De Garmo, in his Essentials of Method, after discussing the question, declared that the teacher has his activity limited to these two things: " First, the preparation of the child's mind for a rapid and effective assimilation of new knowledge; second, the presentation of the matter of instruction in such order and manner as will best conduce to the most effective assimilation." Quick, in his Educational Reformers, after discussing and approving the above, adds that " besides this he must make his pupils use their knowledge, both new and old, and reproduce it in fresh connections."

(5) Just as in the kindergarten which followed it, the infant school at New Lanark brought into play the activity of the children. While, like Froebel, Owen limited the function of the educator to " benevolent superintendence " of the natural unfolding of childhood, yet, like Froebel also, he recognized that since the natural development of

childish powers requires their appropriate exercise, "benevolent superintendence" must both originate and direct childish activity. Some of the games which Buchanan and his female assistant gave to the children at New Lanark were Scottish games peculiar to the Lowlands; some, they devised to teach indirectly important ethical, moral, and physical truths; some, the children themselves invented. All were of a wholesome type and designed, like the games which Froebel bequeathed to the kindergarten, to call forth the spontaneous and untrammeled activity of the children.

It must of course be admitted that these games lacked the efficiency which the theory, and the plan, and the gifts, and the system which Froebel bestowed have given to the play of the modern kindergarten. But they were based upon the same idea and sought to achieve the same purpose. Though Robert Owen did not possess the mysticism which characterizes most of the utterances of Froebel, he showed by his efforts in the infant school at New Lanark that he too believed that "man is primarily a doer"; that "he learns only through self activity"; that "the formative and creative instinct has existed in all children and in all ages"; and that when the activity of the children is properly directed by benevolent superintendence they "render the inner outer," which is the end of all true education.

HIGHER SCHOOL

In the higher school at New Lanark the following subjects were taught: Reading, writing, arithmetic, natural history, geography, ancient history, modern history, sewing, singing, and dancing. No books were used, for "his aim was to train the children to good habits, not to cram their heads with facts." Only amusement in the form of games was offered to those under six years of age. Instruction was made pleasant and agreeable, no lesson being given more than forty-five minutes in length. Much of the instruction was given by the "object method," for William Maclure, who visited the school in 1824, says that " the children are taught by representations in all cases where they can be obtained, the transparent being used only in part for the explanation of the elements of botany, the shape of the leaves, etc." Much attention, and properly so, for it is the basic study in the acquirement of knowledge, was given to reading.

Robert Dale Owen in his description of the school dwells but little upon the course of study, but takes occasion to say, " Children should never be directed to read what they can not understand. Reading should be preceded between the ages of five and seven years by a regular course in natural history, ancient and modern history, chemistry, and astronomy. All this on the plan prescribed by Nature to give a child such particulars as he can easily be made to understand concerning the nature and properties of the different objects around him, before we teach him the artificial signs which have been adopted to represent these objects." Robert Owen doubted " whether in a rational state of society children under ten years old would be taught to read."

Absurd as was Owen's plan to prepare children for intelligent reading, from our point of view, it was made necessary by the exceedingly difficult vocabulary and technical subject-matter in the most elementary readers of that day. In these days when the makers of readers are, in the name of classical literature, filling them with selections that lie beyond the vocabulary, the experience, and the comprehension of the children for whom they are intended, it would be well to remember again and again the simple declaration: " Children should never be directed to read what they can not understand."

The higher school, better than the infant school, perhaps, shows the effects of Owen's visit to Stanz. Through

ROBERT DALE OWEN.

the meager accounts which Robert Owen, his son, and various visitors to New Lanark have written concerning the methods of instruction in the higher school, we can state with safety that in it, with one notable exception, the main features of Pestalozzianism prevailed. Those features as summed up by Morf in his contribution to Pestalozzi's Biography are:

(1) "Instruction must be based on the learner's own experience.

(2) "What the learner experiences must be connected with language.

(3) "The time for learning is not the time for judging, nor the time for criticism.

(4) "In every department instruction must begin with the simplest elements and, starting from those, must be carried on step by step according to the development of the child; that is, it must be brought into psychological sequence.

(5) "At each point, the instructor shall not go forward till that part of the subject has become the proper intellectual possession of the learner.

(6) "Instruction must follow the path of development, not the path of lecturing, teaching, or telling.

(7) "To the educator, the individuality of the child must be sacred.

(8) "Not the acquisition of knowledge or skill is the main object of elementary instruction, but the development and strengthening of the powers of the mind.

(9) "With knowledge must come power, with information, skill.

(10) "Intercourse between educator and pupil, and school discipline especially, must be based on and controlled by love.

(11) "Instruction must be subordinated to the aim of education."

The one tenet of the creed espoused in common by Pestalozzi and by Froebel, which Robert Owen neither accepted nor practised in his various educational experiments was the one which, if added to the declaration of principles given above, would be numbered twelve and reads as follows: " The ground of moral-religious bringing-up lies in the relation of mother and child."

Extremely clear and strong is the attitude of Pestalozzi and Froebel with respect to the necessity of religious influence in education. Pestalozzi placed moral and religious training above the intellectual, and with him moral and religious training were one and the same. He revolted against the prevailing elementary education of his day because " everywhere in it the flesh predominated over the spirit, everywhere the divine element was cast into the shade. Everywhere selfishness and the passions were taken as the motives of action." To him the education which was to lead forth the soul powers as well as the mind powers of the people must be different from this, for " man does not live by bread alone. Every child needs to know how to pray to God in all simplicity, but with faith and love. If the religious element does not run through the whole of education, this element will have little influence on the life; it remains formal or isolated. The child accustomed from his earliest years to pray, to think, and to work is already more than half educated."

With Froebel, all true education was founded on religion. He pointed the way to that halcyon day when " education should lead and guide man to clearness concerning himself and in himself, to peace with Nature and to unity with God "; when the training of the schools " should lift him to a knowledge of himself and of mankind, to a knowledge of God and Nature; and to the pure and holy life to which such knowledge leads." With him always " the object of education is the realization of a faithful, pure, inviolate, and hence holy life."

With Froebel as with Pestalozzi, moral and religious

226

training were one and inseparable. Owen divorced the two by ignoring in all of his educational, as in all of his other attempts at social reform, the religious nature of man. At the time of the New Lanark experiment, he had made at least no public declaration of his religious views. It was not until seventeen years later that, on the very verge of sweeping reforms in English factory laws, which his unceasing agitation coupled with the public confidence reposed in him had made possible, Owen, then the largest figure in the public eye, made such a sweeping attack upon all existing religious creeds and displayed such a bitter hatred toward all existing religious institutions that he astounded the British public, alienated the support of Christian people, defeated his proposed reform measures, and handicapped all his after efforts at social reform by the common public belief that they were the outgrowth of atheistic and anarchistic tendencies. Yet we find that even at the New Lanark school, in the language of Robert Dale Owen, " No religious instruction was permitted, but much moral instruction, some of it direct, but most of it indirect, was given."

Owen's attitude on the subject of religious instruction grew, of course, out of his peculiar religious beliefs, so different from the simple trusting faith of his great educational contemporaries. Though in reality not an atheist in the sense in which we use the term to-day, his God was not the God of Pestalozzi and Froebel, but the God of Huxley—not a living, regenerating force in human hearts touched by His quickening spirit, but a great creative force, which, having endowed life with potential perfection, has left it to be developed by the tender mercies of a chance environment.

The question of religious instruction in the public schools has become a much mooted one at the present day, particularly in the United States. In those lands where church and state are one, the question becomes comparatively easy. There state schools become an arm of the church for the teaching of its creed—a task which, though all other phases of educational training be neglected, must be thoroughly executed. An overwhelming public sentiment approves of the religious instruction given and the voice of a hopeless minority is ignored. But in this country, where freedom of religious thought and speech is guaranteed by Constitutional provision, and where the twenty million children receiving public instruction come from homes where every phase of religious belief and even of unbelief finds enthusiastic supporters, the problem of what to do with religious instruction in the schools becomes exceedingly difficult.

No clearer statement of this problem which confronts legislatures and courts, as well as educators, can be found than that given by Nicholas Murray Butler in the Meaning of Education (McMillan & Co., 1901, pp. 28–31 inclusive). After tersely setting forth the difficulties surrounding religious instruction in our educational system, and showing that the drift in the schools of the United States is away from the simple religious instruction which Pestalozzi and Froebel gave and toward the non-religious instruction of the schools at New Lanark, Butler comments as follows: "Two solutions of the difficulty are proposed. One is that the State shall tolerate all existing forms of religious teaching in its own schools. The other is that the State shall aid by money-grants schools maintained by religious or other corporations. Neither suggestion is likely to be received favorably by the American people at present, because of the bitterness of the war between the denominational theologies. Yet the religious element may not be permitted to pass wholly out of education unless we are to cripple it and render it hopelessly incomplete. It must devolve upon the family and the church, then, to give this instruction to the child and to preserve the religious insight from loss. Both family and church must become much more efficient, educationally speaking, than they are now, if they are to bear this burden successfully."

While Robert Dale Owen wrote but little concerning the methods of instruction and course of study at New Lanark, he has described at length the plan of school government and the moral training attempted there. From this description, the following principles regulating the New Lanark schools may be gathered:

(1) "All rewards and punishments whatever, except such as Nature herself. has provided, are sedulously excluded. By natural punishment, we mean the necessary consequences immediate and remote which result from any action." In his instructions to the teachers Robert Owen declared that, "they were on no account ever to beat any one of the children, nor to threaten them in any manner in word or action, nor to use abusive terms; but were always to speak to them with a pleasant countenance and in a kind manner and tone of voice."

Robert Dale Owen but voiced the sentiments of his distinguished father when he declared all rewards and punishments other than those which Nature bestows to be unjust—" unjust as on the one hand loading those individuals with supposed advantages and distinctions whom Providence, either in the formation of their talents and dispositions or in the character of their parents and associates, seems already to have favored; and on the other, as inflicting further pain on those whom less fortunate circumstances had already formed into weak, vicious, or ignorant, or, in other words, into unhappy beings.

" And prejudicial in rendering a strong, bold character either proud or overbearing, or vindictive and deceitful; or in instilling into the young mind, if more timid and less decided, either an overweening opinion of its own abilities and endowments or a dispiriting idea of its own incompetency—such an idea as creates a sullen, hopeless despondency and destroys that elasticity of spirit from whence many of our best actions proceed, but which is lost as soon as the individual feels himself sunk, mentally or morally, below his companions, disgraced by punishment, and treated with neglect or contempt by those around him."

" Artificial rewards and punishments are introduced; and the child's notions of right and wrong are so confused by the substitution of these for the natural consequences resulting from his conduct—his mind is in most cases so thoroughly imbued with the uncharitable notion that whatever he has been taught to consider wrong deserves immediate punishment; and that he himself is treated unjustly unless rewarded for what he believes to be right; that it were next to a miracle if his mind did not become more or less irrational; or if he chose a course which otherwise would have appeared too self-evidently beneficial to be rejected."

(2) " Every action whatever must be followed by its natural reward and punishment."

(3) " A clear knowledge and a distinct conviction of the necessary consequences of any particular line of conduct is all that is necessary, however skeptical some may be on this point, to direct the child in the way he should go, provided common justice be done in regard to the other circumstances which surround him in infancy and in childhood."

(4) " Whatever in its ultimate consequences increases the happiness of the community is right; and whatever on the other hand tends to diminish that happiness is wrong."

(5) " The happiness of the child is intimately connected with that of the community. Experience aids in this. Artificial rewards and punishments confuse this thought. Rightly understood, the child is led to right action, for he could not deliberately make himself miserable in preference to making himself happy."

(6) " A child who acts improperly is not an object of blame but of pity. The fact of wrong action simply shows

230

that he has not been properly trained." Here Robert Dale Owen draws an analogy between the child who is a wrong-doer and the traveler who, improperly directed, takes the wrong road and fails of his destination. We would not think of chiding or punishing the traveler. Not he, but they who failed to direct him properly are to blame. Rather will we care for his wants, place him upon the right road, and send him upon his way rejoicing. The child who has gone astray is not to blame; but those who have directed him wrong. Like the traveler, he is to be pitied, not censured; cared for; and set again in the path of right action.

Though, as compared with the other schools of the period, the New Lanark school was as successful educationally as the great cotton-mill which maintained it was financially, some of the same difficulties were encountered which confront the public-school administration to-day. Robert Dale Owen recites some of these:

(1) " The children were only five hours at school and under its influence each day; the remaining nineteen hours being spent under the influence of parents more or less ignorant, more or less unrefined, more or less brutal and vicious." The problem of the home handicap is still with us, but it becomes less serious as the home grows better from one decade to another.

(2) " There was great difficulty in securing proper teachers for the work—those possessing the general and particular knowledge, habits, and temper necessary to successful teaching, without the pedantry to which members of the teaching profession are susceptible."

(3) " As soon as the children arrived at the age of ten years, they were withdrawn and placed in the cotton-mills." Child-labor laws and truancy regulations have made this impossible under the age of fourteen years in many of the States of the Union.

(4) Many of the children, because of poor home-train-

231

ing, had formed bad habits which both infant school and higher school found it difficult to eradicate.

Even in that day, when the public conscience had not been quickened in educational matters, the schools at New Lanark attracted wide-spread attention. The visitors who came to New Lanark for the purpose of seeing the schools in operation were very numerous. They arrived by thousands annually. " I have seen," says Robert Owen, " as many as seventy strangers at once attending the early morning exercises of the children in the school." Among these visitors were many of the first persons of the kingdom as well as numbers of illustrious strangers. The Duke of Holstein (Oldenburg) and his brother stayed several days with Owen at New Lanark that they might thoroughly understand the system of infant instruction in operation there. The Grand Duke Nicholas, afterward Emperor of Russia, offered Mr. Owen large inducements to remove his colony to the Russian Empire. Prince John Maximilian of Austria spent some time at New Lanark. Many foreign ambassadors became guests of Mr. Owen, among them Baron Just of Saxony, whose sovereign presented a gold medal to Robert Owen as a mark of approval. An attempt was made by disciples of Owen to establish a similar settlement in London, but unfavorable conditions caused the failure of the experiment.

It is interesting to note that on the 30th of July, 1824, William Maclure, a wealthy retired merchant of Philadelphia, a man destined to play such a leading part in Owen's later educational experiment at New Harmony, visited the New Lanark schools. From this visit there came a friendship between the two men which culminated in their association as partners in the New Harmony venture. Maclure says of the New Lanark schools at this time: " It is really astonishing the order, happiness, and comfort that pervade the whole. His (Owen's) success gives me much pleasure on two accounts: First, for the good it certainly will produce; and, second, for the encouragement it infuses into my long-projected plan of forming experimental schools, which, in so superior a field as the United States, can scarce fail while such an extensively profound and beneficial system seems to flourish in spite of all the opposition both in church and state."

THE SCHOOL AT NEW HARMONY

In less than a year after William Maclure wrote in such enthusiastic terms his approval of the school at New Lanark, Robert Owen had determined to abandon his social and educational labors there and found a " New Moral World " somewhere on the American continent. The very Providence whose interference in human affairs both men denied must have brought about the strange association of Robert Owen and William Maclure in the New Harmony venture; for out of it came not only the greatest experiment in social reconstruction which the world has yet witnessed, but also the firm establishment of Pestalozzian principles of education in this country, a great impetus to the American scientific spirit, and a series of movements which largely affected American educational development.

There was much in common between the two men— more in common between them than there had been between Owen and the hero of Stanz. Both men were wealthy and therefore able to put their schemes for reforming society to the test. Both were philanthropists, willing to give their all for social betterment. Both eliminated religion from their schemes of reform. Both espoused the cause of the productive classes who, in the language of Maclure, "make their living in the sweat of their brows." Both brought a severe indictment against the existing social order. The means by which the reformation of that social order should be consummated was the one serious point of

·difference between them. Owen seized upon every phase of man's environment as a weapon in his fight for the uplifting of his fellows. Interested as he was in the educational ·experiments at New Harmony, the social Utopia he sought to create there claimed the greater part of his enthusiasm and attention. Maclure, on the other hand, believed that " free, equal, and universal schools " were the only means by which the rise of the productive classes could be achieved. Interested only in the educational phase of the New Harmony movement, he manifested little interest and less faith in the dreams which his partner sought to realize.

Both believed in the educational principles enunciated by Pestalozzi. Maclure in his Opinions on Various Subjects, a publication of three volumes, printed and bound in the industrial school at New Harmony, sets forth at length his reasons for approving of the Pestalozzian system of instruction. After criticizing the evils of the social order, he declares that " to rectify as far as education can the foregoing evils, the system of Pestalozzi through all its manipulations is admirably calculated. Having traveled seven summers in Switzerland, and some months of each residing at Pestalozzi's school at Yverdun, I never saw the pupils in or out of school without one of the teachers presiding at their games, etc., all of which were calculated to convey instruction. They were constantly occupied with something useful to themselves or others from 5 A. M. to 8 P. M., with the exception of four half hours at meals, at which all the teachers ate with the pupils; their attention was never fatigued with more than one hour at the same exercise, either moral or physical; all was bottomed on free will by the total exclusion of every species of correction. Their actions were cheerful, energetic, and rapidly tending toward the end aimed at.

" I do not recollect ever to have heard a cry or any demonstration of pain or displeasure nor even an angry word from teacher or pupil all the time I lived among them. One of the most beneficial consequences is the pleasure all of Pestalozzi's pupils take in mental labor and study. Though I often went out of my road fifty leagues to examine young men taught under this system, I do not remember ever finding one of an ill-natured temper or bad conduct of all I saw either in Europe or in this country, and I usually found them greatly superior in all the useful accomplishments to all those educated by other methods."

It was in 1805 that Maclure first visited Pestalozzi's school in Switzerland, where, to use the language of Joseph Neef, " he was soon convinced of the solidity, importance, and usefulness of the Pestalozzian system. Indeed, to see Pestalozzi's method displayed before his eyes and to form an unalterable wish of naturalizing it in his own country were operations succeeding each other with such rapidity that Maclure took them for one and the same operation." On being asked by him to recommend a disciple capable of carrying on the work in America successfully, Pestalozzi named Joseph Neef. Maclure supported Neef for two years while he was learning the English language, after which he established, on the Schuylkill River, five miles from Philadelphia, with Neef as principal, the first Pestalozzian school on the Western continent. After several years of indifferent success the school was transferred to Delaware County, Pennsylvania, where in 1814 the effort was abandoned because of public prejudice against Neef's boldly proclaimed atheism. Neef moved to Louisville, bought a small farm near the city, and renounced teaching altogether. From this retreat he was brought to New Harmony by Owen and Maclure in 1826.

When the partnership between Owen and Maclure gave the latter sole charge of the educational efforts at New Harmony, he gathered together some of the members of the teaching force of his former school and the scientists whom his own distinguished achievements had attracted to the venture and set out with his " Boat-load of Knowledge " down the turbid Ohio. The party arrived at The New Moral World eight months after Robert Owen had established his colony there. Maclure began at once to organize the school system, which he fondly hoped would become the center of American education through the introduction of the Pestalozzian system of instruction. One of his first acts was to publish a prospectus, or " course of study," for the contemplated schools.

MACLURE'S OUTLINE, OR COURSE OF STUDY, FOR THE
NEW HARMONY SCHOOLS

In Silliman's Journal, early in 1826, and before the organization of the schools had been much more than begun, Maclure outlined the system of instruction to be pursued, stating that Phiquepal d'Arusmont, and Madame Fretageot, with Messrs. Say, Maclure, and other educators, " are now prepared to organize at New Harmony a boarding-school on those principles which have for some time been in operation at New Lanark, Scotland."

(1) Great or Fundamental Principle of Education

" The great or fundamental principle is, never to attempt to teach children what they can not comprehend, and to teach them in the exact ratio of their understanding without omitting one line in the chain of ratiocination, proceeding always from the known to the unknown, from the most easy to the most difficult; practising the most extensive and accurate use of all the senses; exercising, improving, and perfecting all the mental and corporal faculties by quickening combination; accelerating and carefully arranging comparison; judiciously and impartially making deductions; summing up the results free from prejudice, and cautiously avoiding the delusions of the imagination, a constant source of ignorance and error."

THOMAS SAY.

(2) Mechanism and Mathematics

" The children are to learn mechanism by machines or exact models of them, arithmetic by a machine called the arithmometer, geometry by a machine called the trignometer, by which the most useful propositions of Euclid are reduced to the comprehension of a child five or six years old; mathematics by the help of the above-mentioned instruments."

(3) Science

" Natural history in all its branches is learned by examining the objects in substance or accurate representations of them in designs or prints; anatomy by skeletons and wax figures; geography by globes and maps—most of the last of their own construction; hygiene, or the preservation of health, by their own experience and observation of the consequences of all natural functions. They learn natural philosophy by the most improved and simple instruments."

(4) Writing and Drawing

" They are taught the elements of writing and designing by the freedom of hand acquired by constant practise in forming all kinds of figures with a slate and pencil put into their hands when they first enter the school, on which they draw lines, dividing them into equal parts, thereby obtaining an accuracy of the eye which, joined to the constant exercise of judging the distance of objects and their height, gives them a perfect idea of space."

(5) Music

" They learn music through the medium of an organ constructed for the purpose, and a sonometer, first learning the sounds and then being taught the notes, or signs of those sounds."

(6) Gymnastics

" Gymnastics, or the exercise of all muscular motions, they acquire by the practise of all kinds of movements always, preferably, those that may lead to utility, such as marching, climbing, the manual exercise, etc. They are taught the greatest part of these branches at the same time, never fatiguing the mind by giving more than an hour's attention to the same thing, changing the subject and rendering it a play by variety."

(7) Languages

" The pupils learn as many languages as there are languages spoken by the boys of different nations in the school, each instructing the other in the vocabulary of his language."

(8) Manual Training

" Lithographing and engraving as well as printing are to be carried on in the school building, as well as other mechanic arts, that the children may receive manual training. The boys learn at least one mechanical art—for instance, setting type and printing, and for this purpose there are printing-presses in each school by the aid of which are published all their elementary books."

In attempting to carry out the course of study announced in Silliman's Journal and outlined above, Maclure patterned the New Harmony educational system closely after the successful system which Owen had abandoned at New Lanark. He not only adopted the same educational principles, but also the same school units and organization. The infant school at New Harmony, receiving children from two to five years of age, was the exact counterpart of Owen's infant school at New Lanark; the higher school, enrolling those from five to twelve years of age, was the reproduction of the night-school which Owen had conducted for the benefit of the operatives of his New Lanark mills.

The schools, though established primarily for the benefit of the children of the community, were open, on payment of tuition, to children from outside the community, and pupils came from as far east as Philadelphia and New York. The terms for non-resident children were: for boarding, lodging, washing, clothing, medical attendance, medicine, and instruction in the various branches taught, one hundred dollars per annum. Girls were received upon the same terms as boys, the course of instruction prescribed for them being the same as that laid down for the other sex. The doctrine of the social system as officially promulgated was: " It is contemplated in Mr. Owen's system, by giving our female population as good an education as our males, to qualify them for every situation in life in which, consistently with their organization, they may be placed."

To an age which coeducation has conquered, Owen's declaration that the females of New Harmony were to receive as good an education as the males seems superfluous, but in the far-off year of 1826 the declaration attracted additional public attention to the educational experiments on the Wabash. While it is true that previous to the New Harmony venture a few private and endowed schools were founded for the express purpose of affording better educational advantages for girls, yet it is also true that the educational system at New Harmony was the first public-school system in the United States which offered the same opportunities to girls as it did to boys. For though the schools at New Harmony were open to non-resident pupils upon the payment of a tuition fee of one hundred dollars per annum, yet, so far as the children of the community itself were concerned, they were public schools in an even wider sense than that in which we use the term to-day, for in them the children were not only trained but fed, clothed, and sheltered.

At the time of Maclure's arrival at New Harmony there were no public schools in the United States save the township schools of New England. In these public schools of the New England colonies some provision had been made for the education of girls before the close of the eighteenth century, but these provisions were meager and unsatisfactory. The training which they received was given either in short summer terms or at the noon hours or at other intervals of the town or boys' school. Boone, in his History of Education, says: " But no such opportunity was offered girls to make the most of themselves as had been forced upon most boys for a half-dozen generations." Even in most of the private schools, where better educational facilities were offered to girls, instruction was confined to writing, reading, spelling, arithmetic, and English grammar. In the very year in which the New Harmony schools were inaugurated, an attempt was made at Boston to establish a high school for girls. In a year, however, it failed because the attempt to give an education to both sexes involved too great a drain upon the public purse. It was not until 1843 that Providence opened its high school for boys and girls. It was several years before another community took up the interest. In 1840 the city of Philadelphia established a separate high school for females. It was not until 1852 that Boston reestablished the girls' high school.

These are the facts in the past history of education in this country which led Boone to say, " By a kind of traditionary blindness, few among the colonial fathers saw the contradiction of the most fundamental of their religious and political principles in disregarding or thwarting the intellectual life of their daughters." The educational experiment at New Harmony then was not only far in advance of the other schools of this country in its methods of government and in its Pestalozzian system of instruction, but also in the provisions which it made for the proper education of the gentler sex.

In Community House No. 2 Madame Neef, assisted by Madame Fretageot, conducted an infant school of over one hundred children. Mrs. Neef was the wife of Joseph Neef and the mother of five of the teachers in the higher school of the community. She was a native of Würtemberg. Her brother became a professor in Pestalozzi's Institute, and she was educated under the supervision of Mrs. Pestalozzi. Professor Neef was her French teacher, and just before his departure for America they were married. The laws of the social system provided that children should become the property of the community at the age of two years, and it was in the infant school that they were first received. The chief work of the teacher was to direct the amusements of the children, who were taught various games, some of them instructive, similar to those employed in the present-day kindergarten. The training of the school was copied very largely after that which Buchanan had given in his crude efforts at New Lanark.

The higher school for pupils between the ages of five and twelve years was taught by Joseph Neef, as principal, assisted by his four daughters and one son, all of whom had been pupils of Pestalozzi and had been brought to the community because of their familiarity with his system of instruction. In the palmy days of the New Harmony experiments the enrolment in this school was between one hundred and eighty and two hundred pupils of both sexes. It was, strictly speaking, the Pestalozzian school of the system. The prospectus published by Maclure in Silliman's Journal constituted its course of study. A portion of the time of the pupils of this school was devoted to some branch of the work of the industrial school, the two schools constituting what we would call to-day a manual training-school.

241

The school for pupils over twelve years of age, called by the New Harmony Gazette the " School for Adults," had at one time an enrolment of eighty. These received, usually at night, special training in mathematics and the useful arts together with lectures on chemistry by Troost, drawing by Lesueur, natural history by Thomas Say, and experimental farming by M. Phiquepal d'Arusmont.

The industrial school was the one innovation which Maclure grafted upon the educational system. Every other feature, as he himself acknowledged in the prospectus of the school, he copied, not from his own unhappy effort on the Schuylkill, but from Owen's brilliant success in Scotland. Maclure was one of the earliest champions of the idea of industrial education. He founded an agricultural school near the city of Alicante, Spain, on an estate of ten thousand acres purchased for this purpose, but an end was put to these plans by a political revolution which resulted in the confiscation of his property. New Harmony afforded another opportunity for an industrial experiment, which he eagerly seized. Though in his eccentric career Maclure championed many ideas with all the vigor of his vehement nature, there was none he espoused more vigorously than he did the educational theories upon which he organized the manual labor work in the schools of The New Moral World. These theories were:

(1) There should be free, equal, and universal schools to which at an early age children should be surrendered and in which they should be clothed, fed, sheltered, and educated at the public expense.

(2) Every child of the productive classes should be taught a trade in order that he may be self-supporting and independent.

(3) Properly managed, the labor of the child at his trade in the industrial department should more than pay for his maintenance and entirely relieve the public from the financial burden of supporting the schools.

When the children who were the property of the community had arrived at the age of five years they passed from the infant school into the higher or true Pestalozzian school. While pursuing the work in this school as set forth in Maclure's Prospectus or Course of Study, they, at the same time, were learning some useful occupation or trade in the industrial school. The child was permitted to choose the branch of industry in which he wished to be trained. Where he made no choice, the management sought to assign him to one for which he had special aptitude. At night the children did not return to the homes of their parents, whom they saw but seldom, but slept in an upper room or loft above the workshop in which their daily manual task was performed. Every child was expected to learn at least one occupation or trade well. When this had been done he might receive permission to enter another workshop and learn a second industry.

It appears certain that at some time or other during the life of the industrial school at New Harmony each of the following useful occupations were taught: Taxidermy, printing and engraving, drawing, carpentry, wheelwrighting, wood-turning, blacksmithing, cabinet-making, hat-making, shoemaking, agriculture, washing, cooking, sewing, housekeeping, dressmaking, and millinery. Whatever may have been the character of the training in other departments, there is absolute proof that the work of the printing-shop was thorough. Maclure's Opinions, a publication in three volumes, was printed and bound by the pupils in it. The typographical work of these books is excellent, and after the lapse of eighty years the binding is in good condition.

We catch a faint glimpse of the industrial system in the diary of the Duke of Saxe-Weimar, who writes of his visit to the community schools in April, 1826: "I found Professor Neef in the act of leading the boys of his school out to labor. Military exercise formed a part of the instruction of the children. I saw the boys divided into two ranks and parted into detachments, marching to labor. On the way they performed various wheelings and evolutions. All the boys and girls have a very healthy look, are cheerful and lively, and by no means bashful. The boys labor in the field and garden and were now occupied with new fencing. The girls learned female employments; they were as little oppressed as the boys with labor and teaching; these happy and interesting little children were much more employed in making their youth pass as happily as possible.

" Madame Neef showed me their schoolhouse, in which she dwelt, and in which places for sleeping were arranged for the boys. Each slept upon a cot frame, on a straw bed. . . . I went to the quondam church, or work-shop for the boys who are intended for joiners and shoe-makers. These boys sleep upon the floor above the church in cribs, three in a row, and thus have their sleeping-place and place of instruction close together. We saw also the shops of the shoemakers, tailors and saddlers, also the smiths, of which six were under one roof, and the pottery, in which were two rather large furnaces. The greater part of the young girls whom we chanced to meet at home we found employed in plaiting straw hats."

The industrial school at New Harmony was the second to be established in the United States. There was at this time but one other manual training-school in this country —the Rensselaer Institute, which was founded two years previously (1824). These two pioneer institutions, so closely associated in point of time, differed widely in cur-riculum. " The Rensselaer school had for that day ex-tensive laboratory advantages in chemistry and physics, and taught the analysis of soils, fertilizers, minerals, and animal and vegetable matter, with their applications to agriculture, domestic economy, and the arts, and as early as 1835 had a department for instruction in engineering and technology." This course appealed only to students of a much greater age than the children who were taught in the workshops of the community.

The Rensselaer Institute was strictly a technical school, while the New Harmony experiment was purely a trade-school. In the latter a trade is taught, in the former both the trade and the technique of the trade are taught. Though the Rensselaer Institute was the first industrial and the first technical industrial school in the United States, Maclure's attempt afforded the first purely trade-school. After reciting a list of manual labor organizations which followed in the wake of these pioneer ventures, Boone, in his History of Education, says truly: " Though many of these efforts to promote industry in connection with literary institutions failed, and most of the schools were closed or reorganized as academies, they served a double and worthy purpose; the function of intelligent labor was magnified and the seed sown for a more fruitful harvest. For how much of the idea of technical education in agriculture and the mechanic arts the present is indebted to these institutions can not perhaps be determined. Enough is known to suggest that the obligation must be large."

But little concerning the workings of the New Harmony educational experiment can be gleaned from the official records of the community. Though still in a remarkable state of preservation, they are almost entirely occupied with the endless bickerings of the social system. The most reliable and interesting information concerning the community schools is to be derived from the accounts given by those who in the days of The New Moral World in the capacity of teacher or pupil or visitor came in contact with them.

Mrs. Sarah Cox Thrall, who died in New Harmony a few years ago, was a pupil in the community schools. She stated that in summer the girls wore dresses of coarse linen, with a coarse plaid costume for Sunday or for special occasions. In winter they wore heavy woolen dresses. At rising, a detail of the girls was sent out to do the milking, and this milk, with mush cooked in large kettles, constituted the essential part of the morning meal, which the children were expected to finish in fifteen minutes. " We had bread but once a week—on Saturdays. I thought if I ever got out, I would kill myself eating sugar and cake. We marched in military order, after breakfast, to Community House No. 2. I remember that there were blackboards covering one side of the schoolroom, and that we had wires, with balls on them, by which we learned to count. We also had singing exercises by which we familiarized ourselves with lessons in various branches. At dinner we generally had soup, at supper mush and milk again.

" We went to bed at sundown in little bunks suspended in rows by cords from the ceiling. Sometimes one of the children at the end of the row would swing back her cradle, and, when it collided on the return bound with the next bunk, it set the whole row bumping together. This was a favorite diversion, and caused the teachers much distress. At regular intervals we used to be marched to the community apothecary shop, where a dose that tasted like sulphur was impartially dealt out to each pupil, just as in Squeers' Dotheboys school. Children regularly in the boarding-school were not allowed to see their parents, except at rare intervals. I saw my father and mother twice in two years. We had a little song we used to sing:

> " Number 2 pigs locked up in a pen,
> When they get out, it's now and then;
> When they get out, they sneak about,
> For fear old Neef will find them out."

Robert Dale Owen also gives us a picture of the New Harmony schools in operation. " In the educational department," he writes, " we had considerable talent, mixed with a good deal of eccentricity. We had a Frenchman, patronized by Mr. Maclure, a Phiquepal d'Arusmont, who became afterward the husband of Frances Wright, a man well informed on many points, but withal a wrong-headed genius, whose extravagance, wilfulness, and inordinate self-conceit destroyed his usefulness. He had a small school, but it was a failure—he gained neither the good-will nor the respect of his pupils.

" Another, of a very different stamp, was Prof. Joseph Neef, from Pestalozzi's school in Switzerland. Simple, straightforward, and cordial, a proficient in modern languages, a good musician, he had brought with him from Pestalozzi's institution at Yverdun an excellent mode of teaching. To his earlier life, as an officer under Napoleon, was due a blunt, offhand manner and an abrupt style of speech, enforced now and then with an oath—an awkward habit for a teacher, which I think he tried ineffectually to get rid of. One day, when I was within hearing, a boy in his class used profane language. ' Youngster,' said Neef to him, ' you mustn't swear. It's silly, and it's vulgar, and it means nothing. Don't let me hear you do so again.'

" ' But, Mr. Neef,' said the boy, hesitating and looking half frightened, ' if—if it's vulgar and wrong to swear, why——'

" ' Well, out with it. Never stop when you want to say anything; that's another bad habit. You wished to know why——'

" ' Why you swear, yourself, Mr. Neef.'

" ' Because I'm a fool! Don't you be one, too! '

" With all his roughness, the good old man was a general favorite alike with children and adults. Those whose recollections of Harmony extend back to the '40s preserve a genial remembrance of him, walking about in the sun of July or August, in linen trousers and shirt, always bareheaded, with a grandchild in his arms, and humming

247

to his infant charge some martial air in a wonderful bass voice, which, it is said, enabled him in his younger days, when giving command to a body of troops, to be distinctly heard by ten thousand men."   ·

Robert Dale Owen thus relates an experience of his own in teaching one of the community schools: "When I first took charge of the school, finding that the teachers occasionally employed corporal punishment, I strictly forbade it. After a time the master of the eldest boys' class said to me one day: ' I find it impossible to control these unruly rascals. They know I am not allowed to flog them, and when I seek to enforce rules of order, they defy me.'

"I sought to show him how he might manage them without the rod, but he persisted. ' If you'd try it yourself for a few days, Mr. Owen, you'd find out that I'm right.'

"' Good,' I said, ' I'll take them in hand for a week or two.'

"They were a rough, boisterous, lawless set; bright enough, quick of observation; capable of learning when they applied themselves, but accustomed to a free swing, and impatient of discipline, to which they had never been subjected. I said to them at the start: ' Boys, I want you to learn; you'll be very sorry when you come to be men if you don't. But you can't learn anything worth knowing without rules to go by. I must have you orderly and obedient. I won't require from you anything unreasonable, and I don't intend to be severe with you. But whatever I tell you to do is what has to be done, and shall be done, sooner or later.' Here I observed on one or two bold faces a smile that looked like incredulity, but all I added was: ' You'll save time if you do it at once.'

"My lessons, often oral, interested them, and things went on quietly for a few days. I knew the crisis would come. It did, in this wise. It was May, the thermometer was ranging toward ninety degrees, and I resolved to take the class to bathe in the Wabash, much to their delight. I told them that by the doctor's advice they were to remain in the water fifteen minutes only; that was the rule. When I called, ' Time's up,' they all came out, somewhat reluctantly, however, except one tall fellow named Ben, a good swimmer, who detained us ten minutes, notwithstanding my order, several times repeated, to come on shore.

" I said nothing about it until we returned to the schoolroom, then I asked the class: ' Do you remember my saying to you that whatever I told you to do had to be done sooner or later?' They looked at Ben and said, ' Yes.' Then I went on. ' I am determined that if I take you to bathe again, you shall stay in fifteen minutes only. How do you think I can best manage that?' They looked at Ben again, and seemed puzzled, never, very surely, having been asked such a question before. ' Has no one any plan?' I asked.

" At length a youngster suggested: ' I guess you'd better thrash him, Mr. Owen.' ' I don't wish to do that,' I replied. ' I think it does boys harm. Besides, I never was whipped myself, I never whipped anybody, and I know it must be a very unpleasant thing to do. Can't somebody think of a better plan?'

" One of the class suggested: ' There's a closet in the garret, with a stout bolt to it—you might shut him up in there till we got back.'

" ' That's better than flogging, but is the closet dark?'

" ' Yes.'

" ' I think Ben would not like to be shut up in the dark for nearly an hour.'

" ' No, but then we don't like to be kept from bathing just for him.'

" Then one little fellow, with some hesitation, put in his word: ' Please, Mr. Owen, wouldn't it do to leave him in the playground?'

" ' If I could be sure that he would stay there, but he

249

might get out and go bathing, and remain in half an hour, perhaps.'

" At this point Ben, no longer able to restrain himself—he had been getting more and more restless, turning first to one speaker, then to another, as we coolly discussed the case—burst forth: ' Mr. Owen, if you leave me in the playground, when they go to bathe next time, I'll never stir from it. I won't. You'll see, I won't!'

" ' Well, Ben,' said I, ' I have never known you to tell a falsehood and I'll take your word for it this time. But remember, if you lie to me once, I shall never be able to trust you again. We couldn't believe known liars if we were to try.'

" So the next time we went in bathing, I left Ben in the playground. When we returned, he met me, with eager face, at the gate. ' I never left, even for a minute. Ask them if I have,' pointing to some boys at play.

" ' Your word is enough. I believe you.'

" Thereafter Ben came out of the water promptly, as soon as time was called; and when any of his comrades lingered he was the first to chide them for disobeying orders.

" Once or twice afterward I had to take a somewhat similar stand (never against Ben), persisting each time until I was obeyed. Then, bethinking myself of my Hofwyl experience, I called in the aid of military drill, which the boys took to very kindly, and when three weeks had passed I found that my pupils prided themselves in being what, indeed, they were—the .best disciplined and most orderly and law-abiding class in school.

" So I carried my point against a degrading relic of barbarism, then countenanced in England, alike in army, navy, and some of the most accredited seminaries."

An account of the formation of the educational society has already been given. With this Mr. Maclure and his associates allied themselves, and the educational interests of the various communities were under its care. In December, 1826, William Maclure forwarded to the State Legislature a petition for the incorporation of the New Harmony Educational Society, and a bill was introduced stating that William Maclure " had bought, in and adjoining New Harmony, one thousand acres of land with suitable buildings erected thereupon, devoted to the establishment of schools, and had furnished a liberal endowment, embracing many thousands of volumes of books, with such mathematical, chemical, and physical apparatus as is necessary to facilitate education, and is desirous to obtain an act of incorporation to enable him more fully to carry out his benevolent designs." This bill was rejected in the State Senate by a vote of fifteen to four, on account of the popular impression that atheism was promulgated in the New Harmony schools. The Gazette, in commenting on the action of the Legislature, says: " We presume, from their conduct, that they have no confidence in our society or its intentions."

In a discussion following the signing of the articles of partnership between the two men, Maclure assured Owen that not only would he guarantee that instructors and professors of a superior type would be enlisted in the proposed educational experiments, but also that by the departmental system of instruction all the children of the schools would be brought into contact with the superior qualifications possessed by all these teachers. Contrary to this understanding, when the schools were organized each principal teacher assumed entire charge of the training of a particular group of children. During the larger portion of the life of The New Moral World Maclure was traveling elsewhere, leaving the New Harmony schools without any leadership save that mildly exercised by Thomas Say, whom he had deputized to assume charge during his absence.

These things, together with the failure of the Pestalozzian school to achieve expected results and of the industrial school to be self-supporting, caused Owen, dissatisfied with the educational experiments of his partner, to establish a separate school system, independent of Mr. Maclure's, under the leadership of a Mr. Dorsey, a short-lived venture that achieved no other result than to inaugurate a quarrel between the two proprietors which culminated in legal complications.

When at last Robert Owen saw the social temple tumbling about his head, with the characteristic blindness of the enthusiast who has failed to achieve his golden dream, he cast about for every reason save the right one to explain the downfall of his ideal social order. Though the real cause of the defeat of his plans at New Harmony lay in the fact that he had trusted too largely to that imperfect human nature which if perfect would make social reform unnecessary and even our present social system ideal, Owen did not hesitate to charge the defeat of his communistic schemes to Maclure's educational experiment.

In his farewell address to the people of New Harmony made in 1827, just before the utter collapse of The New Moral World, Owen said: " If the schools had been in operation upon the very superior plan upon which I had been led to expect they would be, so as to convince parents by ocular demonstration of the benefits which their children would immediately derive from the system, it would have been, I think, practicable, even with such materials, with the patience and perseverance which would have been applied to the subject, to have succeeded in amalgamating the whole into a community.

" You also know that the chief difficulty at this time arose from the differences of opinion among the professors and teachers brought here by Mr. Maclure, relative to the education of the children, and to the consequent delay in putting any of their system into operation.

" Having been led to entertain very high expectations of

the abilities of these individuals, I looked to them to establish superior arrangements for the instruction of all ages, and I was induced to suppose that the population would be compensated by the unequaled excellence of the system when put into operation; and in consequence of the unlimited confidence which I placed in these individuals to execute this most important part of my plan, you all know how much I have been disappointed. Instead of forming one well-digested arrangement, in which all the children of the community should have the benefit of the superior qualifications possessed by each professor and instructor, each principal teacher undertook the entire instruction of a certain number of pupils, by which arrangement they were prevented from associating with other pupils.

" By this error in the practise, the object which I had most at heart could not be attained; the children were educated in different habits, dispositions, and feelings, when it was my most earnest desire that all the children should be educated in similar habits, dispositions, and feelings, and should be brought up truly as members of one large family, without a single discordant feeling.

" It is true that each of the professors and principal teachers possessed considerable abilities, and acquirements in particular branches of education, but the union of the best qualities and qualifications of several of even the best modern teachers is required to form the character of the rising generation as it ought to be formed, and enable children when they attain maturity to become sufficiently rational and intelligent to make good, useful members of the social system."

Though the Educational Society perished in the ruins of the social order and Robert Owen retired broken in fortune from the Waterloo of his efforts as a social architect, Maclure remained in New Harmony and continued his educational experiments. Almost pathetic is the story of his after efforts as an educational architect. In 1827 he published an announcement of "Maclure's Seminary," stating: "Young men and women are received without any expense to them, either for teaching, or food, lodging and clothing. Hours, from five in the morning until eight in the evening, divided as follows: The scholars rise at five; at half past five each goes to his occupation; at seven the bell rings for breakfast; at eight they return to work; at eleven their lessons begin, continuing until half past two, including half an hour for luncheon; then they return to their occupation until five, when a bell calls them to dinner. Afterward until half past six they exercise themselves in various ways; then the evening lessons begin, and last until eight. The basis of the institution is that the scholars repay their expenses from the proceeds of their seven hours' labor, but to effect this will require several years more."

On May 27, 1827, Mr. Maclure announced "The Orphans' Manual Training-School." The Manual Training-School had its laboratory in a separate building, equipped "with such requisites as are necessary for an experimental course of lectures in chemistry. In another building is a small room lately fitted up for containing the philosophic apparatus, for which it is well adapted. The other room of this building has been used for some time as the drawing-school, but it is to be converted into a museum, in which all the natural productions of Harmony and the surrounding country will be accumulated, as well as the collection made by Mr. Maclure during his travels through Europe and America." Mr. Maclure also founded what he called "The School of Industry," which had for its principal motto, "Utility shall be the scale on which we shall endeavor to measure the value of everything." Under the auspices of this organization Mr. Maclure established, on January 16, 1828, the New Harmony Disseminator, "containing hints to the youth of the United States; edited, printed, and published by the pupils of the School of Industry."

When one by one his educational experiments in the training of children, in each of which he placed such high hopes, came to naught, William Maclure, still eager to do something for the cause of education and for the productive classes, " who earn their living in the sweat of their brows," directed his philanthropy toward the formation of an educational society for adults which he dubbed " The Society for Manual Instruction." Announcing its formation, the Disseminator, in 1828, explains that the new society is really a mechanics' institution; that it differs only in name from the mechanics' institutes of the United States and Europe, its objects and means being the same as these; and that its objects are to " communicate a general knowledge of the arts and sciences to those persons who have hitherto been excluded from a scientific or general education by the erroneous and narrow-minded policy of colleges and public schools, which have invariably endeavored to confine learning to the rich few, so that they might tyrannize over the uneducated many."

In 1828 Maclure went to Mexico to recuperate his failing health, leaving his financial and educational interests under the management of Thomas Say. The state of his health finally compelled him to take up his permanent residence there. Within a few years after his departure, the last School of Industry which he established closed its doors because of the withdrawal of the financial support of its founder. The Society for Mutual Instruction led a more or less insignificant and halting existence for several years and then " died for want of breath." Strange to say, after his departure from New Harmony Maclure seems to have lost all his former abundant interest and faith in his educational ventures for children. Not even in his correspondence with Thomas Say and Madame Fretageot does he allude to his former efforts in behalf of Pestalozzianism and self-supporting schools.

Yet within a year before his death in a strange land, we find Maclure still interested in the productive classes at New Harmony, still eager to do something for the education of the children of a larger growth. Through Mr. Achilles E. Fretageot, son of Madame Fretageot, he inaugurated in 1837 a correspondence with the workingmen of New Harmony which resulted in the establishment of a Working Men's Institute and Library, which rose like Phenix of old out of the dormant ashes of the Society for Mutual Instruction. The gifts which he had contemplated for this Working Men's Institute had not been bestowed at the time of his death. They were executed in part by the brother and sister, whom he named as the executors of his will.

This Working Men's Institute, as will be described in a subsequent chapter upon the Maclure Libraries, is in existence to-day, operates the New Harmony Library, was the first of the large group of institutes and libraries which Maclure established through the terms of his will, and is the sole remaining evidence of the educational efforts of the first American geologist. All the other educational ventures perished as perished the social order, leaving no record of their existence save that which they have written by their influence upon the educational methods and systems of the country.

What were the educational principles and aims of the New Harmony schools?

(1) First of all, as has been stated repeatedly, the Pestalozzian system of instruction was followed even more enthusiastically than at New Lanark. Owen advocated this system and Maclure was its devoted apostle. The prospectus for the schools written by Maclure was simply an exposition of the Pestalozzian method of teaching the various branches of study treated in the prospectus. The

eleven postulates of the so-called Pestalozzian creed as given by Morf constituted the chart and compass of the educational experiments on the Wabash.

Morf's twelfth postulate, advocating religious training, was rejected at New Harmony, as it had been at New Lanark. Maclure was a pronounced atheist and opposed even more bitterly than Owen the Christian religion, which he denounced as an institution by the aid of which the non-productive oppressed and held in bondage the productive classes. The peculiar religious opinions of Owen and Maclure attracted to their venture, along with the idle and the vicious and the adventurous, men vehemently advocating every shade and phase of religious belief and unbelief. In such an atmosphere religious training was neither popular nor possible. From the columns of the New Harmony Gazette it is apparent that the two features or phases of the Pestalozzian system most emphasized were:

(a) The object method of teaching.

" Children in course of instruction are not perplexed with words of the meaning of which they have no conception." Models or pictures of the objects to be explained are employed where the object itself can not be immediately presented to the senses of the child.

(b) The concrete in preference to the abstract.

" The whole of the time at school is devoted to demonstrable fact, leaving all abstract studies until judgment is matured by a correct knowledge of them and an extensive acquaintance with the things around them."

(2) The children, in the language of the New Harmony Gazette, " were taught to value virtue for its own sake, without the hope of artificial reward or fear of artificial punishment." The abolishment of all reward and punishment save that arising out of the very nature of the act of the child was the cardinal principle of the New Lan-

ark schools and the feature of the work there in which Robert Owen took the greatest interest. When Robert Dale Owen, while teaching in the community schools, conquered Ben in the manner which he describes on a previous page of this chapter, without the use of the ferule, he was but carrying out the chief educational principle which his distinguished father espoused.

Maclure, strongly approving of the system of school government exploited by the Owens, incorporated it into the educational system of the community. He was especially vehement in his opposition to the methods of punishment prevailing in contemporary schools. In the New Harmony Gazette of March 21, 1826, after stating his objections to those methods of punishment which produce fear, he continues: " Fear is a sensation so humiliating, irksome, and disagreeable to all the feelings of our species (as well probably as to those of all other animals), that the best disciplined temper can not prevent attaching hatred to the cause of it. But of all the manifold and destructive effects that fear has on the human family none is so injurious to the well-being of society and so totally subversive of the true interest of mankind as the fear of the child for the teacher, for, in addition to the innumerable bad consequences inseparable from fear in any stage of life, it closes the mind against receiving instruction from the only source that is accessible to children, their entire attention being occupied in watching the symptoms of anger in their teacher in order that they may be prepared to ward off the blow or contrive some means of escaping punishment."

It is well to remember here that twenty-five years before " Nicholas Nickleby " exposed the brutality of the English boarding-schools and in the very days when the birch rod lay like the sword of Damocles across the desk of every New England schoolmaster, a school system whose only means of government was the love between teacher and pupils, which, permeating every school, would render corporal punishment obsolete, flourished in a Western wilderness.

(3) More of the aims and hopes of the educational experiments at New Harmony are to be gathered from the educational views of the proprietors and teachers than from what little the schools accomplished or failed to accomplish during their brief career. Some of these will be briefly set forth in the paragraphs which follow.

THE RIGHT EDUCATION OF CHILDREN

The ideal training which the educational system of the social scheme hoped ultimately to bestow is described in an article, evidently written by one of the Owens (either Robert or Robert Dale, probably the latter), published in the New Harmony Gazette, May 16, 1827, from which the following is taken:

" *The right education of children*—not that education which teaches the child but a few, to him, unmeaning words and phrases, gives him, perhaps, a knowledge of some of the sciences, or even instructs him to hold converse with men of other days in their own languages, and makes him familiar with the history of ancient nations and people— yet too often leaves him morose, sullen, bigoted, and deceitful or cruel, passionate, and overbearing; a prey to envy, ambition, pride, vanity, and conceit; a being incapable of enjoying life himself and equally a source of misery to others—but that education which watches over the child from its most tender infancy, with a care that knows no intermission; that superintends his instruction and neglects him not in his amusements; that assists him in his difficulties and prevents their recurrence; that seeks to give him such habits, feelings, and desires alone as experience may prove to be a source of happiness; that leaves him not

on his entrance into the world, but ever endeavors to surround him through life with circumstances in unison with
his previous habits and inclinations and thus to make him
an intelligent companion, a pleasing associate, and a happy
being."

*Value of interest and the means by which it may be se-
cured.*—Some of the educational ideas which Maclure sets
forth in the three volumes of his Opinions are ridiculous from the standpoint of the intelligent teacher and lay-
man of to-day. Some of them, however, even the pedagogue of the twentieth century would do well to remember.
After making the query, whose interest has been consulted
in all our old-school operations, Maclure continues: " Attention is the only medium through which instruction
passes into the mind; without it nothing makes a lasting
impression on any of the mental faculties. Can undivided
attention be secured by fear or coercion? This is a query
necessary to be solved, as a principle upon which education
must be bottomed. Does not fear brutalize and paralyze
all the faculties of the mind? Let any one at a mature age
reflect on his feelings when under the impression of fear
and he will find that neither his memory, judgment, nor
any other of his mental faculties were sound. Fear perhaps is the great predisposing cause of many both moral
and physical diseases.

"If fear has so debilitating an influence upon the
physical and moral qualities of men hardened and strengthened by practise and experience, how much more must its
baleful influence pervert and deteriorate the young and
tender minds of children. In a state of fear the attention
is distracted, and can not act in unison with the subject
taught, but is secured by good-will, arising out of the
pleasure and amusement children take in exercises that
interest them. If so, and my experience does not permit
me to doubt it, the essential business and duty of a teacher
is to find out the inclination of his pupils, and teach them

260

any and all the useful lessons he may find they study with pleasure."—Maclure's Opinions, vol. i, page 66.

Reasons why the useful arts should be introduced into the schools.—As has been before stated, Maclure was a thorough-going believer in industrial education. After condemning the pleasures which men derive from sports involving the practise of " tormenting cruelties " (such as fishing, shooting, horse-racing, and bull-baiting), he continues: " If pleasurable ideas can by habit and practise be united with such mortifying exhibitions of human depravity, where every result is annihilated the moment the action is finished, how much more easy would it be for teachers to imprint on the tender minds of children the union of pleasurable ideas with the useful occupation of some mechanical art. This would furnish the necessary muscular exercises so conducive to health, while, at the same time, the gratification would be prolonged by the permanent benefit obtained by the utility of what is produced, and securing pecuniary independence in being capable of practising a productive trade in case of necessity.

" The being taught to make shoes or coats does not force the possessor of such knowledge to be a shoemaker or tailor, any more than learning mensuration or navigation obliges one to become a surveyor or sailor. They are all acquirements good to have in case of necessity, and in no state of society is that necessity more likely to occur than in our system founded on liberty and equality, where the only bar to the most complete equalization of the whole population is the ignorance of the great producing classes, which, however, is vanishing rapidly before the increasing means of obtaining useful knowledge; and children ought to be trained and educated to suit the probable situation which the circumstances of the next age may place them in. Even at present, all our farmers and manufacturers, nine-tenths of our population, would be very much benefited by possessing one or two of the mechanic arts, suitable to their occupations."—Maclure's Opinions, vol. ii, page 147.

The value of natural science as a study.—After discussing the obligation of every parent to give his children an education, Maclure recommends that the pursuit of some natural science be included in the training given, in these words: " While parents are giving their children the useful knowledge to carry them respectably through life, they ought not, on any account, to neglect giving them an occupation or an amusement to fill up their spare time, the want of which is the cause of most of the drinking and debauchery of youth. The best, most useful, and cheapest pastime is the natural sciences, which can be practised in all countries and climates at the least expense of either money or morals; the pursuits of which are productive of health, liberality, and the utmost extension of toleration, as there is room enough for all, without jostling or infringing on each other's rights or property; they banish envy and promote contentment, raising their votaries above the silly squabbles of disappointed ambition and teaching them an accurate mode of examining the properties of substances they are interested in knowing."—Maclure's Opinions, vol. iii, page 224.

" *The senses and the imagination ought to be trained.*"—Maclure believed this with all the radicalism of his strenuous nature. His scientific pursuits had made him thoroughly utilitarian. In his eager search for the accurate knowledge which only the senses can yield, he had lost sight forever of the realm of the spirit, where faith reigns and imagination dwells a handmaiden. Hear the argument by which he exalts the senses and eliminates imagination from the curriculum!

" Nature has given us our senses, through which we receive all our ideas. Nor can the ingenuity of men invent the figure or form of anything that has not come to them either entire or by piecemeal through the medium of their senses. . . . Our senses being the only medium through which we can receive our knowledge of matter or motion, the only channel by which we can receive information of the qualities or properties of animated things, it must follow of course that teaching the correct and rapid use of all our senses and avoiding all abuse and deceptions of them ought to be the principal object of education.

" The delusion of the imagination, being one of the greatest abuses of our sentient faculties, ought to be left at a great distance from all places of instruction. . . . Imagination has been so beaten up, mixed, and compounded with the wisdom of our senses, that it is difficult to draw the line of separation between them; but every vision of the mind, which neither directly nor indirectly has come to us through our senses, may be considered to be the child of the imagination, which sometimes produces pleasure, like an opiate, to end in debility or disappointment; but most frequently it exaggerates imaginary evils, and, perhaps, nine-tenths of the anxiety, misery, and wretchedness of humanity are the fruits of imagination. It is probably not the natural state of man, but the artificial state, engendered by the fallacies of education, and kept up by the rulers of the church and state."

Proper subjects to teach in the school of a free people.— In his Opinions, vol. i, page 48, Maclure declares that education, like mankind, may be divided into two species, the productive and non-productive, the useful and the ornamental, the necessary and the amusing. The productive, useful, and necessary subjects in teaching are those which we acquire through the senses, such as drawing, chemistry, natural history, mineralogy, geology, botany, zoology, arithmetic, mechanics, natural philosophy, geography, and astronomy. The non-productive and ornamental subjects are those which train the imagination, such as literature, mythology, etc. " It is the productive, useful, and necessary that constitute the comfort and happiness of the millions, and ought alone to occupy the care and attention of all representative governments, elected by the majority of the millions, who produce all that is consumed under the domination either of public or private revenue. The millions have a right to what they produce; and all appropriations out of the public treasury, for teaching the non-productive knowledge which is merely ornamental or amusing to the possessor, may perhaps be considered as a deviation from right and justice, in expending the fruit of the labor and toil of the productive classes, to teach the children of the idle and non-productive how to consume their own time and the public property in learning to amuse themselves and kill time agreeably."—Maclure's Opinions, vol. i, page 48.

FREE, EQUAL, AND UNIVERSAL EDUCATION

The persistency with which both Owen and Maclure throughout their stormy careers advocated the establishment of a system of State schools, supported by the public purse, wherein without cost every child might receive an education equal to that of his fellows, constitutes their greatest claim on public gratitude. When the social experiment opened its doors invitingly to the discontented of the Republic, there were no public schools, in the sense in which we use the term to-day, outside of New England. " Public schools " in the Middle and Southern States were either " free schools " or " pauper schools." It was not until 1871 that some sections of the Eastern States ceased to charge a fee for the fuel consumed by the pupil. In our own time the public-school idea in some portions of the South is compassed by the care which it is thought the State should take of the dependent and unfortunate classes. It required the constitution of 1852 to establish in Indiana the principle that the property of the State should educate the children of the State and that all the common schools should be open to pupils without charge. Even the township schools of New England, though bestowing an education that was " free and equal," were not " universal," for, basing their moral and religious training upon the narrow creed of the dominant sect, they often alienated the support and the patronage of the followers of other faiths.

Yet in 1825, nine years before the first free school supported by taxation on Indiana soil opened its doors, and at least half a century in advance of the prevailing thought of the era, Robert Owen and William Maclure established upon the very frontier of civilization an educational system for all where instruction could be obtained " without money and without price." Though the non-residents were charged tuition, to the children of the community the schools were indeed and in truth free, equal, and universal; and it was hoped they would become self-supporting, for it was expected that their industrial training would ultimately relieve The New Moral World of the expense of maintaining the educational system. Just as Owen held up before the eyes of the nations a new social order, which, convinced of its benefits, they were expected to adopt in their respective civilizations, so Maclure hoped through the educational experiments within that social order to guide the human race toward the blessings of schools " free as the living waters."

The public utterances and writings of both men are replete with the sturdy assertion of the idea that schools ought to be " of the people, for the people, by the people." After maintaining that public schools furnish the most effective means of shaping character, Robert Owen declares that " the national plan for the formation of character should include all the modern improvements of education without regard to the system of any one individual and should not exclude the child of one subject in the empire." Equally vehement is Maclure, who says: " One of the most sacred duties of a free people, the first time they exercise the right of universal suffrage, is to elect into power none but such as will enact such laws as will secure to all free, equal, universal, and general instruction, at the expense of the public, which is the people's purse. Once secure an equality of knowledge by placing the whole population by free schools on the same footing, the equality of the two other essentials of freedom, property and power, must follow as certainly as light and heat follow the rays of the sun."

The sons of Robert Owen caught the spirit of free schools from their father. In an address delivered at New Harmony in 1840 Richard Owen said: "It should be our strenuous endeavor to give an education free and universal to the son of the poorest farmer as to the son of the chief magistrate. It may require much time and patience to attain the desirable result, but it should never be lost sight of. Let our first patriotic object at all times be—equal and universal education."

Though a subsequent chapter presents the invaluable services which Robert Dale Owen rendered to the cause of free schools in the formative days of the Indiana educational system, we can not forbear to mention here his attitude on the question of equal and universal education. Years after the educational experiments went down in the ruins of the social order, Robert Dale Owen still breathed their spirit, when, through the editorial columns of the Free Enquirer, he declared: "We desire to see our public schools so endowed and provided that they shall be equally desirable for all classes of society. To effect this the means of instruction which are offered to the poor should be the very best which can be provided. This is no mere fanciful theory. I object, therefore, to all exclusive establishments for education in a republic; and exclusive every school or university is which denies admittance to the son of the poor on account of his father's poverty. I desire to see the

266

RICHARD OWEN,

living waters of knowledge bought without money and without price; for, so should they be in a commonwealth like this."

Startling to the age in which they were proclaimed as were the declarations of the founders of New Harmony concerning free public schools, they were no more so than the innovations which Maclure read into them, and by which he proposed to secure and perpetuate them. To a people vigorously debating the very legality of " pauper schools," he proposed and sought, through the educational experiments at The New Moral World, to demonstrate the wisdom and the feasibility of a Spartan system of education.

SPARTAN SYSTEM OF EDUCATION

Like Pestalozzi, Maclure believed that in education lay the only hope of uplift for the working classes, whose cause he always championed. That this education might be open to them, he contended for free, equal, and universal schools. That such schools when established might reach the productive classes and serve them most efficiently, he proposed that in them all the children of the State, whether of low or high degree, " should be fed, clothed, and instructed at the expense of the people's purse, formerly called the public treasury." Not since the days of ancient Sparta had a system of instruction been advocated which was predicated upon the surrender of children of tender years to the absolute care and control of the State. Under the Spartan *régime,* home control did not cease and that of the government begin until the child had attained the age of seven. In Maclure's system, the infant at the age of two years must be transferred from parental to State care. The aim of the system of instruction in Sparta was bodily strength and agility. Maclure sought for the children of his care utility and mechanical skill. The original Spartan system of instruction was designed to prepare the male youth for the pursuit of war. Maclure hoped through its revival to prepare both the male and female descendants of the productive classes for industry and for an "independence of the oppression which their ancestors had suffered from the worthless classes of society."

Maclure gave numerous reasons for "pressing a revival of the ancient Spartan school organization upon the people of North America."

(1) The children would be divorced during their formative years from the handicap of ignorant and immoral homes.

(2) The productive classes, relieved of the burden of maintaining the children, would be better able to work out their own redemption.

(3) The forcible removal, if necessary, of children to the State schools would defeat the indifference of parents toward education.

(4) By making the surroundings as well as the instruction of children the same, a greater equality of opportunity of all social classes would be secured.

(5) By the grouping of the children in large numbers, they could be instructed and maintained for less than the cost under the present arrangement either to the parents of supporting them or to the State of educating them.

(6) Only by a system wherein the State commands the entire time of a child can he be properly taught a useful trade that will insure his industrial independence as a citizen.

(7) Through the useful trades and occupations taught the pupils, "free, equal, and universal schools" could be made self-supporting, thus "relieving the productive classes of the burden of maintaining them."

(8) Best of all, the complete surrender of all children to the care of the republic would settle, once and forever, in the affirmative the question of State responsibility for the education of its wards.

THE EDUCATIONAL EXPERIMENT

Robert Owen accepted Maclure's innovation because it afforded an opportunity to transplant the offspring of rude, debased, often vicious homes into the refining atmosphere of the system of instruction which he hoped to see established at New Harmony. When he drew up the plans of organization for The New Moral World, he provided therein for the absolute surrender of all its children, at the age prescribed by his partner, to the educational system. During the brief life of the new social order no feature of its educational work was so rigidly enforced as that, which, for want of a better name, we may term Maclure's New Spartan System. Robert Dale Owen became a firm convert to the idea, for many years later he declared through the editorial columns of the Free Enquirer, " I hold it befitting a republic that the State should furnish throughout the land, at public expense, State institutions where every young citizen should be educated and maintained from youth to manhood."

Self-supporting Schools

While the educational experiments at New Harmony were in progress, the people between the Connecticut and the Wabash were opposed to the maintenance by public taxation of free schools wherein the pupils received instruction only. Maclure's innovation added maintenance to the burden of instruction which the populace had already refused to bear. In order to secure the coveted free training to which the majority had not yet granted support, and fearful lest the burden of taxation, even if shouldered, might fall too heavily upon his favorite " producing classes," Maclure revived Pestalozzi's scheme for self-supporting schools, and during the educational experiments in community days made repeated efforts to demonstrate their feasibility. Though his industrial schools fell as far short of self-support as did the less

ambitious effort of the Swiss schoolmaster at Neuhof, yet
Maclure, nothing daunted, still stoutly contended that the
foremost reason for the introduction of the useful arts into
the schools was " the great economy of enabling children
to feed, clothe, and educate themselves by their own exertions; thus rendering them independent of the labor of
others and establishing an equality founded on each ad-
ministering to his own wants from the most early age."

Consolidation or Centralizing of Schools

Modern advocates of the consolidating or centralizing
of rural schools will be interested in knowing that three-
quarters of a century ago William Maclure recommended
for the schools patterned after the New Harmony experiment, which he confidently expected to be established
throughout the land, the same procedure.

At a period when educational affairs in the country
west of the Appalachians were in a chaotic state, Maclure
strenuously and repeatedly urged that the newly formed
States adopt a civil township of the New England type as
the local unit for the administration and support of the
schools.

When these townships had been so created by process of
law, Maclure hoped to see erected, at the center of each,
one of his " Spartan systems of self-supporting free public
schools." With extreme care he locates and describes the
schoolhouse. " The locality must be chosen in a healthful
situation, removed from swamps or stagnant water, on or
near canals, great roads, or navigable rivers, surrounded at
least by two acres of land for every child, as a productive
farm from which they might obtain wherewith to feed
them." " Buildings must be erected expressly for the purposes of the school." " The arrangement and commodious
position of the workshops, houses, courtyards, gardens,
etc., are necessary to successful execution of the plan."

. . . " Materials used in construction ought to be solid and durable." " Wood to be avoided because of perishable quality and liability to harbor noxious insects."

" Pisé, a mixture of gravel, sand, and clay, rammed solidly between a shifting frame, might perhaps fulfil all the requisites of durability, health, and economy for buildings." . . . " With a coat of whitewash it has the solid and handsome appearance of a stone building and might be roofed with tiles or slates that would make it fireproof." " It might be heated by hot air or steam by the latest improvements in the construction of the kitchens." . . . " A parallelogram or square may be thought the best form for centralizing all the inhabitants, that the least time might be lost in changing place. A courtyard would occupy the center and all around the buildings would be the gardens, both for the convenience of culture and collecting the fruits."

With the characteristic confidence of the reformer, Owen's partner describes the benefits to be derived from such a plan of centralization:

(1) " In a township six miles square, the school situated at its center would be only three miles from its distant parts, bringing the scholastic operation within the reach of the inspection of all the inhabitants who are to benefit by the good management or suffer by the bad.

(2) " All being fed and clothed by the establishment, the vicinity of parents is not necessary and the schools may collect the children of a large district to the number of some hundreds, and each would serve in place of twenty or thirty small district schools, when the children eat and sleep at home.

(3) " An immense saving would be effected in time in a country so thinly peopled as the United States, where the greatest part of the children's time is wasted in going and coming at least once a day to a school necessarily at a considerable distance.

(4) " The grouping of the children as to age, capability, or aptitude would be facilitated, which is utterly impossible in the present method of small schools.

(5) " Such a centralized system of schools would render possible the employment of more and better teachers, the teaching of a wider range of subjects, and the purchase of models, prints, and instruments incalculably superior to anything that the parish schools can possibly afford to buy.

(6) " Best of all under such a system, free, equal, and universal schools could be operated successfully at a minimum of expense, if not entirely without expense to the productive classes."

NEEF'S PLAN OF EDUCATION

No discussion of the methods of instruction or the principles of education which dominated the experiments at New Harmony would be complete which failed to set forth at least some of the views of Joseph Neef. Preceding pages of this book have sketched briefly the career of the man who was principal of both the early schools founded for the purpose of perpetuating the Pestalozzian system of instruction in this country. No man since the great Swiss schoolmaster has possessed either a greater devotion to his principles or a more unselfish allegiance to the cause of education.

In the introduction to his book, published seventeen years before the birth of Robert Owen's Utopia, and styled a Sketch of a Plan of Education Suited to the Offspring of a Free People, wherein the author exploits at length his peculiar educational principles and methods, Neef humbly acknowledges that the training of children and the rearing of vegetables are the only occupations for which he feels any aptitude. " I have, therefore, seriously inquired in which of these two spheres of activity I should produce the greatest advantage to the society of which I am a member, whether by clearing and tilling some secluded spot of land, or by cultivating the pretty bewildered field of education. After mature examination, I became fully convinced that in the latter capacity my faculties will be more likely to be beneficial to my fellow citizens. . . . Hear it, ye men of the world! To become an obscure, useful, country schoolmaster is the highest pitch of my worldly ambition!"

The meaning of education. While Socrates, Plato, and many of the profound thinkers of the Christian era had uttered related truths, it remained for Pestalozzi to define education, as he does many times in different phraseology, to be " the natural progressive and symmetrical development of all the powers and faculties of the human being." When Joseph Neef, transplanted to the Western continent by William Maclure, became the first great American apostle of Pestalozzianism, he brought with him, as the cardinal tenet of his creed, the same conception of the meaning and purpose of education which the author of his faith had proclaimed. In an age in which the cramming system sat enthroned in the boasted New England schools and threatened a triumphal march westward, Neef announced to the people of the United States through his Sketch that according to his humble opinion " education is nothing else than the gradual unfolding of the faculties and powers which Providence chooses to bestow on the noblest work of this sublunary creation, man. This definition may appear new, but I trust that its newness will not prevent its being as solid and true as just and plain. Certainly it requires no superior degree of acuteness to discover that Nature gives every human being physical, intellectual, and moral capacity. The new-born infant contains the germines of those faculties as the acorn comprehends the future majestic oak. Teach and accustom the young mind to make a just use of these faculties and your task

273

as an educator is done. This unfolding of these powers is the real object of education, or, rather, education itself. Our arts and sciences, by the means of which that display is effected, are but accessory things."

While the definition of the meaning and purpose of education given by Pestalozzi and Neef was too broad for the age to which it was uttered, it has become too narrow for our own. Education has always been a subject having many phases. Successive reformers in its fields have re-defined it in terms of the phase which each wished to emphasize; in terms of the reform which each sought to achieve. The scholars of the Renaissance, aglow with enthusiasm for the glory that was Athens and the power that was Rome, declared learning and culture to be the sole aim of instruction and made education and knowledge synonymous. This view emphasizes the content of the course of study. Pestalozzi and Neef, attacking the system of instruction in the schools of the Humanists, maintained education "to be not knowledge, but the unfolding of childish power." This view emphasizes education as a *process*. It addresses itself to the method of instruction rather than to the content of the curriculum. By it one may determine better how to teach than what to teach out of the wealth of possible subjects that confront the twentieth-century pedagogue. These definitions of the meaning of education, asserted by the Humanists and by Pestalozzi, are, within certain limits at least, phases of the truth. Yet, both fall short of the lofty purpose which the twentieth century is breathing into the educational process.

All previous ages, in attempting to state the purpose of the schools, have focused their attention upon the child as an individual. The definition of education which they framed emphasized the ego and read into the educational process only an individual purpose. To the worshipers of the New Birth the *summum bonum* of instruction was to bestow learning *upon the child;* to Pestalozzi and Neef it was to unfold the powers and faculties *of the child.* Though both realized to some extent that the welfare of the social order was dependent upon the training of its future citizens, both made the interests of the child the center and circumference of all educational effort. There is a large element of truth in this view. All instruction must be individualized, since it must be comprehended and absorbed, not in social groups but personally and individually. Just, and only, in the proportion that the children of the Republic are made individually better and wiser will the society which they are to constitute become better and wiser.

These latter days have become more altruistic in stating the mission of the schools. The educational thinkers of the twentieth century have focused their eyes upon the child as a factor in society. They see both the child as an individual, who must be unfolded; and the social order for which he must be fitted, and wherein he should play his part as a citizen, touch elbows with his fellows, live to their fulness the measure of his days, work out his own individual destiny and be a weapon for good in the fight for social uplift. From the broad view-point of twentieth-century altruism the supreme duty of the schools is not to perfect the ego, but to fit it to play well a part which throughout life it must play in the struggle for the betterment of the race. By common consent we are seeking to rewrite the definition of education in altruistic phrase, are restating its meaning in terms of life, and reading into the very web and woof of the educational process a great social purpose.

What is the new meaning and purpose of education? Many would answer, " preparation for life," and many, " training for citizenship." Excellent as are these replies, they have grown so gray in the service of writers on educational topics that they have degenerated into meaningless catch-phrases.

Nicholas Murray Butler would answer, " A gradual adjustment to the spiritual possessions of the race." While Columbia's president would doubtless read and probably has read into his answer much, if not all, that the critics find wanting, nevertheless, in its wording his definition seems inadequate and one-sided. The schools must not only bring the child into an adjustment with his spiritual possessions; they must prepare him to be a thinker and a worker, who shall so react upon those possessions that they shall be transmitted, enlarged and enriched, to posterity. Otherwise, progress would be impossible.

These, and many other similar definitions, reflect with a greater or less degree of accuracy the educational thought of the hour. Language is always more limited than thought. Any attempt to state in words the aim of the schools must necessarily fall short of the high mission which this altruistic age has assigned to them.

Conceding these things to be true, many believe that so far, at least, Paul Hanus has made the best statement of the aim of education when he declares it to be " preparation for complete living." " To live completely is to be as useful as possible and to be happy." To be as useful as possible one must be a worker, striving with skill and earnestness. " To be happy one must enjoy both his work and his leisure."

This description of the educational process is best because it encompasses all that the other definitions emphasize, and more. To prepare for complete living is certainly to inculcate learning and culture, since without these life must needs be narrow and fragmentary; is certainly to unfold completely every childish power and faculty; is certainly to prepare for life in its fulness; is certainly to train for citizenship, since one could not live completely who was deficient in civic duties; is certainly to bring the student into adjustment with the spiritual possessions of the race, since one could not even begin to live

276

completely until he had been brought into the ownership of his scientific, his literary, his esthetic, his institutional, and his religious inheritance.

If each generation be prepared to live completely, it must be a testator as well as an heir, receiving from the educational process both the priceless inheritance which its forefathers have bequeathed, and the power to make that legacy still more priceless for generations yet to come.

School Republics for Self-government of Children

The last few years have witnessed numerous attempts in the United States to demonstrate the wisdom and the feasibility of managing schools through no other authority than that exercised by juvenile republics organized for the purpose of training their members in self-government. These attempts have been heralded as distinct departures in school management. Yet, in 1808, Joseph Neef outlined and subsequently attempted, both on the Schuylkill and on the Wabash, to execute successfully an elaborate plan for a self-governed school.

It was Neef's thought that the organization of the republic should be preceded by a very elaborate course in ethics, dealing with rights and duties, most of which must have been beyond the comprehension of the children. At the completion of this preliminary preparation for citizenship, Neef stepped before his pupils and inaugurated the republic in this language:

" Hitherto, my dear little friends—hitherto, my will was your law; it was the supreme rule to which you were obliged to conform your actions; I was your despot; your government was despotic. But you have now discovered the eternal laws of reason, which are to be the supreme regulators of your future behavior; that is, of all your actions; you are capable of being your own legislators, your own governors; you are, therefore, worthy of a free government; you are worthy to be governed by your own laws, or rather by the dictates of universal reason, which the Almighty has made a constituent part of your nature, and which you have now discovered; you are no longer my subjects, but you are, and must ever be, subject to your duties. To be a member of your society, a citizen of your little republic, is my ambition; it is your business to determine whether, by my preceding deportment toward you, I deserve to be your fellow citizen and fellow student."

The first business in order after the "inaugurating speech" was the formation of a constitution for the doubly infant republic. With characteristic enthusiasm and confidence, Neef describes the growth of the written instrument of government to which he had assigned his "gubernatorial authority."

"Do unto others that which thou wouldst have done to thee. This shall be the first statute, or rather the basis and foundation of our constitution. On one side we shall set down our unalienable rights, on the other our immutable duties, correlative to and resulting from our rights. All our laws will be nothing else but corollaries from and further explanations of our first and supreme law.

"Regulations of police will soon be found indispensably necessary, and of course they shall be made.

"The first transgression of a law or regulation will convince us that our little republic wants a court of justice and an executive power, and they will, of course, be established; a penal code will be wanted, and consequently created.

"That punishment and trespass ought to be rigorously proportional will not be liable to the least doubt; and this exact proportion we shall, therefore, strive to explore and to establish.

"If one of us happens to be accused, he shall enjoy all possible liberty to defend himself against his accuser; and, should his fellow citizens declare him to be not guilty, his accuser shall suffer the same punishment to which the accused would have been liable had he been found culpable.

"In framing our laws, statutes, and regulations we shall take peculiar care to make as few as possible, and exert all our skill to remove from them the least shade of baneful equivocation. All the citizens of our republic shall know and understand all their own laws."

Classical Education Unnecessary

Neef was in hearty sympathy with the utilitarianism of the New Harmony curriculum and shared in Maclure's violent antipathy toward the learned languages. "It is universally believed," says Neef, in his Sketch, "or at least pretended, that in order to render a boy's education liberal, learned, and classical he must absolutely learn that the Athenians called a fox ἀλώπηξ, and the Romans *vulpes*. Against this sufficiently ridiculous belief I make no great opposition, because I care very little about what is called a liberal, learned, and classical education, and because I believe that the education of a rational man ought to be rational, and nothing more. I shall raise against me the tremendous outcry of all our learned Hellenists and Latinists; I shall be charged with barbarism and vandalism, but I can not help starting the following question: Is the knowledge of those languages necessary, and consequently useful? Is it reasonable, is it comfortable to common sense, to lose, nay, waste, from six to ten precious years in acquiring those languages? Are the advantages flowing from that knowledge a competent requital for the loss of time and of better knowledge that might be acquired in that time?

"I have maturely weighed and reflected on the matter and my answer to these questions is decidedly in the negative. I can not find the least necessity, nor consequently the least utility, in learning those learned languages. I am wholly unable to discover any real advantage which they bestow on the learner. I conclude, therefore, that it is repugnant to common sense to lose so many years as is usual in studying them."

Neef's radical opposition to the study of the Greek and Latin tongues was an attack upon the narrow curriculum of contemporary schools. In them the classical course constituted the one course of study required of all. The educational experiments on the Wabash were a revolt against the content as well as the method of the prevailing system of education. But in their eagerness to offer and do full justice to the utilities which the New England schools ignored, Maclure and Neef eliminated the cultures from the New Harmony course of study and made their boasted curriculum as narrow as that which it came to conquer.

Both the group of educators in The New Moral World and their contemporaries were right and yet wrong—right in that each emphasized an important phase of the twentieth-century curriculum, and wrong in that each failed to recognize the value of that which the other advocated. Few, if any of us, will agree with Neef that the so-called learned languages ought to be entirely eliminated from the curriculum. There is still a place, and that place a very important one, for a classical education in the affairs of men. Such a training provides unsurpassed mental discipline; is an unchallenged badge of scholarship and culture; leads, as no other road can, to the mastery of language, to skill and distinction in oratory and literature; and girds the learned with the open sesame by which the inner life of the ancient world is being laid, a priceless treasure, at the feet of these latter days.

Many, however, have come to believe that differences in taste, aptitude, ability, and prospective calling in life make the enforced pursuit of a classical course in many cases "unnecessary, useless, and unjust." Moreover, many will live to see the day when the hurdle of a foreign tongue will no longer be thrust across the path of the pilgrim seeking light; when the entrance requirements of all our schools will be as broad as the tastes and the aptitudes of the children of men; when the fittest shall be all those who have even the one talent which our educational system may enroll in the service of the republic.

NEW HARMONY'S FAILURES

What features of the New Harmony schools were objectionable? What features has the evolution of schools demonstrated to be either erroneous or impracticable?

(1) First of all, though Maclure never completely abandoned the hope that they might be successfully operated at a later day, the self-supporting schools of the new social order fell of their own weight. Neither then nor since has any type of industrial school been self-maintaining. No modern trade-school attempts as did Maclure's to feed, clothe, and shelter as well as train all its students. Yet, so little has the labor product aided in meeting the expense budget, that, in most, if not all, our technological and trade-schools, no pretense is made of placing upon the market the handiwork of the pupil. Not even in the modern reformatory, where needs are the simplest, cost of maintenance the lowest, and the workmanship of the inmates better than that of immature children can ever hope to be, do the receipts from either the labor or the products of the institution lift from the shoulders of the taxpayers of the State more than a small portion of the burden of maintaining it. A self-supporting factory is a commonplace thing. But if it were continuously and solely dependent upon the labor of an ever-shifting body of promiscuous children, unskilled, immature in strength and experience, as well as years, and often lacking taste as well as aptitude for the work, then the self-supporting factory, like the

self-supporting school, would become an unattainable dream.

(2) The Spartan system of education, which Maclure hoped to revive, eliminated the home as a factor in the training of the child. His scheme, providing as it did for the surrender of the infant to the community as soon as he could be safely taken from the arms of the mother who bore him, would rob the home of its sociological and educational importance.

In that little masterpiece, Through Nature to God, John Fiske shows conclusively: (1) That in the enormous increase in duration of infancy, or the period when parental care is needed, lies the fundamental difference between man and any of the higher mammals, such as dogs, horses, and apes; (2) that this prolonged period of infancy is necessary to bring the child into proper adjustment with his environment; (3) and that this long period of helplessness and dependence, by knitting the parents together around a common center of interest, lies at the foundation of the human family and therefore at the foundation of society and of *institutional life*.

History demonstrates it to be equally true that as civilization has become more complex and life richer, deeper, and more far-reaching, we have extended further the period of infantry or tutelage, " until now, while the physiological period of adolescence is reached in perhaps fourteen or fifteen years, the educational period of dependence is almost twice as long." (The Meaning of Education, Nicholas Murray Butler, page 12, Macmillan Company, New York, 1901.) This is but saying in other words that the length of the period of infancy has kept step with the progress of the race and that the duration of parental care furnishes an accurate barometer of the civilization of any given epoch.

Maclure's proposition to transplant the weanling from its mother's breast to a motherless school system was a blow at the very vitals of the institution of the family, for since it arose only to care for the child during the years of his adjustment, without him the home has neither meaning nor purpose. Nor is it any the less true that the surrender of the infant at the tender age of two years to a hard-and-fast industrial system was a retrograde movement, a turning back of the hands of the clock of civilization, since such a procedure practically abolished the all-too-short period of dependence and parental care prevailing in the days when Maclure sought to revive the custom of ancient Sparta.

It is no answer to this last criticism to argue that in Maclure's proposed *régime* the State was to stand *in loco parentis* to the child. For that institution we call the government can no more be father and mother to the human offspring than the incubator can perform all the functions and duties of motherhood. Both the home and the school are necessary factors in the process of adjusting the child to his environment. To eliminate either is to rob him of a portion of his heritage.

(3) Enthusiastic over the evident efficiency of Pestalozzian methods and devices, the New Harmony group of educators ascribed to them power in the teaching of abstract conceptions and difficult processes which they did not possess. The prospectus of the school promises that "by an instrument called the trignometer the most useful propositions of Euclid are to be reduced to the comprehension of a child five or six years old." (!) After a very detailed description of the construction of Pestalozzi's three arithmetical tables, Neef cites triumphantly a series of problems which—though he declares that with the aid of the tables they were solved with ease and rapidity by children nine years of age—are beyond the intelligent comprehension of any class short of second-year algebra to-day. These instances are typical of the confidence with which it was expected that the Pestalozzian system of instruction

would make every branch of the scientific course of study as plain and easy to little children as the road to market. The mistake lay not in the system of instruction, but in ascribing to that system the impossible. The inevitable consequence was a curriculum which throughout its length and breadth was beyond the capabilities of those for whom its various studies were intended. Against the New Harmony course of study the criticism may be urged, just as it has been rightfully urged against many of the educational practises of later days, that "all instruction should be adapted to the capabilities of the learner. The important thing is not what children can be made to do, but what they ought to do at their stage of development."

(4) The course of study in the schools of the new social order bestowed upon the child only one of the five spiritual inheritances which successive ages have transmitted, enriched and enlarged, to posterity, and which it is the privilege and duty of the educational process to bestow.

These five inheritances to which the child is entitled are: *(a)* His scientific inheritance. The child is entitled to be armed with the modern scientific method and the results of modern scientific research. Thus prepared, he is entitled to go out into nature "to love it, to come to know it, to understand it," above all, to commune with it and to master it.

(b) His literary inheritance. This is the richest legacy because it is the one to which, for twenty-five hundred years, the race has given the most attention. The child is entitled to dip deeply into the storied lore of the ages, for through it will he quicken his imagination, enrich his vocabulary, master his own mother-tongue, think the thoughts of the prophets, seers, and sages of old, and acquire the learning and culture which the Greeks best describe by the use of "that fine old word Humanitas."

(c) His esthetical inheritance. The child is entitled to be brought into a feeling of appreciation and love for

284

the beautiful, the artistic, the picturesque and the sublime. He is entitled to the cultivation of that dormant esthetic sense which, whatever be his vocation, will lift his thought and taste above the sordid things of life into the realm where the soul revels in the true and the beautiful; and transform him from a hewer of wood and a drawer of water into a king with a destiny.

(d) His institutional inheritance. The child is entitled to know how the human institutions, which are to play such a large part in his life-story, came to be; to receive a clear insight " into his rights, which are so easy to teach, and into his duties, which are so easy to forget "; to be brought into sympathy and harmonious relationship with the institutional life enveloping him, which, if he understands it aright, will teach him needed lessons concerning the duties and responsibilities of citizenship and " the necessity of cooperation in the working out of high ideals."

(e) His religious inheritance. Somewhere, either in the schoolroom or in the home, the child is entitled to know the wondrous story, freed from creed and dogma, by which that branch of the human family to which he belongs explains its own origin and destiny. Call that story a superstition, if you will, it is the only superstition which time has strengthened. Leaving out of consideration even the acceptance of its truth, the child is yet entitled to the Christian story, since it is so closely interwoven with the last nineteen centuries of racial progress that it is absolutely essential to their interpretation.

NEW HARMONY'S SUCCESSES

What features of the New Harmony educational experiments merit our approval? Though in 1826, Albert Gallatin, then ambassador to Great Britain, declared " the New Harmony system of education to be the best in the world,"

even the special pleader in their behalf must concede that
the early educational ventures on the Wabash (1) failed
to meet the expectations of Owen and Maclure; (2) failed
as institutions as dismally as did those of the social order;
and (3) failed to influence the few contemporary schools
surrounding them. The value of the educational efforts in
The New Moral World must be measured not by what they
achieved in themselves, for they accomplished little and
perfected nothing; but rather by what they attempted—by
the precious seed which they sowed on a frontier soil; and
by the results which came from them in after years—by
the golden harvest into which after many days that seed
has ripened.

*(a) The precious seed sown by the New Harmony educa-
tional group.* To describe this is to enumerate almost all
the innovations, to recapitulate almost all the educational
fields in which, both in thought and practise, the reformers
of the new social order were pioneers. They advocated
and embodied into institutions educational ideas half a
century in advance of contemporary thought. To Owen,
Maclure, and Neef, and to the group of distinguished scientists and lesser educational lights aiding and abetting them,
we must thankfully rest debtor for those priceless contributions:

(1) *The first infant school established in America.*
This was in 1826. It was not until three years later that
a school for children of tender years was inaugurated in
New York City—a school to which Boone erroneously gives
the credit of being the first infant school on this side of
the Atlantic—an error not surprising, in view of the absence of any published account of the New Harmony educational experiment at the time his interesting and valuable work was written.

(2) *The first kindergarten of any type in the Western
World.* To the extent that the play-school at New Harmony, like Buchanan's earlier efforts at New Lanark, was a

THOMAS SAY'S TOMB AT NEW HARMONY.

forerunner of Froebel's more efficient organization, the kindergarten of the New Harmony schools preceded the first kindergarten of the Froebel type by thirty-four years, for it was not until 1860 that Miss Peabody, "without a knowledge of the details of Froebel's system," opened in Boston a school based upon the kindergarten idea.

(3) *The first use of the kindergarten as a part of the public-school system.* Though the Froebel kindergarten was introduced in 1860, its recognition and adoption by the public-school systems of the country was tardy. It was not until 1873 that Dr. W. T. Harris, then superintendent of the public schools at St. Louis, after years of agitation of the question, induced that city to be the first in the United States to introduce the kindergarten into its public educational system.

(4) *The first distinctively trade-school* and the second industrial school in point of time inaugurated in the United States.

(5) *The first industrial school of any type to be made a part of a free public-school system.*

(6) The first noteworthy American attempt and the second American attempt of any character to introduce and perpetuate the Pestalozzian system of instruction which has conquered the schools of this nation.

(7) The first public-school system, free or unfree, offering the same educational advantages to both sexes.

(8) *The first free public-school system* in a land in which to-day the blessings of an education, "free as the living waters" (as Robert Dale Owen so earnestly hoped that it might become), forces itself upon the American children, if need be, by due process of law.

(9) The first real public-school system west of the Appalachians.

(10) The first formidable revolt ever made by a public-school system in this country against that so-called "liberal" education, which, regardless of taste and aptitude,

ability and prospective calling, persist in thrusting the classics down the throats of all its unwilling victims.

(11) The most humane and enlightened system of school government to be found anywhere—for it was not equaled even by that in the schools of the tender-hearted Pestalozzi himself.

(12) The most enthusiastic and determined advocacy and support of " free, equal, and universal schools " that history records.

(13) The most ambitious and pretentious educational experiment which the world *had* yet witnessed and, with the exception of Pestalozzi's earlier effort, the most courageous and unselfish educational experiment which the world *has* yet witnessed.

(b) The results that came from the sowing. Immediate results there were none. It was not to be expected that there would be. Owen and Maclure and the " Boatload of Knowledge " were prophets and seers upon the mountain-top, their backs to the wilderness, their faces turned toward a fleeting vision of the promised land. The New Harmony educational experiments were half a century in advance of their times. The educational principles and practises of that all-too-brief golden age on the Wabash did not lie within the comprehension of either the frontier pedagogue or the New England schoolmaster. Both followed blindly and implicitly in the footsteps of Master Cheever. The prejudice with which the sturdy pioneer from New England viewed the social and religious ideas of the Commune extended to its educational system and all pertaining to it. Schools were few and far between, poorly equipped and poorly attended, uncertain in duration and taught by poorly paid, poorly prepared backwoodsmen or roving adventurers from the East. The rough frontiersmen, engaged in a life-and-death struggle with the forces of the wilderness, had little time and less thought for the affairs of the schoolroom. The

few who, in that age of slow communication between widely scattered settlements, had heard the story of the educational ventures at New Harmony associated them with the " other social vagaries " by which the new social order astonished, and yet at the same time amused the practical pioneers of the Western country. When the last, lingering school of the Commune closed its door it was apparent, even to an unprejudiced observer, that, measured by the immediate effect upon contemporary education, the New Harmony group of educators had labored and given of their substance entirely in vain.

But one " can not see, 'neath winter's field of snow, the silent harvest of the future grow." If Owen and Maclure, standing on the ruins of their golden dream for the betterment of their fellows and vouchsafed one clear vision into the future, could have seen the seed seemingly fallen among thorns and on stony ground grow, as it did grow, into a golden harvest of methods and measures and institutions for the educational betterment of men, they would have exclaimed in unison, " It is well." For, measured by its after-effect, the educational experiment at New Harmony deserves to rank among the most important educational movements in this country.

A subsequent chapter tells, in detail, the story of the chain of public libraries, modeled after the Society for Mutual Instruction of community days, which Maclure by the generous provisions of his will, established in one hundred and sixty frontier settlements of the West. Given at a time when there were few private and no public libraries, it is impossible to overestimate the impetus which this wise benefaction gave to intellectual development in every one of the one hundred and sixty communities which enjoyed the benefits of Maclure's liberality.

Subsequent pages describe the attainment and distinguished services of the noted group of scientists who, drawn to The New Moral World originally by the first American geologist, made the scene of Maclure's disastrous educational efforts a rendezvous and Mecca of scientists for many years. By their labors New Harmony became not only the first important scientific outpost in the West, but also the strongest scientific center in America.

The closing chapter of this book deals with the life and distinguished services of Robert Dale Owen. He was the very incarnation of the spirit of the founders of the new social order. In him both his father and William Maclure lived again, for his act was their act, made more effective by his talent. Whether as editor of the Free Enquirer or law-maker, we find him always the earnest, effective champion of " free, equal, and universal schools," and of wise measures for their betterment. As a member of the National Congress, he became the legislative father of the Smithsonian Institution. As a member of the legislature of the very State from which his distinguished father had withdrawn in chagrin over the failure of his educational, as well as his social schemes, Robert Owen, filled with the ancient enthusiasm of his house for popular education, formulated and brought to a successful passage the school-law whose enactment marks the natal day of the Indiana educational system. Robert Dale Owen was truly the legislative father of the Indiana common-school system. Through the wise legislation for which he must be credited, most of the educational principles and plans for the organization of common schools which the New Harmony group of reformers advocated, triumphed throughout the Middle West.

Though denied immediate consideration by contemporary schools, the educational doctrines of the New Harmony group found entrance to them in other ways. Neef's Plan and Method of Education and his Methods of Teaching, both published almost a generation before Hall's Lectures on School Keeping and Page's Theory

and Practise of Teaching, were among the first pedagogical treatises in America. The New Harmony experiments gave these two books for the first time the
recognition and prestige which made them one of the
authorities in school management and methods throughout
the country west of the Alleghanies for fully a quarter of
a century after the collapse of the educational ventures of
The New Moral World. Through the writings of his first
American disciple Pestalozzi influenced the pioneer teachers on the frontier of civilization.

During their brief career the New Harmony educational experiments afforded the first training-school for
teachers in all the West. Boone says that " the Pestalozzian theory found admirable exposition in the community
school for both young men and young women, to whom it
was more than a model school in their later teaching; it
was at once an inspiration and a liberal training." When
Owen's social system dissipated into thin air, there went
forth from brief homes on the Wabash men and women
who, scattering in every direction through the Ohio and
Mississippi valleys, and becoming the instructors of the
pioneer youth, sowed in almost every isolated hamlet the
tenets of the educational creed which Pestalozzi and Neef
and Maclure had espoused.

The eminent scientists who made New Harmony a
rendezvous were themselves bearers of good seed and glad
tidings. Their achievements and contributions drew renewed attention to the best features of the educational
" light that had failed." Most of them, enthusiastic be-
lievers in the methods and aims of the New Harmony
group, carried with them on their scientific explorations to
every remote spot the new educational faith. Climbing
to eminence in every Western State as surveyors and geologists and university instructors, their advocacy of the free
public school and the Pestalozzian system of instruction
commanded the attention which their distinguished attain-

ments merited. They secured, after many days, the tardy recognition for which the New Harmony group of educators had asked, and asked in vain.

When the social system went to pieces, hundreds of its most enthusiastic devotees turned their backs upon the scene of the great disappointment and sought permanent homes elsewhere. Some returned to the country east of the Appalachians, while a greater number scattered themselves through the promising hamlets of the Ohio and Mississippi valleys. All carried to the new habitation an enthusiastic support of the free public school and the Pestalozzian creed. Who can estimate the influence which they have exerted in molding the spirit, the method, and the organization of the public-school systems both north and south of Mason and Dixon's line?

The second distinctive Pestalozzian movement in this country invaded the conservative atmosphere of staid New England. It numbered in the list of its enthusiastic champions such men as Horace Mann and Barnas Sears and George Boutwell and Lowell Mason and Agassiz and David Page and E. A. Sheldon, and a host of others almost as illustrious. No more distinguished group of educators has blessed any epoch in our career as a nation. Their achievements constitute one of the brightest pages in our educational history. Combining with the enthusiasm that characterized the New Harmony group the conservatism and intellectual balance necessary to permanent reform, they gave the Pestalozzian faith a firm foothold on American soil, wrote its spirit into wise laws and enduring institutions, and sent it westward to complete the work that New Harmony had inaugurated. Whence came the first inspiration of this second Pestalozzian group? From the East or from the West, or from both? Who can answer with safety? Would it not be pardonable, at least, if the teachers of the Middle West should elect to believe that the traditions and the influence of the New Harmony experiments, working silently through the years, played at least a small part in the awakening of New England and served in some slight degree to turn the minds and hearts of its educational thinkers in expectant faith to the teachings of the master of Burgdorf?

Most of the educational doctrines of the New Harmony group of educators have triumphed and a national free public-school system, for which they so strenuously contended, more far-reaching and efficient than pictured in their fondest dream, is consummating that very equality of opportunity among the classes which the social experiments of The New Moral World sought to achieve. Robert Owen and William Maclure did not fail, for in the fulness of time they have come into their own.

CHAPTER XXI*

JOSIAH WARREN

" A remarkable American, Josiah Warren."
—JOHN STUART MILL.

AMONG the most remarkable characters attracted to
New Harmony in community days was Josiah Warren,
equally notable as an inventive genius, a social philosopher,
and a peaceful revolutionist. He was born in Boston in
1798, of historically famous Puritan stock. Of his parents
and early life but little is known. At an early age he
displayed musical talents, and, with his brother George,
played professionally in local bands. At the age of twenty
he married, and soon after set out from his native place
to improve his fortunes in the West. He settled in Cincinnati, and gained an honorable repute as an orchestra leader;
but he had other interests besides music. Mechanical pursuits occupied his leisure hours, the earliest fruit of which
was the invention of a lamp, patented in 1823, which sub-
stituted lard for tallow as fuel, giving a better light at a
lower cost. Its success was such that the inventor before
long was running a lamp manufactory in Cincinnati.

More pressing problems than those of illumination
were, however, shortly to arise and absorb the active mind
and generous heart of the ingenious young New Englander.
There came to Cincinnati in 1824 a visitor whose reputa-

---

* This chapter is the contribution of Mr. William Bailie, of Boston,
who has made a searching study of the life and services of Josiah
Warren, and is the best informed authority on the philosophy of that
remarkable man.

JOSIAH WARREN.

tion as the boldest and most successful social reformer of the age was world-wide. When Robert Owen, with a fervor of conviction and inspiring enthusiasm which have never been surpassed, unfolded his plans for the inauguration of The New Moral World, Warren was so much impressed that he decided to join the grand experiment which was about to begin at New Harmony. So, after disposing of his lamp factory, Warren, with his young family, joined Owen and his enthusiasts on the Rappite property, hoping to assist in founding the ideal community which was to usher in a millennium of peace and plenty, brotherhood and happiness, ultimately to embrace all mankind.

Here Warren found a field in which to study the problems of government, property, and industry, together with the relation of the individual to society, such as never before was given to man. During two stormy years of vicissitudes, disappointments, and failure Warren remained with the community, and bore his share of the burdens incident to so pretentious an undertaking. And when he finally departed it was not, like so many others, as an embittered reactionary, but as an earnest, hopeful student who had spent his time to good purpose. As one who had with painful solicitude witnessed the inadequacy of communism to correct the evils of property; and the failure of paternal authority, as well as of majority rule, to solve the problems of government, he had learned an invaluable lesson, and stored up pregnant experience for use in future efforts to grapple with the same vital issues. With Warren the failure of communism was simply a reason for trying another plan of attack upon the existing institutions of society. Like Owen, he never doubted that the " emancipation of man " was possible, and human happiness only a question of suitable social adjustment and the application of what he deemed to be right principles.

Chief among the causes which, in Warren's mind, led to disaster at New Harmony, were the suppression of individuality, the lack of initiative, and the absence of personal responsibility. When everything was decided by authority, or by the will of the majority, each was prone to ascribe the faults of the system to the shortcomings of his neighbors. These defects Warren believed to be inseparable from any social scheme based upon government and community of goods. Even under the most favorable conditions failure would in the long run be assured. He concluded, therefore, that the basis of all future reform must be complete individual liberty. Every one should be free to dispose of his person, his property, his time, and his reputation as he pleases—but *always at his own cost;* this qualification of the principle is inseparable from it, the core, as it were, of his philosophy.

The New Harmony experience had convinced Warren that any theory of reform, however perfect or plausible, should be put to the test before being offered to the world as a remedy for existing evils. To this end, therefore, he undertook his first experiment, the Time store.

On the 18th of May, 1827, there was unpretentiously opened at the corner of Fifth and Vine streets in Cincinnati a small country store, conducted on a plan new to commerce. It was the first Equity store, designed to illustrate and practicalize the cost principle, the germ of the cooperative movement of the future. When the advantages of the store became known, it proved to be the most popular mercantile institution in the city. The people called it the "Time store" because a clock was used by the merchant to determine the amount of compensation for his service in waiting upon the customers. The storekeeper exchanged his time for an equal amount of the time of those who purchased goods from him. The actual cost of the goods bought was paid for in cash, the labor note of the customer was given to the merchant to pay for his service. It ran something after this fashion: "Due to Josiah Warren, thirty minutes in carpenter work.—John

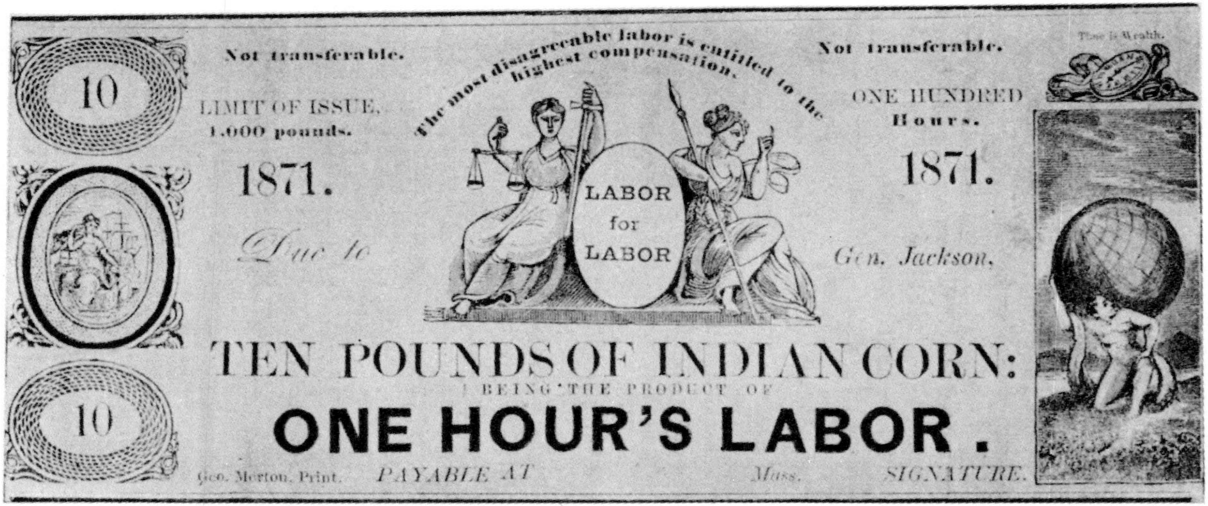

LABOR NOTE ISSUED BY JOSIAH WARREN.

Smith." Here was the application of the principle of labor for labor, the cost principle, in its most primitive form, which was subsequently modified to allow for the different valuations of the various kinds of labor.

The idea of labor notes originated with Robert Owen, but Warren's application of it was original and proved entirely successful. Though at the beginning the Equity store met with scant encouragement, it was but a short while until it taxed all the reformer's time and energies. The merchant on the next corner soon found himself without occupation, and requested Warren to explain to him the method of conducting business on the equity plan. The founder of the movement was only too happy to assist his rival to convert his place into a " Time store," and delighted to see so quickly an instance of what competition could do in enforcing the adoption of more equitable methods of exchange.

Warren's store was a labor exchange where those who had products to sell could dispose of them, provided the goods were in demand, without having to give the lion's share as profit to the middleman. It was also a bureau for labor seeking employment, and thus served to direct the reformer's attention to the long and useless apprenticeships by which the common trades were hedged around. He wished to disprove the need for long terms of industrial servitude, and this desire led to the idea of a cooperative village. Full of enthusiasm for the principles which he was now convinced would solve the deeper economic problems of society, having tried them in regard to the distribution of wealth, he longed to see them applied to its production.

Robert Dale Owen at this period became interested in Warren's plans, but after much waiting, and a visit to New York in 1830, the Cincinnati reformer decided to prepare, unaided, for a village experiment. He set himself to learn many practical arts, including wagon-building, wood and metal working, printing and type-founding. The first village of Equity was commenced in Tuscarawas County, Ohio, and after a two years' trial was abandoned, owing to the malarial and unhealthful condition of the locality. Many interesting experiments in the industrial and practical education of the young were carried out by Warren, which showed that in this field he was a true pioneer, for it is only to-day that his views are finding realization in the manual training-schools and technical institutions for practical education.

The Peaceful Revolutionist, Warren's first periodical, appeared in January, 1833, but survived only a few months. It was a four-page weekly of conspicuously neat typography, and was devoted to expositions of the principles of equity. So primitive at the time were his resources, and so marvelous his skill and ingenuity, that the plates from which the paper was printed were cast over the fire of the same stove at which the wife cooked the family meals. The printing-press he used was his own invention, and with his own hands he made type-molds, cast the type and the stereo-plates, built the press, wrote the articles, set them up, and printed off the sheets.

The years prior to 1842 were devoted mainly to mechanical pursuits and printing inventions. About 1840 Warren constructed the first press that was ever used to print newspapers from a roll. The following description of this mechanism is from an editorial which appeared February 28, 1840, in an Evansville paper:

" The first number of the Southwestern Sentinel is the first newspaper probably in the world which was ever printed on a continuous sheet. Our press or printing machinery is the invention of Mr. Josiah Warren, of New Harmony. He has brought a series of experiments extending through nine years to a successful close, and this machine, which he calls his speed press, is one of the results."

Unfortunately the innovation was opposed by the printers, who saw in its labor-saving power a menace to their interests. They deliberately threw the press out of gear at every opportunity, and at length so exasperated the inventor that he came one day to the Sentinel office, had the press hauled away, and deliberately broke it to pieces.

Typographical inventions continued, however, to occupy Warren's attention. His purpose was to extend his stereotyping inventions to all varieties of printing, illustration, and artistic reproduction. His improvements in this field he termed " universal typography."

The Indiana Statesman, of New Harmony, under dates of October 4, 1845, and March 7, 1846, contains flattering accounts of the progress and utility of Warren's inventions. His typographical plates were durable, cheap, and had a smooth, glassy surface, so like stone that the inventor termed them " stone-types." He claimed that the facility with which illustrations could be got up, the rapidity of stereotyping and printing them, together with the durability of the plates, justified the expectation that they would ultimately supersede woodcuts, steel-plate and copper-plate engraving and printing, and lithography. The process included printing in colors, besides a result similar to what is now known as half-tones.

While it is doubtful if Warren ever received an equivalent for his ingenuity, labor, and outlay on these inventions, at which he worked during the larger part of his life, it is certain that his methods were utilized by others, and the world is accordingly the gainer by his improvements. The processes now in use for the finer class of stereotype work are based upon his discoveries. The latter years of his life were devoted to studies and experiments with a view to perfecting his inventions, and his final results, it is believed, were not made known to the world, nor rendered available when death terminated his labors.

The New Harmony Time store was opened in 1842. At

first it encountered strong opposition at the hands of interested rivals, but its beneficial influence was soon felt in
a fall of retail prices throughout the surrounding country.
Of this, his second store experiment, Warren wrote:
"Whatever may be thought of the hopelessness or the un-
popularity of reform movements, I will venture to assert
that no institution, political, moral, nor religious, ever
assumed a more sudden and extensive popularity than the
Time store of New Harmony. But it was principally
among the poor, the humble, and the downtrodden. None
of those who had been accustomed to lead, none who had
anything to lead with, offered the least assistance or aid,
nor scarcely sympathy, though they did not attempt to
deny the soundness of the principles. . . . When all
the stores in the surrounding country had come down in
their prices to an equilibrium with the Equity store, the
custom naturally flowed back again to them, and the next
step was to wind up the Time store and commence a village."

Warren next turned his ingenuity to the production in
1844 of an original system of music, denominated by him
"Mathematical Notation," designated on scientific principles to accomplish in the representation of harmonic
sounds a similar service to that performed by phonography
in the representation of the elements of speech. The
author printed the book by his newly perfected universal
typography, and, as may still be seen by a copy preserved in
the library of the New Harmony Working Men's Institute,
it was a beautiful example of his stereotyping process, reproducing his own handwriting in delicate copper-plate.
Dr. Mason, a musical authority of that day, admitted the
comprehensiveness and simplicity of Warren's musical
notation, but believed it would be a hopeless undertaking to attempt to supersede the universally accepted
system.

About this period Warren received seven thousand dol-

EXPLANATION OF THE EQUITABLE MONEY.

THE MONEY TAKEN FOR LABOR OUGHT TO ENABLE THE HOLDER OF IT TO GET AS MUCH LABOR AS HE OR SHE GAVE FOR IT.

Labor is here understood to be, All kinds of services that would not be performed for the pleasure of it.

The Note promises a certain, DEFINITE QUANTITY of LABOR embodied in the article promised : so that the receiver of it can know what he is doing when he takes it : which he cannot know when he takes common money — he can never tell how much of any thing he can get for a dollar twenty four hours after he has taken it : and this is the great defect of all money as now known and used. The Notes are made " NOT TRANSFERABLE", at first, because the use of them requires a new training of the understanding, and we do not want them to fall into the hands of those who have not had this. — Therefore, the name of the payee is at present inserted with a pen, when the note is issued : and if the holder of it passes it to any other person, it is because he thinks that the payer would not object if he was present : and thus the note becomes a medium of introduction to the payer of it. Notes for large amounts being lost, if payable only to the person named, (on the face or by endorsement), secures the non payment of them. : but very small amounts (for change) can be made payable to "Bearer", as the occasional loss of them might not be of serious consequence.

Instead of these notes being, like bank notes, made of the thinnest paper, on purpose to be easily lost, they can be made of Parchment or Card paper, which is more safe, more easily handled, and even in the dark they can be distinguished from each other by their sizes. With a coating of bleached Shell Lac, after they are printed, they will bear a good deal of circulation.

These notes have been made to promise Carpenter work, Mason work, Iron work, Needle work, Washing, &c. &c. The notes of the store keeper circulate very freely : But notes that promise some Staple Article that every body uses,— one that will keep from year to year,— an article that can not become worthless by the over-supply of it :— an article that is easily divisible into minute quantities, and one that cannot be monopolised, is best for general purposes. IRON, STEEL, and INDIAN CORN are articles answering all these demands, particularly Indian Corn. It can be kept of uniform quality from year to year. Every one who has land can raise his own banking capital. It is too bulky to be stolen. It can be converted into some Thirty different kinds of food, besides Beef, Butter, Milk, Cheese, Hides, Tallow, Pork, Lard, Mutton, Wool, Poultry, Eggs, Oil, Starch, Alcohol, Molasses, Fuel &c., all without passing into any speculator's hands : "LIMIT OF ISSUE" A Record is kept at the printing office of all the notes given out, and which Record is open to public inspection and the amount issued to any one can be publicly known.

The Issuers of these Notes can advertise on the backs, any different kinds of Labor in which they can redeem them, attaching a price to each kind in pounds of Corn, as we now do in dollars and cents : and the value of the notes to the holders of them will be greater in proportion to the different kinds of valuable services they will command. For farther particulars, see "TRUE CIVILIZATION".

This is a very small and very simple thing to the eye ; but, considered as a New Element in human affairs, no mind can measure its magnitude ?

LABOR NOTE ISSUED BY JOSIAH WARREN

lars for his stereotyping patents, and such a wave of financial prosperity revived his desire to found another Equity
village. For this purpose he secured land near New Harmony, but abandoned it for more favorable prospects in
Ohio. The village of Utopia was founded by Warren in
1847 about a mile above Claremont, a Fourierist community which had just then come to grief. Unlike the
latter, there was no common ownership of property in
Warren's experiments. Each family owned its own lot and
house (after it was erected), but the members of the village
cooperated in all cases where it was mutually advantageous
to do so. Warren's efforts were for those whose only means
was their labor force, and his purpose was to demonstrate
that such people, with free access to natural resources,
could, by exchanging their labor on equitable terms, by
means of labor notes, build their own houses, supply their
prime necessities, and attain to comfort and prosperity
without dependence on capitalists, or any external authority, for the means of life.

Utopia went on progressing in a quiet way for many
years. It was the policy of the settlers to avoid publicity,
and to refrain from encouraging outsiders to visit or to
join them. One of the pioneers, E. G. Cubberly, in October, 1872, while still residing in his original home in
Utopia, wrote: " The labor notes put us into a reciprocat-
ing society—the result was, in two years twelve families
found themselves with homes who never owned homes before. . . . Labor-capital did it. I built a brick cottage, one-and-a-half stories high, and all the money I paid
out was nine dollars and eighty-one cents—all the rest was
effected by exchanging labor for labor. Mr. Warren is
right, and the way to get back as much labor as we give is
by the labor cost prices; money prices, with no principle
to guide, have always deceived us."

It may naturally be asked what became of the village.
Why did equity villages not multiply? Why did the pio-

neers keep from the public as far as possible all information concerning them? To such questions no satisfactory answer in a few words can be given. Owing to the high price of the surrounding land, most of the settlers, after about four years, moved from Utopia into Minnesota, where land was cheap and abundant.

Leaving the scenes of his labors in Ohio and Indiana, Warren in 1850 visited New York and Boston, and, by means of a quiet propaganda, succeeded in arousing the interest of many earnest people in the individualistic form of cooperation advocated by him. He met the brilliant writer and reformer, Stephen Pearl Andrews, who henceforth became Warren's most ardent disciple, and the literary exponent of equity. Andrews' Science of Society, an exposition of the sovereignty of the individual, and cost the limit of price, has probably done more toward calling the attention of independent thinkers and reformers to Warren's philosophy than anything ever put forth by himself, and is by far the ablest statement of the "principles" which has yet appeared.

As a result of Warren's activity the Village of Modern Times was founded in 1851. The site was on Long Island, forty miles by railroad from New York City. The soil was considered worthless, but this did not deter the enthusiasts of equity. They came by ones and twos, and gradually began to clear the ground for market-gardening, meanwhile building themselves houses of such pretensions as their limited resources permitted. About a hundred souls had settled on the ground when the New York Tribune began to feature the colony and create a publicity as undesirable to the settlers as it proved to be annoying. The newspaper notices brought many visitors, some to stay, mostly ignorant of the ideas on which the village was founded. True to their principles, which allowed equal rights to all in natural opportunities, the pioneers refrained from taking any steps to exclude the newcomers,

302

so long as they did not invade the rights of others. This devotion to principle had, however, its drawbacks, though in the end it proved a self-corrective. One man began to advocate plurality of wives, and started a paper to support his views. Another believed clothing to be a superfluity and not only personally practised his Adamic vagaries but inflicted them upon his helpless children. A woman who would not have passed for a model of physical perfection, displayed herself in male attire, which gave rise to the newspaper comment that "the women of Modern Times dressed in men's clothes and looked hideous." Still another woman had the diet mania so severely that, after trying to live on beans without salt until reduced almost to a skeleton, she died within a year. Whereupon the newspapers declared: "The people of Modern Times are killing themselves with fanatical ideas about food." These were some of the burdens the real settlers had to bear because they acted on the non-invasive principle, and accorded liberty to do even the silliest things, believing that experience, and the application of personal responsibility in allowing things to be done at each one's own cost, would work the surest and most effectual cure.

Despite the persistent misrepresentations and the withering slanders to which the colony was subjected during its earlier years, the pioneers prospered. But after reaping so much of the undesirable fruits of notoriety, the name was changed to Brentwood, under which appellation it is still known.

Writing to an English friend in 1857, one of the settlers, Edward Linton, asks: "You have been here, sir, and I ask you, considering the natural obstacles to overcome, if you ever saw greater material success attained in so short a time by the same number of people without capital, and with only their hands and brains to operate with, under all the disadvantages of habits formed by a false education and training. . . . And as it regards individual and social happiness and the entire absence of vice and crime, I am confident this settlement can not be equaled. This is, emphatically, the school of life. It is what has been learned here, infinitely more than what has been done, that constitutes what I consider the greatest success of the settlement. What has not been done is, I think, of far more consequence than what has been done. . . . I would rather that my children would live here and have the advantages of the society and practical lessons taught here, than for them to have what is called an education in the best institutions of learning in the world."

Linton's tribute to Warren in the same letter can not be omitted: " But whether I ever live to see the practical realization of the principles or not, here or elsewhere, I never can feel sufficiently grateful to the unostentatious man whose remarkable and peculiar constitution of mind enabled him to discover the most subtle and sublime truths ever made known to man for his self-government and the regulation of his intercourse with his neighbors. In my own person and in my own domestic affairs I have been incalculably benefited."

Broad avenues, tree-shaded streets, pretty cottages surrounded by strawberry-beds and well-tilled gardens, formed the outward appearance of Modern Times. The occupants were honest, industrious, and had learned to mind their own business, while readily cooperating with their neighbors for mutual advantage. They were free from sectarian dissensions, law-courts, jails, rumshops, prostitutes, and crime. No one acquired wealth save by his own industry. Long afterward the people who lived there during the years that the principles of equity were the only law among citizens, looked back with regret mingled with pleasure on those pioneer days of effort to achieve a higher social ideal.

It should be remembered that the equity villages did

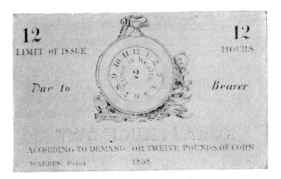

LABOR NOTE ISSUED BY JOSIAH WARREN.

not fail in the sense that New Harmony, Brook Farm, and numerous other similar experiments failed. The Modern Timers had no trouble over property or forms of government. Each owned his house and land, and by mutual understanding political or civic authority was dispensed with. None felt responsible for the failure of his neighbors, and only aggressive or invasive action was resented by combined action. The panic of 1857, which in New York City alone threw upward of twenty thousand people suddenly out of work, shattered a manufacturing enterprise that had been successfully begun in Modern Times. Before the effects of the ensuing industrial depression had cleared away, the country was in the throes of civil war, and all hope of success was for the time dissipated.

In July, 1854, while living at Modern Times, Warren began the publication of his Periodical Letters, a record of the movement and further exposition of the principles, which were issued with more or less regularity until the end of 1858. He spent the winter of 1855–'56 visiting his old friends in Ohio and Indiana. After 1860 he returned no more to the Long Island village.

The reformer's activity declined with advancing age. Several years were spent quietly at Cliftondale, near Boston, and in 1873 he went to reside with his friends, the Heywoods, in their home at Princeton, Massachusetts. Here he wrote and printed his last production, Part III, of the True Civilization series, giving " practical applications " and the " facts and conclusions of forty-seven years' study and experiments in reform movements through communism to elementary principles found in a direction opposite to and away from communism, but leading directly to all the harmonic results aimed at by communism." Equitable Commerce, his first book, containing practically all his views, was first published in 1846, and was several times reprinted.

THE NEW HARMONY MOVEMENT

The last months of Warren's life were passed in Boston at the house of his early friend, Edward Linton, where he was cared for in his last illness by kindly hands. Kate Metcalf, one of the pioneers of Modern Times, nursed him to the end, which came on April 14, 1874.

CHAPTER XXII

ROBERT OWEN'S LATER LIFE

"He originated and organized infant schools. He secured a reduction of the hours of labor for women and children in factories. He was a liberal supporter of the earlier efforts to obtain national education. He labored to promote international arbitration. He was one of the foremost Englishmen who taught men to aspire to a higher social state by reconciling the interests of capital and labor. He spent his life and a large fortune in seeking to improve his fellow men by giving them education, self-reliance, and moral worth. His life was sanctified by human affection and lofty effort."—*Inscription on monument to Robert Owen in Kensal Green Cemetery.*

In the autumn of 1827 Robert Owen arrived again in England. Through negotiations with the minister from Mexico to the Court of St. James he projected a plan for communistic colonization in the provinces of Texas and Coahuila. Immense tracts of land in these provinces were to be set apart for Mr. Owen's use, though remaining under Mexican control, and here he was to be given an opportunity to establish a vast communistic commonwealth, colonized from all quarters of the globe. Mr. Owen went to Mexico in order to complete these plans, but the negotiations came to an end when he discovered that the degree of religious toleration he demanded would not be granted. In the spring of 1829 he was again at New Harmony, and in April of that year he met Alexander Campbell in a famous debate on religious questions. The discussion was held in Cincinnati, and lasted several days, before immense audiences. It was a veritable

307

battle between giants; for years the printed report of these debates was read and reread throughout the West.

From Cincinnati he journeyed to Washington, where he interested himself in bringing about a better feeling between the United States and Great Britain. As he became intimately associated with President Jackson and Secretary of State Van Buren, his labors were not without effect. The same year he returned to England and began the campaign in behalf of cooperation which he continued to the end of his life. His systems of "labor exchange" and "equitable commerce" attracted wide attention, and have developed into the great labor cooperative system of Great Britain.

Robert Owen frequently crossed the Atlantic to visit his sons and daughter in America, and to urge his plans on this side of the ocean. As late as 1844, while Fourierism was planting its phalansteres in America, he arrived in New York and published an address to the people of America, declaring that he had come "to effect in peace the greatest revolution ever yet made in human society." He called a world's convention to consider reform movements, in 1845, but this was a failure. Adin Ballou, as quoted by Noyes, said of him at this time:

"Robert Owen is a remarkable character. In years, nearly seventy-five; in knowledge and experience, superabundant; in benevolence of heart, transcendental; in honesty, without disguise; in philanthropy, unlimited; in religion, a skeptic; in theology, a Pantheist; in metaphysics, a necessarian circumstantialist; in morals, a universal executionist; in general conduct, a philosophic non-resistant; in socialism, a communist; in hope, a terrestrial elysianist; in practical business, a methodist; in deportment, an unequivocal gentleman. . . . Mr. Owen has vast schemes to develop, and vast hopes of speedy success in establishing a great model of the new social state, which will quite instantaneously, as he thinks,

308

bring the human race into a terrestrial paradise. He insists on obtaining a million of dollars to be expended in lands, buildings, machinery, conveniences, and beautifications for his model community. He flatters himself he shall be able, by some means, to induce capitalists, or perhaps Congress, to furnish the capital for this object. We were frankly obliged to shake an incredulous head and tell him how groundless, in our judgment, such splendid anticipations must prove. He took it in good part, and declared his confidence unshaken and his hopes undiscourageable by any man's unbelief."

Robert Owen spent the following winter in New Harmony. In June, 1846, he addressed the Constitutional Convention of the State of New York on Human Rights and Progress.

" Six times," says Noyes, " after he was fifty years old, and twice after he was seventy, he crossed the Atlantic and back in the service of communism. Let us not say that all this wonderful activity was useless. Let us not call this man a driveler and a monomaniac. Let us rather acknowledge that he was receiving and distributing an inspiration, unknown even to himself, that had a sure aim, and that it is at this moment conquering the world. His hallucination was not in his expectations, but in his ideas of time and methods."

Ralph Waldo Emerson makes some interesting allusions to Robert Owen as he appeared to him in 1845. " Robert Owen of New Lanark," he says, " came hither from England in 1845 to read lectures or hold conversations wherever he could find listeners—the most amiable, sanguine, and candid of men. He had not the least doubt that he had hit on the plan of right and perfect socialism, or that mankind would adopt it. He was then seventy years old, and being asked, ' Well, Mr. Owen, who is your disciple? how many men are there possessed of your views who will remain after you are gone to put them in practise?' replied, 'Not one.' Robert Owen knew Fourier in his old age. He said that Fourier learned of him all the truth that he had. The rest of his system was imagination and the imagination of a visionary. Owen made the best impression by his rare benevolence. His love of men made us forget his ' three errors.' His charitable construction of men and their actions was invariable. He was the better Christian in his controversies with Christians.

" And truly I honor the generous ideas of the socialists, the magnificence of their theories, and the enthusiasm with which they have been urged. They appeared inspired men of their time. Mr. Owen preached his doctrine of labor and reward with the fidelity and devotion of a saint in the slow ears of his generation.

" One feels that these philosophers have skipped no fact but one, namely, life. They treat man as a plastic thing, or something that may be put up or down, ripened or retarded, molded, polished, made into solid or fluid or gas at the will of the leader; or perhaps as a vegetable, from which, though now a very poor crab, a very good peach can by manure and exposure be in time produced—and skip the faculty of life which spawns and spurns systems and system makers; which eludes all conditions; which makes or supplants a thousand Phalanxes and New Harmonies with each pulsation.

" It would be better to say, let us be lovers and servants of that which is just, and straightway every man becomes the center of a holy and beneficent republic which he sees to include all men in its laws, like that of Plato and of Christ.

" Yet, in a day of small, sour, and fierce schemes, one is admonished and cheered by a project of such friendly aims and of such bold and generous proportions; there is an intellectual courage and strength in it which is superior and commanding; it certifies the presence of so much truth in the theory, and in so far is destined to be fact.

" I regard these philanthropists as themselves the effects of the age in which they live, in common with so many other good facts the efflorescence of the period and predicting the good fruit that ripens. They were not the creators that they believed themselves to be; but they were unconscious prophets of the true state of society, one which the tendencies of nature lead unto, one which always establishes itself for the sane soul, though not in that manner in which they paint it."

In his later years Mr. Owen came to recognize a truth which he had overlooked in all his schemes for social regeneration—the controlling influence of the spiritual nature. As he himself confessed, while he had provided for the physical, the intellectual, and the moral needs of man, he had overlooked the spiritual. " Yet, this, as he now saw," says Sargent, " was the most important of all in the future development of mankind. . . . Owen says that in looking back over his past life he can trace the finger of God directing his steps, preserving his life under imminent dangers, and impelling him onward on many occasions."

" For the last ten years of his life," says Lloyd Jones, " the proceedings of Robert Owen had ceased to be discussed in the newspapers and on the platform. It need not be concluded from this, however, that he was entirely inactive. He republished a considerable portion of his earlier writings, among other things his plan for dealing with the wretched condition of Ireland. He restated his views on national education, maintaining that ' the great want of the world was a good training from birth, and a sound, practical education for all, based on true principles.' He drew up proposals for a treaty of federation between Great Britain and the United States of North America—the gist of which is that Great Britain and

America should declare their interests to be the same; should agree to a federative union to which all other nations should be admitted, and recognize it as a duty to terminate war and live in the abundance of a peaceful industry and friendly exchange." Thus Robert Owen anticipated by fifty years propositions which have in recent years been made for a permanent treaty of arbitration between the United States and Great Britain.

As late as 1857, while in his eighty-sixth year, Mr. Owen attended a meeting of the Social Science Association at Birmingham, and read a paper on The Human Race Governed without Punishment. Attempting to read a paper at the meeting of the association at Liverpool the following year, he broke down and was carried from the platform. He was taken to his native town of Newton, where he secured accommodations in the house next to the place where he was born. Robert Dale Owen was summoned from Naples, where he was *charge d'affaires* for the United States, and, holding the hand of his distinguished son, the great philanthropist breathed his last. His last words were, " Relief has come."

" The agitation of Owen," writes his friend and follower, Lloyd Jones, " was unsuccessful in its immediate results, but though the immediate consummation of our hopes be denied, it is for us to work on as wisely and as faithfully as we can, trusting the fulfilment will come, perhaps in a better way and at a time more suitable than he could appoint. For everything done by Robert Owen and his friends in founding cooperative villages and workshops, there is ample recompense in the present success of the cooperative idea. I think it constitutes an especial claim on our gratitude that Owen brought into practical activity for the public good the energies of the humblest and the poorest, to augment the vast popular power by which the present cooperative movement is maintained. It is only since Owen's influence has been felt that it can truly be said the masses of the people have been brought collectively into action for the promotion of objects which have been attended by results that are likely to be permanent; because, while they secure general advantages, they confer a general discipline and strength. The cooperative movement is rapidly becoming a national movement, sustained by the development and activity of an ever-increasing popular knowledge. . . . In every effort he made for the benefit of society his aims were honest, his industry unimpeachable, his generosity unbounded, his sacrifices great and unhesitatingly incurred. He labored for the people; he died working for them, and his last thought was for their welfare."

CHAPTER XXIII

NEW HARMONY'S LATER HISTORY

WHEN Robert Owen's splendid social bark went to wreck upon the rocks and shoals of human nature at New Harmony, the company of genius which in part composed its crew was left stranded on what then seemed a desert island in the illimitable wilderness. But that little center of progressive thought and philanthropic spirit became a lighthouse destined to diffuse its guiding rays far beyond the limits of the frontier State of which it was a part. Through William Maclure New Harmony was to give a vast impetus to popular education, particularly throughout the West; through David Dale Owen and his coadjutors it was to accelerate the development of American science; through Frances Wright it was to fix its indelible impress upon American popular sentiment; through Robert Dale Owen it was to become a potent factor in American institutional development; through Josiah Warren it was to affect the trend of economic thought, and through Robert Owen, his views modified in the great school of experience he had set up at New Harmony, it was to exert an influence in fixing the tendencies of the cooperative movement in England and the United States.

The residence in New Harmony of William Maclure, Gerard Troost, Thomas Say, Charles A. Lesueur, and the younger Owens, made it the rendezvous of scientists for many years. Prince Maximilian von Neuweid, with his corps of scientific explorers, spent the winter of 1832 at

314

New Harmony, making a careful study of local natural history in company with Say and Lesueur. Prince Maximilian was one of the most indefatigable scientific explorers of the first half of this century. He left the Prussian Army after attaining the rank of general and set out on an expedition through the interior of Brazil, studying especially the natural history, geology, and ethnology of that region. He published the results of this expedition in several volumes. In 1832–'34 he traveled in the United States " under the title of Baron Braunberg, accompanied by his artist Bodmer and his taxidermist Dreidoppel." After visiting the larger Eastern cities, he embarked from Pittsburg for New Harmony on October 9, 1832. He arrived at New Harmony on October 19th. In the following spring he descended the Wabash and Ohio rivers to Cairo by steamboat, thence ascending the Mississippi to the mouth of the Missouri and the Missouri to the Rocky Mountain region. In May and June, 1833, he was again at New Harmony. Early in June, 1834, accompanied by C. A. Lesueur, he went by wagon from New Harmony through Owensville, Princeton, Vincennes, " thence eastward very near the route now followed by the B. and O. S. W. Ry. across Indiana; thence northward to Lake Erie; thence eastward via Niagara Falls to Boston." His observations during his American journeys were embodied in two large volumes, entitled Reise Durch Nord Amerika, published at Coblentz, 1838–'43 —" one quarto volume of texts and illustrations and another folio volume of maps and texts." " An English version of this text was published in 1843," says Dr. Schnack, " but the translation is a very free one, and therefore not accurate or available for scientific purposes. His journal contains many valuable observations in almost all departments of physical and natural science, being especially interesting on birds, reptiles, and flowers, not omitting geology, and the habits and manners of the natives. The Maximilian Collection of Birds is in the possession of the American Museum of Natural History, in New York City, and is regarded as a valuable collection. In his journal he gives a list of fifty-eight trees and mentions a large number of shrubs he had observed in the vicinity of New Harmony."

In June, 1839, Dr. David Dale Owen, who, since the close of the community experiments, had returned to Europe in order to pursue his studies in geology, in 1835 had taken a medical degree from the Ohio Medical College, and in 1837 had been commissioned to make a preliminary geological survey of Indiana, was appointed United States geologist. His headquarters were established at New Harmony, and he was given instructions to make a survey of the Northwest, including what is now Minnesota, Wisconsin, Iowa, and the northern part of Illinois, with a view to locating mineral lands preliminary to the sale of the public domain. This great work was completed in two months. Dr. Schnack thus describes Dr. Owen's interesting method of work: " A large number of men, many of them eminent scientists, were employed. The entire corps was divided into two companies, each having an intelligent head to look after the work; and to each company was allotted a district, in which every section was to be visited and samples of the rock, etc., collected.

" At stated points Dr. Owen would meet each camp and study the work accomplished. The country was almost without settlements, and each camp had to be supplied with hunters, whose duty it was to furnish game for subsistence. In looking over Dr. Owen's report one can not fail to appreciate the skill and fidelity with which this great geologist performed this extensive survey under immense difficulties and in such a short time. He carried with him, on the trip up the Mississippi River, supplies of the most important rocks, minerals, and reagents. These were exposed on a table in the cabin of the steamboat, and he would daily give his men instruction in geology and point out the characteristic rocks of the leading formations, and the minerals likely to be found in them."

In this way, by the time they reached the place to disembark they had been made acquainted with the first principles of geology. "In after years," continues Dr. Schnack, "this region was more systematically surveyed by Dr. Owen. The headquarters of the United States Geological Survey continued at New Harmony up to 1856, when, at the completion of the Smithsonian Institute building at Washington, they were conveyed to that building. A part of the immense collection was taken to Washington, another to the Indiana State University at Bloomington, and a third to the American Museum of Natural History in Central Park, New York. In passing through the first and last of these institutions, I have been surprised to find such a large proportion of the specimens in all departments labeled as coming from the New Harmony collection."

When New Harmony became the headquarters of the United States Geological Survey the old granary-fortress of the Harmonists, which had been equipped with gratings and loopholes by the Rappites for protection against marauders, was turned into a museum. In this were stored not only the specimens collected by surveying parties, but the collections made by Thomas Say in the surrounding States, and by William Maclure in Spain, Portugal, Italy, France, Mexico, and the West Indies. Over the old desk at New Harmony Hall lectures on chemistry, geology, and biology were delivered by the leading scientists of the country and the foreign travelers attracted to New Harmony by its international reputation as a scientific center.

One of Dr. Owen's most valuable assistants in the

prosecution of the geological surveys undertaken from New Harmony was Richard Owen, who was a young man of eighteen, "fresh from the schools of Europe," at the conclusion of the community period. Another was the coworker of Thomas Say, Charles A. Lesueur, who lived in New Harmony many years, exploring the mounds of southern Indiana, writing voluminously on the fishes and mollusks of the West, and "making his living largely with his pencil in painting and making sketches." Lesueur finally returned to France and spent the last years of his life as curator of the museum at Havre. John Chappelsmith, "a wealthy Englishman, an artist and engraver," drew many of the cuts of fossils for the geological reports, and made meteorological observations for a number of years. Mrs. Chappelsmith was an enthusiastic student of entomology, and had some reputation as a lecturer.

James Sampson, who came to New Harmony in 1828, was another scientific student of the David Owen *régime*. " After making in the dry-goods business a sufficient income," wrote Colonel Richard Owen, " he devoted himself to collecting objects of natural history, by hunting and fishing as well as by exchange, until he had accumulated quite an extensive collection, more especially of land and fresh-water shells and archeological specimens, his whole residence being virtually a museum."

Alexander Maclure, brother of William Maclure, lived in New Harmony many years, engaged in study and the administration of his brother's affairs. He was especially interested in social science.

Connected with the geological survey, to again quote Dr. Schnack, were "Colonel Charles Whittlesy, the veteran geologist; F. B. Meek, the eminent paleontologist, who determined and sketched most of the fossil animals for the reports of the Illinois geological survey; Leo Lesquereux, the noted fossil botanist, who has described and sketched more fossil plants of North America than all the rest of the authors combined; . . . Dr. Elderhorst, author of a standard work on the Blowpipe, and Dr. C. C. Parry, who served on Dr. Owen's geological survey of the Northwest in 1848, and whose knowledge of the Western flora was probably exceeded by none." Robert Henry Fauntleroy, of the United States Coast Survey, spent several years at New Harmony, where he made some interesting experiments in magnetic declination and intensity. He married, in 1835, Miss Jane Dale Owen, Robert Owen's daughter. Samuel Bolton, an English chemist, lectured frequently on his specialty in New Harmony, beginning as early as 1828. Evidence of the importance of New Harmony as a scientific center is found in the number of State geologists appointed from that place. David Dale Owen occupied this position in Kentucky from 1854 to 1857, in Arkansas from 1857 to 1859, and in 1859 and 1860 was State geologist of Indiana, his service being terminated by his death. He was succeeded in Indiana by Richard Owen, who later became colonel of an Indiana infantry regiment during the civil war, and for fifteen years, beginning in 1864, was professor of natural science in the Indiana State University, —the first of a series of great students and teachers who have given this institution wide repute as a center of instruction and research in natural science. Richard Owen survived all other members of the famous Owen second generation, dying in his eighty-first year at New Harmony on March 24, 1890. Dr. Gerard Troost became a professor of chemistry and mineralogy in the Nashville University, and was later State geologist of Tennessee. Major Sidney Lyon superintended the geodetic and topographical survey of Kentucky. Professor A. H. Worthen served as state geologist of Illinois from 1858 until his death nearly thirty years later, during which time he published seven volumes of reports, " constituting probably the most complete geological survey that has been made of any Western State." Prof. E. T. Cox, son of one of the Owenite communists, was State geologist of Indiana from 1868 to 1880. Dr. J. C. Norwood conducted an early State geological survey of Illinois.

Among the visitors to New Harmony while it was a scientific Mecca were Audubon, the ornithologist, then a storekeeper at Henderson, Kentucky, forty miles distant, and Dr. George Engelman, who rode to the place on horseback from St. Louis in February, 1840, only to miss seeing the coterie of scientists he had expected to meet there. He chronicles as the result of his trip the sight of a " broad-fruited maple in bloom."

Sir Charles Lyell, the eminent Scottish geologist, was one of the last of the many European scientific explorers who visited New Harmony during its scientific golden age. On his second tour of the United States in 1845–'46, he came by boat from New Orleans up the Mississippi and Ohio to Mount Vernon, thence by stage to New Harmony. In his notes he says: " We spent several days very agreeably at New Harmony, where we were most hospitably entertained by Dr. and Mrs. David Dale Owen. . . . Some large buildings, in the German style of architecture, stand conspicuous, . . . the principal edifice being now appropriated as a public museum, in which I found a good geological collection, both fossils and minerals, made during the State survey, and I was glad to learn that by an act of the Indiana Legislature, with a view of encouraging science, this building is exempt from taxation. Lectures on chemistry and geology are given here in the winter. Many families of superior intelligence, English, Swiss, and German, have settled in the place, and there is a marked simplicity in their manner of living which reminded us of Germany. They are very sociable, and there were many private parties, where

NEW HARMONY AS IT NOW APPEARS FROM INDIAN MOUND.

there was music and dancing, and a public assembly once a week, to one of which we went, where quadrilles and waltzes were danced, the band consisting of amateur musicians. . . .

" We found also, among the residents, a brother of William Maclure, the geologist, who placed his excellent library and carriage at our disposal. He lends his books freely among the citizens, and they are much read. We were glad to hear many recent publications, some of the most expensively illustrated works, discussed and criticized in society here. We were also charmed to meet with many children, happy and merry, yet perfectly obedient; and once more to see what, after the experience of the last two or three months, struck us as a singular phenomenon in the New World, a shy child. There is no church or place of public worship in New Harmony, a peculiarity which we never remarked in any town of half the size in the course of our tour of the United States. Being here on week-days, only, I had no opportunity of observing whether on Sunday there were any meetings for social worship. I heard that when the people of Evansville once reproached the citizens of this place for having no churches, they observed that they also had no shops for the sale of spirituous liquors, which is still a characteristic of New Harmony."

CHAPTER XXIV

THE MACLURE LIBRARY MOVEMENT

IN the person of William Maclure, New Harmony gave to the United States its first great founder of libraries. Though the earlier gifts to public libraries from the "Father of American Geology" lacked the munificence of those by which the Master of Skibo Castle has startled the world, yet they were equally as generous and even more timely, for they were given in pioneer days, when standards of culture were being established, when frontier manhood and womanhood were being formed, when the foundations for the public-library systems of to-day were being laid.

Though the utter collapse of his educational experiments at New Harmony during and after the Owen *régime* discouraged Maclure from any further attempts to establish self-supporting schools for children, not even old age and failing health abated his interest in the productive classes nor his conviction that education was the only means by which those classes could be rescued from the oppression under which he believed them to be suffering. Feeling the rapid approach of death, Maclure determined to attempt one more venture for the education of those who "earn their living in the sweat of their brows."

Nine years after his departure from New Harmony to Mexico, Maclure, a stranger in a strange land, sick unto death, focused a renewed benevolence upon the little town that had been the scene of bitter defeat to

322

WILLIAM MACLURE.

his former educational experiment; and upon his native land, whose social and industrial system he had so often and so bitterly denounced.

The Working Men's Institute was the only one of Maclure's pathetic educational efforts at New Harmony which weathered the collapse of The New Moral World successfully. This institute, modeled after the noted Mechanics' Institutes then so much in vogue in the British Isles, was a club of laboring men holding stated meetings from house to house for the discussion of social, political, and religious questions and for mutual instruction. A few years after Maclure's departure the institute "went to sleep." He determined to resurrect the organization, give it a permanent home, add a library to it, and make it a model for other and similar institutions to be established by him in other parts of the country.

As a result of a vigorous correspondence between Maclure and the citizens of New Harmony "who labor with their hands," the Working Men's Institute was rejuvenated and incorporated under the laws of the State. He immediately gave the organization an order upon a London bookseller for books to the value of one thousand dollars, and conveyed to it as a permanent home a wing of the old Rappite church.

Death cut short his further plans. While returning to the Wabash country for the purpose of executing a trust providing generously for this, his anticipated "model library and institute," he expired near the little village of San Angel, Mexico, after a short illness, on the 27th of March, 1840.

In his last will and testament, drawn and signed before the United States Consul in the City of Mexico, Maclure provided for the inauguration of a system of libraries. Though his estate was but a pittance as compared with the holdings of Mr. Carnegie, yet it was both formidable and peculiar for the age in which it was accumulated. "It seems strange to read in the will of an Indianian (for such we must hold Maclure to be)," writes Jacob P. Dunn, in an interesting monograph on the history of the Indiana library system, "the disposition not only of some thirty buildings at New Harmony and about ten thousand acres of land in that vicinity, but also over a million reals in Spanish securities, his house No. 7 Calle del Lobo, in Alicante; his Convent of St. Gines and accompanying estate of ten thousand acres in Valencia; his convent and estate of Grosmano, near Alicante; his estate of Carman de Croix; the Valley of Murada; forty-one thousand francs in French securities; notes and mortgages on properties scattered from Big Lick plantation in Virginia to various parts of England, France, and Spain; the total remaining editions of Michaux's Sylvia, Condillac's Logic, and Garner's Dictionary; more than one hundred boxes of minerals, prints, etc., and near two thousand copper plates of engravings and illustrations of various kinds."

The will by which Maclure hoped to create permanent libraries for the working people of his native country sets forth, with its maker's characteristic vehemence, hatred for the non-productive classes, respect for labor, confidence in the worthiness of the common people, and an abiding faith in the regenerating virtue of education. "The power and influence of the classes who live by the ignorance of the millions has prevented the spread of knowledge." "Industry and persevering manual labor puts the last finish to every species of property before it can enter into the value of either individual or national wealth." "In all the countries I have had access to I have found the laborers the most honest, upright, and useful classes, and the only class that can make a good use of knowledge to diminish the immorality, vice, and crime producing poverty, ignorance, misery, and wretchedness."

The will made the testator's brother, Alexander Maclure, and his sister, Anna Maclure, his executors, and directed among other things that they should donate " the sum of five hundred dollars to any club or society of laborers who may establish in any part of the United States a reading- and lecture-room with a library of at least one hundred volumes." The instrument proceeds to define " laborers " as " the working classes who labor with their hands and earn their living in the sweat of their brows."

Being advised that the trust in favor of these libraries was void because created for the benefit of bodies not in existence, Maclure's brother and sister, though generously remembered in the will, proceeded to consume the entire estate, of which, in the failure of the provisions respecting libraries, they were the sole heirs.

But a young attorney of Posey County, A. P. Hovey, afterward governor of Indiana, believing the trust to be good in law, fought the cause of the libraries through the Supreme Court of the State, which established the trust and made Hovey its administrator. In 1855 the estate was finally converted into funds and the distribution began. Organizations styling themselves " Working Men's Institutes," " Mechanics' Associations," and " Literary Societies " pretended at least to comply with the provisions of th› will respecting both the personnel of their membership and the collection of books. To these donations of five hundred dollars each were made. The following table gives in order the Maclure libraries thus established in Indiana, the location being given by county, with the name of the town following in parenthesis when shown by the records:

Posey Co. (Mt. Vernon); Floyd (New Albany); Owen (Gosport); Parke (Annapolis); Posey (Poseyville); Huntington (Huntington); Spencer (Liberty); Grant (Marion) ; Posey (Farmersville) ; DeKalb (Vienna) ; Switzer-

land (Vevay); Owen (Spencer); Ohio (———); Henry
(Knightstown); Hancock (Greenfield); Wayne (Center-
ville); Bartholomew (Columbus); Decatur (Greens-
burg); Lawrence (Bedford); Fayette (Connersville);
Posey (Stewardsville); Dearborn (Aurora); Gibson (Barren); Martin (Mt. Pleasant); Adams (Decatur); St. Joseph (South Bend); Fulton (Rochester); Knox (Vincennes); Boone (Thorntown); Elkhart (Goshen); White
(Monticello); Clay (Brazil); Miami (Peru); Greene (Linton); Gibson (Princeton); Hamilton (Westfield); Hen-
dricks (Danville); Crawford (Leavenworth); Fountain
(Covington); Tippecanoe (Lafayette); DeKalb (Au-
burn); Clinton (Frankfort); Blackford (Hartford City);
Lagrange (Lima); Parke (Rockville); Whitley (Columbia
City); Starke (Knox); Noble (Albion); Putnam (Green-
castle); Kosciusko (Warsaw); Greene (Bloomfield); Jackson (———); Porter (Valparaiso); Warrick (Boonville);
Lagrange (Lagrange); Jay (Portland); Martin (Dover
Hill); Fountain (Attica); Pike (Petersburg); Benton
(Oxford); Posey (Wadesville); Jefferson (South Han-
over); Sullivan (Sullivan); Gibson (Snake Run); Hamil-
ton (Noblesville); Wabash (Wabash); St. Joseph (Misha-
waka); Monroe (Bloomington); Tippecanoe (Farmers);
Shelby (Shelbyville); Perry (Cannelton); Rush (Rush-
ville); Madison (Anderson); Dearborn (Lawrenceburg);
Union (Liberty); Howard (Kokomo); Floyd (New Al-
bany); Orange (Paoli); Orange (Lost River); Washington
(Salem); Jennings (Vernon); Johnson (Franklin); Delaware (Muncie); Wayne (Richmond); Posey (Cynthiana);
Floyd (New Albany); Union (Cottage Grove); Morgan
(Mooresville); Harrison (Corydon); Clark (Jefferson-
ville); Tipton (Tipton); Spencer (Rockport); Ripley
(Versailles); Scott (Lexington); Sullivan (New Lebanon); Randolph (Winchester); Allen (Fort Wayne);
Franklin (Springfield); Posey (New Harmony); Vander-
burg (Evansville); Clark (Charlestown); Morgan (Mar-

tinsville); Henry (Newcastle); Wayne (Cambridge City); Vermillion (Eugene); Jackson (Seymour); Putnam (Bainbridge); Jefferson (North Madison); Greene (Worthington); Vigo (Terre Haute); Sullivan (Carlisle); Crawford (Alton); Pulaski (Winamac); Carroll (Delphi); Steuben (Angola); Montgomery (Crawfordsville); Clay (Bowling Green); Gibson (Patoka); Montgomery (———); Gibson (Marsh Creek); Franklin (Brookville); Cass (Logansport); Boone (Lebanon); Lake (Crown Point); Warren (Williamsport); Vermillion (Newport); Wells (Bluffton); Putnam (Portland Mills); Elkhart (Elkhart); Parke (Bloomingdale); Posey (Smith Township); Gibson (Black River); Daviess (Washington); Brown (Nashville); Jasper (Rensselaer); Marshall (Plymouth); Howard (Poplar Grove); Johnson (Edinburg); Laporte (Michigan City); Jackson (Uniontown); Vermillion (Clinton); Johnson (Greenwood).

One hundred and forty-four of these libraries were inaugurated in Indiana through Maclure's benefactions. Eighty-nine out of ninety-two counties were the recipients of donations. Sixteen organizations in Illinois were aided, making in all one hundred and sixty libraries created by the distribution of eighty thousand dollars under the provisions of the will.

Though it suffered many vicissitudes, the New Harmony Working Men's Institute has been the only successful and permanent library established through the well-meant but misdirected benevolence of the first American geologist. The organization realized but little from the aid which Maclure had planned for it. Death prevented an endowment from his hands. The London bookseller against whom the order for books to the value of one thousand dollars was drawn became a bankrupt, and the order was only partially honored. The old German church, at best a crude library home, tumbled into ruins above the aspiring head of the " model library and

327

institute." Nor did the rejuvenated organization seek
to avail itself of the provisions of the will. But while
Maclure failed to render to his first and best beloved
library the aid which he had so fondly planned, yet he
did breathe into the dead institute the breath of life,
turn its activities into the direction of library work, and
set its feet in the paths of permanency. For from the
date of the Maclure grant the New Harmony Working
Men's Library has maintained a continuous existence.
To quote the words of Mr. Dransfield, the present librarian, it "has grown slowly but surely."

Permanent itself, the Working Men's Library, on the
site of so much that had proved visionary and futile,
profited by the demise of neighboring organizations. A
Maclurean Institute, organized under the provisions of
the will which Hovey had so faithfully labored to establish, after a two-years' struggle gave up the ghost and
turned its books, some three hundred volumes, over to
the older society. At the close of the war, an old township school library of six hundred volumes was absorbed.

Others emulated the earlier generosity of Maclure.
In the year 1854 a member of the corporation, limited
by the terms of its charter to twenty-six members, died
leaving one thousand dollars for the purchase of books
"treating of science and fact." Twenty years later, out
of an abundant prosperity and in grateful remembrance
of the early struggles of their society, the later followers
of George Rapp, then known as the Economy Society, purchased the dilapidated old church, tore it down, converted
it into a school building, which they presented to the town
of New Harmony, and at an expense of two thousand
dollars repaired the wing owned and occupied by the Working Men's Institute and Library.

By far the most substantial aid received by this
library, however, came through the repeated generosity
of Dr. Murphy, a citizen of New Harmony, and one

of the twenty-six members composing the library corporation. Dr. Murphy was a waif, born in the city of Cork, Ireland, in December, 1813. At a tender age he was brought to Louisville, Kentucky, by a brutal man who claimed to be his uncle. Mistreatment forced him to run away. His wanderings brought him barefooted and starving to New Harmony shortly after the inauguration of Owen's new social order. The people of the Commune received him with open arms, supported him, and educated him in the model schools with which Maclure hoped to revolutionize the educational systems of a continent, and in which Murphy was taught the trade of a tailor.

After the collapse of Owen's scheme Murphy plied his trade in the little town that had proved a haven of refuge to him. Unsuccessful in this vocation he attempted farming, in which he likewise failed. Returning to New Harmony he engaged in the general clothing business, in which his financial failure was complete. Leaving New Harmony he attended a medical school in Louisville, graduating with distinction. Returning to the scene of his former misfortunes Murphy entered upon a successful career as a general practitioner. Fortunate investments added to the lucrative income which he received from his professional work, until he and his wife, a childless couple, had amassed a considerable fortune.

With the characteristic loyalty and gratitude of his race Murphy sought some method of discharging his debt to the community to which he owed so much. From its earliest revival he had been deeply interested in the affairs of the Working Men's Library, and it became the object of his generosity.

In 1893 he induced the Library Society to sell its old quarters and assisted it to erect the building now occupied. This is a handsome brick structure containing in addition to its excellent library quarters a large auditorium, a museum, and a very creditable art gallery. Dr. Murphy made contributions of books and specimens for the museum and filled the art gallery with costly paintings purchased in Italy. In 1899 he made a further donation of forty-five thousand dollars. In 1900 the gift was increased to seventy-six thousand dollars. At his death, in December, 1900, the sum total was increased to one hundred and fifty-five thousand dollars.

The present estimated wealth of the society is two hundred thousand dollars, from which is derived an annual income of six thousand dollars. Two thousand dollars per year is spent for books and periodicals, and a lecture course costing twelve hundred dollars is offered each winter. From four hundred and twenty-five volumes in 1847, the number upon the open shelves of the library has grown to more than seventeen thousand, to which the yearly additions are in excess of twelve hundred books. No other town of even double the same population can boast such library facilities as can the site where the stolid Rappites toiled and dozed away their narrow lives in ignorant contentment. The number of books per capita in the New Harmony library is probably greater than that of any other public library. Better still, the circulation per capita exceeds that of all competitors. Best of all, it is claimed that the per cent of illiteracy on the site of the first great Pestalozzian school is less than at any other point in the United States.

Two features of the New Harmony library merit special commendation. One is the rare good judgment constantly displayed in the purchase of new books. Mr. Carnegie advises that the novel of the hour be subjected to a three-years' test at the hands of the reading public before it is given recognition by a free library. The book committee of the sole surviving institution founded by the earlier Carnegie has obeyed this injunction almost to the very letter. The shelves of no public library are freer from the worthless fiction by which, in an effort to pander to the popular clamor, the intellectual standard of too many communities has been lowered and the literary tastes of too many readers perverted.

The other commendable feature of the Working Men's Institute is the extraordinary care and diligence which, for many years, has been exercised in the collection and preservation of local history material. The New Moral World was not only the most ambitious communistic experiment which the world has yet witnessed, but it was also the effort to found an ideal social order which has bequeathed to posterity the most complete record of its own proceedings. The older Owen and his followers believed that the experiments which they were conducting on the Wabash would be imitated by other community groups, and ultimately lead to the peaceful revolution of society. Hence a faithful account of the proceedings of the parent community must be kept, both because of the success and fame that was destined to attend its philanthropic efforts, and because it was to serve as a prototype and guide for other communities certain to follow in its wake. The records of no municipality of these latter days surpass in fulness and accuracy those which the semivisionary, semipractical citizens of The New Moral World made for their Utopia.

These records ultimately became the property of the Working Men's Institute. From the day on which Maclure breathed into the defunct organization a new spark of life, its chief pleasure and pride has been to preserve and to augment them. Every publication, every newspaper, every scrap of material treating of any phase of the problems which The New Moral World sought to solve, or throwing additional light upon any phase of the Rapp and Owen *régimes,* have been carefully culled and filed. The very ends of the earth have been searched for additional facts concerning the unfortunate social ventures of which the New Harmony library has constituted itself the historian. This labor of love has widened until it has included within its scope the traditions and early struggles of the county of which the site of the labors of the Rappites and Owenites was formerly the county seat. To-day the library is a repository of valuable sociological and historical material, much of which can not be duplicated elsewhere. No other known library approaches it in the completeness of its local history collection. Valuable both in quantity and quality as are the general publications upon its shelves, by far the most precious asset, measured from any standpoint which this library possesses, is the record of memorable early days in the Pocket, which have been so faithfully and intelligently compiled, especially during the *régime* of the present secretary of the Working Men's Institute, Mr. Arthur Dransfield.

This is a feature of library work which every similar institution would do well to emulate. Reminiscences of the rapidly disappearing pioneer, records yellow with age, old and current newspaper files, publications and contributions of every type reciting any fact or achievement of the community or its citizenship—all these should be gathered and preserved in some archive. If need be, money should be appropriated out of the common treasury of the library to further this worthy duty. No similar amount spent for any other given feature of the work will confer as much ultimate value and benefit upon the institution and its patrons. Where the vicinity is not blessed with a public library, or, though so blessed, the library fails to rise to the mark of its high calling as local historian, then some other local group or organization should undertake the task. And who so competent to discharge this necessary labor of love as the teachers, through their township and county organizations?

How different the fate of the Maclurean libraries

332

created by the will! " There was nothing in their formation to insure and but little to encourage perpetuity."
The preliminary library of one hundred books collected
as a condition precedent to the bestowal of the testator's
bounty usually consisted of old books of all sorts, hastily
gathered together and possessing neither value nor durability. The books purchased through Maclure's generosity were almost exclusively standard works of a scientific and technical character, designed for a limited
coterie of readers, and possessing little or no interest for
the majority of the very class which their donor sought
to reach. For this strange collection of books there was
neither a competent custodian nor suitable quarters. What
with lack of supervision and rough usage, they melted
away. And there was neither taxation nor endowment,
a testator nor a " good angel " in the flesh to replace them!
What books survived the perilous ordeal of a brief circulation were in many instances divided among the remaining members and became their individual property.

In 1854, under the provisions of a law for which
Robert Dale Owen stood sponsor, township libraries were
organized by the State of Indiana. These, separate and
independent from the Maclure libraries, gradually absorbed such of the latter as had remained intact. Here
the earlier Carnegie planned better than he knew; for
the books by which his will so pathetically sought to
found libraries for the benefit of a distinct class in
society, became the nucleus of many of the free public
libraries of township and city which, with their doors
wide flung to rich and poor, constitute such a proud
feature of American life to-day.

So rapidly, however, did the Maclure books disappear
that, as early as 1890, the special reports made by the
county superintendents of schools on the various libraries
of the several counties of the commonwealth mention
but two Maclure libraries in addition to the formidable

one which the citizens of New Harmony have maintained so creditably. These are located at Williamsport,
Warren County, and Princeton, Gibson County. "At
Williamsport one hundred and forty-five volumes of a
Maclure library are deposited in the high-school building, and the public is privileged to use them." At
Princeton an old collection of books purchased by a gift
which Hovey made possible, initiated the present town
library of three thousand six hundred and seventy-three
volumes.

It is possible that a thorough search would reveal
the presence of a few Maclure books in other libraries.
The remainder of the one hundred and sixty collections
have become less than a tradition. Outside of the town
and county in which he exercised his greatest philanthropy the name of Maclure is known to but few of the
most intelligent citizens of his adopted State. "Where
known, it is usually connected with a vague recollection
of some sort of library of which very little knowledge
is had."

The New Harmony library is a monument of which
the great Scotch ironmaster, were he the founder, might
well be proud. If the life of the earlier Carnegie has
accomplished no other good he has not lived in vain, for
in the Working Men's Institute his philanthropic efforts
have reaped a posthumous success granted to the labors of
but few men. It is difficult to assign to Maclure's other
benevolent experiments their true place and worth.
Measured by their permanency, failure must be writ in
large letters across the face of all of them, from the Pestalozzian School to the remotest Maclurean institute. Measured by their influence upon men and institutions, success
must be written across the face of his benevolence; for the
far-reaching results radiating in every direction from
them, furthered better than he had hoped, and in ways
which he had not anticipated, the uplift of humanity.

Measured by the spirit which prompted them, their unselfishness entitles the " Father of American Geology " to an honored place in the long list of benefactors who have dedicated their time and their substance to the betterment of men.

CHAPTER XXV

ROBERT DALE OWEN

" Although Owen failed to make his community successful, his opinions spread far and wide. The courts of law, the halls of legislation, and the family government have been modified and influenced by the opinions taught by Mr. Owen in the early days of New Harmony, and afterward promulgated by his son, Robert Dale Owen."

—GEORGE FLOWER.

ROBERT DALE OWEN, the most distinguished of the four talented sons of Robert Owen, first saw the light of day in Glasgow, Scotland, November 7, 1801. Born to wealth, every possible educational advantage was thrust upon him by his father. At the age of sixteen he was sent to Fellenberg's School at Hofwyl, where, like William Maclure, he became an enthusiastic believer in the Pestalozzian creed. When he returned to Scotland Robert Dale entered with hearty and intelligent sympathy into his father's social and educational experiment at New Lanark. His influence cast into the scale determined the purchase of Harmonie from the Rappites. In that golden age on the Wabash, as editor, teacher, or assistant to his illustrious father in the management of the affairs of the Commune, he played a conspicuous and creditable part.

Early in life Robert Dale Owen began the literary labors that won for him fame little less than that achieved as a statesman. His first production was a play called Pocahontas, which was performed at New Harmony by the Thespian Society. This society was formed in 1828, and continued as an organization for nearly fifty years,

336

ROBERT DALE OWEN.
September, 1875.

in that time graduating a large number of young people to the professional stage. The scenery for the plays produced by this society was for many years painted by Charles A. Lesueur.

Following Frances Wright's lecturing tour in 1828, Robert Dale Owen became associated with her in the publication of the Free Enquirer, which was removed to New York City. In this journal these two brilliant editorial writers advocated many of the social and educational reforms which had been exploited at New Harmony. One outcome of their agitation was a political movement in the State of New York, organized by George H. and Frederick W. Evans, two of their converts. As the result of the efforts of the Evans brothers a working men's party was formed, demanding, among other things, "the abolition of chattel slavery and wage slavery." In 1830 a convention was held in Syracuse and Ezekiel Williams was nominated for governor. He received nearly three thousand votes, and by a fusion the party elected one member of the legislature. It was called the "Fanny Wright party" by its opponents.

The agitation extended to Massachusetts, and numbered Edward Everett among its supporters. The organization was finally merged into the "Locofoco" party, and had no small influence in developing the antislavery movement. All over the country organizations, composed largely of working men advocating the principles promulgated by the Free Enquirers, were formed, marking the first organized participation of working men in American politics. The movement was, however, soon overshadowed by the great issues which divided the country into two hostile camps, and ultimately were settled by the arbitrament of war.

In 1836 Robert Dale Owen entered Indiana politics as a member of the State legislature. In the same year he was nominated as a Van Buren elector and went upon the stump in Indiana to become a political orator of wide renown. His speeches were models of logic and free from the taint of personal abuse.

In 1842 he was elected to Congress, and was returned in 1844, but in 1846 was defeated. He impressed himself upon the leaders of his party in Congress as a man of unusual ability, and his advanced views exercised a marked influence in determining the trend of Democratic thought on public questions. While in Congress he originated and introduced the bill providing for the application of the neglected Smithson bequest to the founding of the Smithsonian Institution. This bill was introduced by Mr. Owen on December 14, 1845, and on the same day it was referred to a select committee of which the distinguished Indianian was a chairman. On February 28, 1846, the bill was reported to the House by him, and on April 22d it was taken up by the Committee of the Whole. During the same session it was passed by both the House and Senate.

In a speech of characteristic force Mr. Owen advocated the passage of the bill, outlining the nature of the work which it was intended this institution should undertake, and which it is still pursuing. At this time it had been ten years since the United States Government accepted the bequest of Smithson, and numerous suggestions as to the manner of its application had come to naught.

Mr. Owen referred to the various plans proposed by distinguished scholars upon whom the President had called for advice. Professor Wayland suggested the founding of a university exclusively for higher research—an institution something like that for which Mr. Carnegie has made provision at Washington by a gift of ten million dollars. A bill in line with this suggestion was introduced in the Senate, but was laid on the table. Dr. Cooper proposed an institution for original research in higher mathematics, chemistry, and agriculture. Richard Rush advocated the establishment of a college to undertake about the same work now being done by the department of agriculture, his plans including buildings and grounds of sufficient size to make possible the propagation of seeds for general distribution, and the delivery and publication of courses of lectures on scientific topics of popular interest. John Quincy Adams proposed a Government astronomical observatory—the Government now maintains one at Washington. Senator Choate, of Massachusetts, advocated the establishment of a library to rank with the largest institutions of similar character in the Old World—an idea which has in later years been developed in the Library of Congress. It is a rather remarkable fact, indeed, that every one of these suggestions has been carried out by the Government.

As an associate of Mr. Owen's on the select committee declared, the bill providing for the institution was " an anthology from all the plans submitted, though possessing valuable original features, the credit of which belongs to the chairman of the committee, Mr. Owen." Mr. Owen's idea was to make the institution of value not merely to a few scholars but to the whole people, developing fully Smithson's desire that it should be devoted to " the diffusion of learning."

In view of the lifetime of effort which Mr. Owen devoted to the advocacy of the common-school idea, it is not strange that one of his plans, which has never been developed, anticipated the establishment of a national normal school for the training of teachers for State normal schools, two of which had already been founded in the United States. " I hold it to be a democratic duty," he said, " to elevate to the utmost of our ability the character of our common-school education."

The Smithsonian building is said to represent peculiar ideas of architecture held by Robert Dale Owen and his brother, David Dale Owen, who was United States geologist when the structure was erected. Robert Dale Owen became a member of the first board of regents of the Smithsonian, and was influential in determining the nature of its future work, concerning which there was much discussion among American scientists of that period.

Creditable as was his all too brief congressional service, Mr. Owen's well-merited reputation for unselfish and far-seeing statesmanship must rest upon his action as a member of the lower house in the Indiana Legislature during the twenty-second and twenty-third assemblies; as a member of the Indiana Constitutional Convention of 1850, and as a member of the State legislature which met in the capital city of the Hoosier State close upon the heels of the newly adopted constitution.

Elected a member of the Indiana Constitutional Convention in 1850, he entered upon the period of his greatest usefulness, for at last there arrived the opportunity for writing into law some of the advanced doctrines for which his father stood, and which the younger Owen had been eloquently and forcibly advocating during all the years succeeding the collapse of the New Harmony communities. In that body, as Mr. John Holliday says, " He was beyond all comparison the most laborious, fertile, and efficient member. The law reforms and the provisions for woman's rights and free schools were especially his work, and leave upon our statute-books the ineffaceable marks of his father's inculcations, modified and strengthened by his own talent and observation."

Nor could Robert Dale Owen be other than a valiant fighter for free schools and be loyal to his father, to William Maclure, and The New Moral World. Sturdy as was his defense of the property and social rights which he believed ought to be enjoyed by the women of a nineteenth-century civilization, he was, if anything, more enthusiastic and certainly more successful in his efforts to consummate on Indiana and neighboring soil a public-school system that should afford to the children of all classes an education " without money and without price." His writings and public utterances are replete with brave and wise arguments favoring the establishment of schools " free and universal " " to the son of the poorest farmer as to the son of the chief mayor." It is difficult to cull from his declarations concerning the free public school those which all would agree upon as being the wisest—the most striking and prophetic.

When the New Harmony Gazette, rescued from the ruin of the " social system," became the Free Enquirer, Robert Dale Owen, as editor-in-chief of the rejuvenated publication, employed its columns as zealously in the cause of free schools as he did in the interest of the peculiar social and religious views with which he and Frances Wright astonished and angered the country.

Detecting in the educational legislation of the newly formed States of the Middle West a tendency to discriminate against the children of the ignorant and the vicious, Mr. Owen in the Free Enquirer, hastened to declare that " all poverty is not caused by misconduct. Many men are poor because they are more scrupulous than their neighbors; such poverty is honorable; and if the father's worth is to be the measure of the son's deserts, the child of such a poor man merits as good, nay, a much better education than the son of the fortunate speculator whose coffers groan under a half million. But we deny the position that because the parent is worthless the child ought to be neglected. The child of the greatest criminal in the Republic has as good a right to a rational education as that of the most disinterested patriot. Does a child make its parents or choose them? According to what principles of justice then can it be punished with ignorance for their crimes? "

Just before the Constitutional Convention Mr. Owen but voiced the feeling of the people of his adopted State when he declared its educational organization to be chaotic and its schools far behind other and younger Western States in efficiency. In urging the necessity of a constitutional provision under which the school system might be properly reorganized, he declared a truth which it has required twenty centuries to impress upon a small portion of the race:

" We hold that there is no object of greater magnitude within the whole range of legislation, no more imperative demand for public revenue than the establishment of competent schools. We hold that, in the nature of things, nothing can be better entitled to a share of the public revenue than that from which private and public wealth derive all their value and security. In short, our schools are the very foundation upon which rest the peace, good order, and prosperity of society."

Though it denied the efficiency, as an instrument of social regeneration, of the very religion to which his talented daughter declares that Mr. Owen turned in expectant faith in his failing years, the creed which he proclaimed in the lusty days of his young manhood was noteworthy, for it breathed in every line a stirring confidence in the efficiency, as an agent of social redemption, of a national system of education, which for over a quarter of a century through the editorial columns of the Free Enquirer he persistently urged upon the American people. That creed follows:

I believe in a National System of Equal, Republican, Protective, Practical Education, the sole regenerator of a profligate age and the only redeemer of our suffering country from the equal curses of chilling poverty and corrupting riches, of gnawing want and destroying debauchery, of blind ignorance and of unprincipled intrigue.

By this, my creed, I will live. By my consistency or inconsistency with this, my professed belief, I claim to be judged. By it, I will stand or fall.

ROBERT DALE OWEN.

During his first term as a member of the Indiana Legislature, on William Stillwell's farm, three miles east of New Harmony, he spoke from the bed of a rude farm wagon drawn within sight of the grounds upon which the farmers of the vicinity had at their own expense just completed the building of a small one-room school. Amid these picturesque surroundings Mr. Owen terminated his address with this eloquent tribute to the country schoolhouse:

"Do you ask me what manner of temple these Temples of Liberty may be? There, behind those trees, recently erected by the citizens of this very neighborhood and soon to be open and filled with those who when we are gone are to maintain or to forfeit the inheritance of their fathers—there is one of them. You will find no polished marble, no massive pillars curiously carved, none of the ornaments of architecture or luxuries of taste. That Temple of Freedom is but an humble schoolhouse. And a country schoolhouse, men will say, is but a small matter. Aye, so also is a cool drink from the spring but a small matter, yet it has saved human life ere now! And so is a summer shower a small matter, yet without it would our grain grow or our corn ripen? And what a draft of pure water is to the traveler dying of thirst, or a refreshing shower to the ground parched with drought, that is Education to Liberty.

"Yes, in such unpretending institutions as the country schoolhouse are the liberties of our great Republic preserved and protected. If not there, they can find protection nowhere. Just in proportion as such buildings abound among us and are managed by enlightened teachers and filled by willing scholars—just in proportion are our liberties secured and our independence established on a rock foundation. Any other foundation apart from the intelligence of the people is but of sand, and if thereupon the national edifice be founded the storms of party and the floods of misrule will beat upon that edifice and great will be the fall thereof. . . . If we neglect even so small a matter as common schools, let us not complain of

343

the unhappy consequences. We shall have brought them all upon ourselves.

" The mind of a child is like the rich land before us. Something that land must produce. Rank and luxurious growth must be of tangled weeds and bushes if it be neglected and thrown open, but of the best fruits of the earth if it be carefully fenced and diligently cultivated. *It* is not neglected. See, it has been carefully tilled. The promise of an abundant harvest is all over it. And shall those fields of far richer promise, of far more valuable harvest—the fields of intellect—shall they be left to run to waste, unprotected, uncultivated, forsaken?

" Every parent will answer, No. Let him do more than so answer. Let him act as well as resolve. If there be no school in his neighborhood, let him use his best exertions to establish one. If he succeed and procure a teacher, his labor will not be in vain. It will return to him a hundredfold."

In legislative hall and Constitutional Convention Robert Dale Owen's utterances and services in the cause of free schools were no less wise and brilliant.

Mr. Owen was a member of the lower house in the Indiana legislature, session of 1838, representing the county of Posey. One of the chief causes of contention during this session was the Surplus Revenue Fund of the common schools. In 1836 the National Treasury had a very large surplus. As there was no national debt to be discharged, Congress determined to distribute a large part of this surplus among the several States of the Union, according to the population of each. The share of Indiana amounted to $806,254. The legislature of 1837 set apart $573,502.96 of this sum for the use of the common schools and made it a part of the permanent fund under the title " Surplus Revenue Fund."

A formidable attempt was made during the legislative session of 1839 to divert this Surplus Revenue Fund from the Common School Fund in which the Acts of 1837 had placed it, and in which it would be used as an interest-bearing principal for the benefit of the schools of the State, into an Internal Improvement Fund, where it would be dissipated in the construction of canals and the deepening of rivers. Worthy and necessary as are internal improvements, the friends of the public schools regarded the proposition to divert any portion of the Common School Fund of the State to any purpose, however meritorious, as but the entering wedge in a series of assaults by which the fund which has made the Indiana educational system possible would be dissipated.

When the overzealous champions of the internal improvement program introduced a " Bill Transferring the First and Second Instalments of the Surplus Revenue from Common Schools to Internal Improvements," the partizans of the free public-school system of the State fought it with all the vigor and bitterness of which they were capable, both because it proposed to reduce the Common School Fund, which they regarded as the most precious asset possessed by the Commonwealth, and because it established a dangerous precedent for the future.

None fought this assault upon the resources of the common schools of his adopted State with such skill and earnestness as the representative from Posey. When it appeared that the assault would be successful, Owen, in what was practically his maiden effort as a legislator, made a speech which stemmed the tide, defeated the proposition to divert the Surplus Revenue, hurled confusion into the ranks of the enemies of free schools, and perpetuated the Common School Fund of Indiana. He said:

" The gentleman from Wayne says that if this bill were well explained and fully understood among the people it would be popular.

" Strange, most strange and baseless doctrine! If the people understood it! Ah, sir, if the people truly under-

345

stood it—if they knew and felt what their children gain when they receive a liberal education and what they lose when it is denied them—they would rise up, yes, in mass, against a law so unjust, so unrepublican, so subversive of knowledge and equality as this!

" Yes, sir, talk of democracy and equality! They are idle, powerless words without education to give them substance and spirit.

" In the mind is the true seat of inequality. If the mental resources of one man be abundant and of his neighbor be scanty, of small avail is it that their purses are of equal length. Mind commands and ever has commanded both wealth and power.

" If I believe, as I do believe, that I can procure for my children advantages beyond those that may fall to the lot of some others whose parents happen to be somewhat less favored by fortune than myself, it is not because I may chance to have a few extra dollars to leave them—for the advantage of wealth to young people just starting in the world is very problematical—but it is that I have the same means and the desire to give my children those advantages of education which no reverse of fortune can ever take from them; those advantages of education, which, let their purse be light or heavy, will insure to them, with moderate industry and prudence, consideration and a standing among the favored classes of the land. And, while I know that my circumstances permit me to obtain such knowledge for my own children, shall I vote for a law cutting off others from similar advantages?

" We have decided this matter once. We have done well. The people have approved our course. They cherish this fund. They look upon it as their own and their children's. Never with my vote shall it be taken from them. Never, without my protest, shall it be diverted to any other from the sacred cause to which it is now devoted. Never, I am sure, can it be so diverted with the people's consent, And never, if I know anything of the feelings of this house, will they countenance this project for its diversion.

" Now at the very outset, in its first stage, do I hope that the bill will be rejected. I am not satisfied to have it defeated. I am unwilling to see it even for a moment countenanced by the house. I wish and hope to see it put down at once; and by such a majority that it shall be evident to the public and to all future legislatures that such efforts ever will be, as they ought to be, idle and unavailing."

Valiant as was his lifelong advocacy of free public schools, it was as a member of the Indiana Constitutional Convention of 1851 and the legislative session immediately following that he was able to render the most efficient and most conspicuous services to the cause of an education " free as the living waters." No intelligent comprehension of the education reforms inaugurated by that second Constitutional Convention and no adequate appreciation of the large part which the younger Owen has played in laying the foundations of the public-school systems of Indiana and the Middle West are possible without a knowledge of the history of education in the Hoosier State previous to 1850. This will be briefly sketched.

The first Constitutional Convention of the newly made State of Indiana, convened at Corydon in 1816, adopted the following provision respecting education:

" Knowledge and learning generally diffused through a community being essential to the preservation of a free government . . . it shall be the duty of the General Assembly as soon as circumstances will permit, to provide by law for a general system of education, ascending in a regular gradation from township schools to a State university, wherein tuition shall be gratis, and equally open to all."

Commenting on this in an address before the students

of Indiana University in later years, Robert Dale Owen said:

"With pride and pleasure may we read in our State constitution the provision which the provident wisdom of the Corydon convention therein established for the promotion of public education. You may look through the constitution of every State in the Union and you will not find in one of them a prospective provision for public education so liberal and comprehensive as this of our own young State. Read aright, that single paragraph should attract as settlers to the forests of Indiana every emigrant who feels, as parents ought to feel, the engrossing importance of the subject. . . . Education is the noblest object, the most important work that ever occupied a legislature's time or a nation's thoughts; that shall make the world in its coming generation a happy or a miserable one; the only rock foundation of political liberty and public order; the Great Moral Arbiter of the future destinies of our race!"

The provisions of that natal Constitution were unique and without precedent among the older States. "Previous to Indiana, no State had in its constitution declared for a graduated system of schools extending from the district schools to the university, equally open to all on the basis of gratuitous instruction." The dictum of the first instrument of government for the infant State battling against the strenuous forces of the wilderness was a distinct advance and departure in educational thought and procedure.

If to do were as easy as to know what it were good to do, the duty of providing by law for a general system of education which the constitution had imposed upon the pioneer people of a frontier commonwealth would have been easily and efficiently discharged. It was one thing, however, to command by the stroke of the pen the building of an effective school system; it was a much more difficult thing, as the early fathers of Indiana soon dis-

348

covered, to conceive and enact such legislation as should consummate a system of public instruction at once State controlled, uniformly administered, and uniformly available.

The history of the educational legislation between the first and last Indiana Constitutional Conventions is but the story of repeated efforts, some of them spasmodic, many of them mistaken, all of them unsuccessful, to create a State system of schools in keeping with the ideas of the makers of the early constitution.

The difficulties against which that early school legislation labored were: (1) The lack of an overwhelming public sentiment such as we enjoy to-day supporting the schools; (2) the lack of funds with which to maintain them; (3) the lack of competent teachers; (4) the lack of systematic organization of the educational system of the State.

Education was a secondary consideration during pioneer days. The rough backwoodsmen, struggling with the Indian and the forest, prized muscle more than culture, and internal improvements more than the public-school system, for which a faithful few never ceased to labor. Theoretically all admitted the advantages and benefits of education both to the individual citizen and the State. " The objection was not so much to schools as to free State-controlled, State-supported schools."

The arguments against a State public-school system were varied and ingenious. It was urged that the funds of the State, however large, could not support schools operated upon such a vast scale. Bachelors blessed with property, and parents whose children attended private schools, maintained that the support which they would be compelled to render by taxation to free schools would be entirely out of proportion to the benefit which they received from them. Sectarianism denounced the public school as " godless," while the enemies of religion declared the real object of the proposed free educational system to be the union of church and state. Rejected by the rich because they could afford the luxury of private instruction for their offspring, the free school was spurned by the less fortunate as a "pauper institution." It was contended that "education is a private responsibility of the parent, and if not of the parent then of the church"; that the "real purpose of taxation is to support the Government"; that "taxation for free schools sets limits to individual rights, for the industrious ought not to be taxed to support the indolent"; that "taxes are a drain in any case, but that educational taxation is larceny"; that the free school propaganda is "undemocratic," dangerous to the state and subversive of the general good, "a usurpation of local rights and an infringement of personal and family liberties." As late as 1837 a member of the State Legislature declared that he desired for an epitaph the words, "Here lies an enemy of free schools." Within two years of the Constitutional Convention which founded our present educational system, citizens otherwise in good standing in their respective communities sought by the display of armed force at the polls to prevent the passage of educational measures which the legislature had submitted for ratification to the voters of the commonwealth.

Intimidated by such strenuous opposition, successive legislatures, despite the devoted efforts of the faithful friends of education, notable among whom was Robert Dale Owen, cringed and temporized and compromised with the enemies of the free public school.

In the wake of cowardly compromise came a train of evils. State school funds, created largely through the generosity of the National Government, though bearing promise for the future, yielded but little aid to the free schools of the commonwealth. Failure to assert the right of the State to control, or the duty of the State to assist in maintaining them left the public schools at the caprice of isolated communities. Some of these elected not to maintain "pauper

350

schools." Where established, " the schools free as the living waters," of which Robert Dale Owen had so fondly
dreamed in those halcyon days at New Harmony, were in
reality pay schools, a monthly fee being exacted for the
niggardly support of a short-term school of uncertain
duration. Ignorance and indifference on the part of the
people, coupled with the beggarly pittance which these
crude struggling schools yielded to the pedagogue, attracted to the work of teaching only the indolent, the adventurous, and the incompetent. Since there was no State
supervision and no local organization of the schools worthy
the name, what little educational system, if system it may
be called, which the State possessed or claimed to possess,
was in a chaotic state. As a result of these conditions, when
the second Constitutional Convention met in 1850 the per
cent of illiteracy in Indiana was greater than that of any
other State north of Mason and Dixon's line and almost
twice as great as the average per cent of illiteracy in all the
twenty-six States that then composed the Union.

In 1843, led by the Hon. Caleb Mills, to whom Indiana
owes a debt of gratitude as great as that which Massachusetts owes to Horace Mann, the friends of education began
a crusade in favor of the complete reorganization of the
schools of the State. Spurred to action by startling rev-
elations concerning both the dangerous and wide-spread
illiteracy and the utter inefficiency of the educational system of the commonwealth, the legislatures of 1848 and
1849 submitted wise educational measures, meeting the
approval of Mills and his associates, for ratification by the
people. In each instance the vote showed a large and increasing majority of the citizenship in favor of free schools
and their proper support.

The second Constitutional Convention followed close
upon the heels of this ratification of " public schools
wherein tuition shall be gratis and open to all." Though
its provisions respecting education superseded the measures

which the popular vote had but just ratified, yet that ratification declared the true attitude of the State, strengthened the hands of the devoted friends of the schools, and wrote the educational provisions of the new instrument of government.

Though his experience in the schools at New Lanark and New Harmony, his devotion to the free public school, his wide knowledge of educational affairs, and his tact and ability as a debater and parliamentarian clearly entitled Robert Dale Owen to the position of chairman of the Committee on Education in the Constitutional Convention, public prejudice against the very name of Owen rendered his appointment impossible.

Though not even a member of the special committee to which they were entrusted, Owen was the dominant force of the convention in educational matters. He early convinced the delegates that the Constitution must provide for the establishment of a general and uniform system of common schools wherein tuition should be without charge and equally open to all. He pointed out to them and to the special committee the general provisions by which the new instrument of government should pave the way for a complete reorganization of the educational machinery of the State. Upon his motion, prominent educators addressed the convention concerning the condition of the educational affairs of the commonwealth and suggested legislative remedies for the same. Owen himself appeared before the committee repeatedly, urged upon it the sections of the article on education in the present Constitution, induced the committee to report that article favorably, and aided in bringing the article to a successful passage. It rests in the Constitution to-day, partly the handiwork of Owen.

The first section of the constitutional provisions relating to education declares that, " Knowledge and learning, generally diffused throughout a community, being essential to the preservation of a free government, it shall be the duty of the General Assembly to encourage, by all suitable means, moral, intellectual, scientific, and agricultural improvement, and to provide, by law, for a general and uniform system of common schools, wherein tuition shall be without charge, and equally open to all."

The Constitution of 1816 had contained substantially the same provision couched in much the same language, save that in it the duty of the General Assembly to provide by law for a *general* and *uniform* system of common schools was qualified by the use of the words " as soon as the circumstances will permit." The clash of selfish and sectional interests had never permitted the performance of this duty, and the State was without a general and uniform system of schools when the Constitutional Convention assembled. By a majority of eighty thousand the people of the State ordered that the provisions of the Constitution of 1850 be carried into effect. Armed with this ratification, Robert Dale Owen, as chairman of the Committee on Education in the lower house of the legislative assembly that immediately followed the Constitutional Convention, pressed to a successful issue the school law of 1852 that gave form and substance to the constitutional provisions relating to education.

By successive grants both before and after the adoption of the Constitution of 1816, the National Government had bestowed upon the young commonwealth, battling against the forces of the wilderness, both land and money for educational purposes. The early Constitution did not attempt to define or dispose of these assets but left them to the tender mercies of annual legislation. Since the funds that grew out of these successive congressional grants were entirely at the caprice of legislative enactment, the repeal or amendment of the statute under which any given fund had been applied for the benefit of the free schools could easily arrest, divert, or dissipate it. Though these funds were in the strictest sense of the word trust funds for the use of the schools, repeated attempts were made between the two Constitutions to annul or divert them. Only the honor of the State and the never-to-be-forgotten vigilance of the unselfish friends of education defeated the combined assaults of the enemies of free schools and the misguided friends of other and less worthy enterprises upon the noblest trust fund which history yet records.

Robert Dale Owen had been the leader in two of the successful legislative fights by which the partizans of the public schools had brought confusion upon the assailants of these schools funds. Recognizing that as long as they were the creatures of the General Assembly they would be in perpetual danger from attacks like those from which he had aided in rescuing them, he induced the special committee and the convention to define these funds in the Constitution itself and by so doing made them inviolate.

The second section of the educational provisions of the Constitution declares the Common School Fund of the State to consist of the following:

1. The Congressional Township Fund.
2. The Surplus Revenue Fund.
3. The Saline Fund.
4. The Bank Tax Fund.
5. The Seminary Fund.
6. The Contingent Fund.
7. The Swamp Land Fund.

Though the Constitution by defining and dedicating the various educational resources of the State to the common fund had made that fund a perpetual principal for the benefit of the public schools of the State, yet Robert Dale Owen, fearful lest the interpretation of the courts might defeat the plain intent of the Constitution, induced his colleagues to insert among the educational provisions of the Constitution a declaration that all the funds which go to make up the Common School Fund of the State should forever be a trust fund to be held sacred and inviolate during the perpetuity of the State government. In the opinion of many able lawyers this provision, for which Owen is to be given the greater meed of credit, places the common fund of the State even beyond the influence of a modification or repeal of the Constitution by which it was created.

After several wise provisions concerning the distribution of the Common School Fund and the duties and responsibilities of the various county governments with respect to the same, the article on education terminates by creating the office of State Superintendent of Public Instruction. The educational affairs of the State were in a chaotic condition, largely because of the lack of a strongly centralized administration of the same. The younger State of Wisconsin had already provided for such an executive officer as the State Superintendent. Mr. Owen urged his colleagues to profit by the example which Indiana's less mature sister State offered the convention. To the creation of this office and to the ability in which it has been administered in all its history, much of the present efficiency of the Indiana educational system must be attributed.

The legislative assembly of 1852, recognizing the services of Robert Dale Owen in the cause of education in the Constitutional Convention, bestowed upon him the chairmanship of the Committee on Education which the latter body had denied him, and afforded him the supreme opportunity of his life to render valiant service in the cause of free public schools.

The provisions of the Constitutions of 1816 and 1850 with respect to the character and organization of the schools of the State were almost identical. So nearly do the provisions and the language of the two instruments resemble each other that they suggest the deadly parallel.

355

Yet the Constitution of 1816 did not succeed in creating a general and uniform system of public schools while the Constitution of 1850 was the natal note of the system which has been perpetuated into our own day. That under substantially the same provisions the Constitution of 1850 should succeed in doing what the Constitution of 1816 failed completely to achieve is due to the genius of Robert Dale Owen. As chairman of the Committee on Education in the lower house, he realized that the first section of Article 8 of the new Constitution was a dead letter in the absence of wise legislation carrying out its general provisions; that the section in question, like its sister section in the Constitution of 1816, was a mere skeleton which the General Assembly must by successive statutes clothe with flesh and blood; and that if the legislative assembly of 1852 did not immediately proceed to the task of making the constitutional provision just described effective, the schools under the new instrument would be as lacking in uniformity and efficiency as the schools had been under its predecessor.

Owen impressed this view upon his colleagues of the committee and upon the members of both Houses of the General Assembly. As chairman of the Committee on Education of the lower house and chairman of the joint committee for both houses, he brought to a successful issue the School Law of 1852, with which his name must ever be associated.

In the new school law the old tone of compromise and apology was superseded by a spirit of hope and earnestness. Some of its provisions were revolutionary in purpose and scope. A State tax of ten cents on each one hundred dollars' worth of property was levied. This established the principle that the property of all the State should be taxed for the education of all the children of the State. True to the teachings of William Maclure, who had strenuously advocated the civil township as the unit of school government in all the Western States, the old congressional township system was abolished and each civil township was declared a township for school purposes, the township trustee being given full control of its educational as well as its civil affairs. This innovation, copied in modified form by other Western commonwealths, has given Indiana perhaps the best organization of rural schools in the nation. Provision was made for the formation of township libraries and their maintenance. This was the beginning of the present public-library system of the State. Incorporated cities and towns were declared school corporations separate and independent of the civil townships in which they were located. They were empowered to appoint school trustees, to build schoolhouses, and to levy taxes for their support. This was the beginning of the present town and city school systems of the State. Provision was made for the election of a State Superintendent of Public Instruction and for the establishment of the State Board of Education, the duties of each being clearly defined. To the ability with which these two factors in the educational administration of the State have been administered the schools of the commonwealth owe much of their efficiency.

In accordance with the mandate of the new Constitution, all the permanent school funds defined in the new instrument of government were consolidated and wiser measures enacted for the safe and profitable investment of the principal, and the equitable distribution of the proceeds arising from it. To-day, as the result of the legislative provisions of 1852, for which Owen and his associates upon the Educational Committee deserve the credit, Indiana is blessed with a permanent school fund of nearly eleven million dollars. Only three States—Texas, Illinois, and Missouri—have a larger productive school fund.

It has been the custom for years to attribute to the honored Caleb Mills the credit for the laws which really formed the public-school system of Indiana. To detract one jot or tittle from the great amount of praise which has been and will continue to be bestowed upon that eminent educator for the part which he played in creating and organizing the educational machinery of the commonwealth would be neither just nor possible; but if Mr. Mills was the professional father of the Indiana educational system, Robert Dale Owen was its legislative ancestor, and the two working together as educator and statesman were the architects who laid broad and deep the foundation of all that is worthy in the educational organization of the Hoosier State. Both created and fostered an enthusiasm for the free public school. One suggested a superb plan for the organization of the schools of the State and the other wrote that plan into enduring legislation.

Such were the contributions of Robert Dale Owen to the educational history of his adopted State. Through him Robert Owen and William Maclure labored and spoke in convention hall and legislative assembly. Had they been there, clothed in the flesh, they would have cried " Bravo ! " to all of his efforts as delegate and legislator in the cause of education. In him the spirit of humanity and the great love which the founders of New Harmony bore for free schools, which are after all the chief hope of those who earn their living in the sweat of their brows, perpetuated itself in the educational system of the commonwealth of Indiana.

The Constitution of 1850 and the School Law of 1852 are, through Robert Dale Owen, the handiwork of Robert Owen and William Maclure. Though the educational experiments of the Commune failed as signally as did the social order, who dare say that the master of New Lanark and the Father of American Geology lived in vain?

The School Law of 1852, with some important additions, constitutes the school law of Indiana to-day. Temporarily annulled by a decision of the Supreme Court, the provisions of the Act of 1852 were incorporated into the School Law of 1865. Into that law, some new features were in-

troduced, one of the most important being that of teachers'
institutes. The law of 1865 has been supplemented by
others, each one calculated to perfect the system and to
widen its scope. The power of taxation has been increased
and trustees have been empowered to issue bonds to procure funds for the erection of new and more commodious
buildings. Successive statutes have provided for the education of colored children; for the important office of
county superintendent; for the present State text-book
law, and for the creation and support of an efficient State
Normal School.

The departures from precedent which marked the era
of Robert Dale Owen's activity in Indiana legislation excited wide discussion and comment, much of it unfavorable,
but in succeeding years other States followed the example
of Indiana, not only in making the most generous provisions for free schools, but in emancipating woman from
legal bondage. In the formation of public sentiment along
these lines Robert Dale Owen was an active agent. As
writer and speaker his genius was equal to any attack upon
the laws for which he stood sponsor, and in the period of
discussion which followed the adoption of these advanced
measures he was the most conspicuous and brilliant figure.
Commenting on the legislation enacted through his influence, a contributor to the London Times said: " Indiana
has attained the highest civilization of any State in the
Union."

In 1853 Mr. Owen was appointed, by President Pierce,
chargé d'affaires at Naples, and at this post he remained
for nearly six years. During this period he followed his
father in becoming an advocate of spiritualism. " From
the first avowal of spiritualistic notions," to quote a biographer, " he led the numerous hosts of the new faith with
undisputed superiority. Into the work of propagating,
defending, and expurgating spiritualism he put the remainder of his life. He attended spiritualistic conventions

all over the country, shaped the doctrines, explored the phenomena, and defended the honesty of his, the new faith, and really converted it from a loose assemblage of notions into a system and a religion. His works, Footfalls on the Boundary of Another World, and The Debatable Land Between this World and the Next, were widely read and discussed, the first causing a literary sensation."

Robert Dale Owen from his boyhood was opposed to slavery. His keen sympathy with the oppressed of every type and the radical notions concerning human equality which he held in common with his illustrious father, brought him at a tender age into an intense hatred of the institution of human bondage.

In England slaves were exceedingly rare, and the younger Owen saw but little of the commerce in the bodies of black men. The New Moral World was projected upon soil which the Ordinance of 1787 had forever dedicated to human liberty. But there was no lack of opportunity to observe the workings of the slave traffic. Robert Dale Owen saw the negro on Indiana soil a fugitive from a brutal master; a beast of burden on primitive flatboats plying Western waters; a human chattel in the slave market at New Orleans; and joined with Frances Wright at Nashoba in a noble but misguided effort to rescue him and solve the slavery question by colonization.

Each succeeding contact with slavery in any of its phases increased the already deep-seated antipathy of his early years. Maintaining as he did the equality of all men, irrespective of color or sex, to him slavery was an intolerable injustice against which every fiber of his splendid young manhood cried out in protest. Realizing the utter hopelessness of any save a peaceable resistance to the traffic in human bodies then, like Lincoln he made a solemn resolve that if an opportunity should ever come he would strike a valiant blow against slavery.

There was a strange connection and resemblance be-

THE OLD FORT—PRESENT CONDITION.

Headquarters United States Geological Survey under David Dale Owen.

tween the life of the younger Owen and that of the mar-
tyred President. Though Owen was eight years the senior
of Lincoln, the two were contemporaries in public life for
over a third of a century. Lincoln was reared on Pigeon
Creek, Indiana, within less than fifty miles of the site
upon which the elder Owen sought to found a social order
that should achieve human equality. While the younger
Owen was being reared in luxury in a well-ordered English
household, Lincoln grew to young manhood, almost in
squalor, in a dilapidated frontier cabin.

While Robert Dale Owen, grown to man's estate, entered with the enthusiasm of the true humanitarian into
his father's social and educational experiments, Lincoln,
spurred on by poverty, vigorously navigated with flatboat
and raft the Ohio and its tributaries. It is more than
probable that his craft, ascending the Wabash, touched at
the then flourishing port of New Harmony and that he
and Owen met, like ships that pass in the night, beneath
the classic shades of The New Moral World.

At approximately the same time both left the "Indiana
Pocket" for wider fields of usefulness: Owen to enter
upon an editorial career in the metropolis of the country,
by which he sprang almost at once into national prominence
as the foremost advocate of "human equality irrespective
of color or sex"; Lincoln to rise by sheer force of hard
work and strength of personality from obscurity to acknowledged leadership of the antislavery sentiment in the
Middle West.

There was much in common between the two men.
Both had deep-seated convictions of right and wrong.
Both were unswerving in their devotion to a principle.
Both were men of pure private life and irreproachable
public conduct. Both were singularly gifted with that fine
moral courage which would rather be right than be President. Both were misunderstood and maligned by their
contemporaries. Both in the fulness of time came into a

tardy recognition of the unselfishness and the value of the services which each in his own place had rendered for the betterment of men and the relief of the oppressed.

Hatred of the institution of human slavery was common to the two men. Both had registered in early manhood a resolution to fight it to the bitter end. Yet neither was an Abolitionist as the term was used in their day. Neither believed that Congress had any constitutional right to interfere with slavery in the Southern States. Neither countenanced the idea of the forcible emancipation of the negro. Both pinned their hope to colonization, to compensated emancipation, to an educated ballot, to constitutional amendment. When the awful form of disunion darkened the national threshold, both were willing to submit to slavery, if need be, in order to preserve our national existence intact. With both the paramount object then became " to save the Union and neither to save nor destroy slavery." " If they could have saved the Union without freeing any slaves, they would have done so. If they could have saved it by freeing some and leaving others, also they would have done that." It was not that they hated slavery the less but that they loved the Union more.

By the Compromise Measures of 1850 Henry Clay postponed secession and the civil war for ten years. He offered five propositions, all of which by separate bills were enacted into laws: (1) to admit California as a free State; (2) to apply the principle of Squatter Sovereignty to New Mexico and Utah; (3) to purchase the claim of Texas to a portion of New Mexico; (4) to abolish the slave-trade but not slavery itself in the District of Columbia; (5) to pass a more effective fugitive slave act.

The passage of the new Fugitive Slave Act aroused the most intense excitement throughout the North. Memorials poured in upon Congress from all the free States demanding the repeal of the law as " revolting to the moral sense of the civilized world." Webster, who had upheld the act, was denounced as a traitor to liberty. Fourteen Northern States practically nullified the new act of the National Congress relating to runaway slaves by passing laws to protect them. Underground railroads grew in number and in zeal, while over all the Northland excited Abolitionists publicly counseled armed resistance to their Southern brother seeking by due process of law to reclaim his dusky but human chattel.

Within a month after the passage of Clay's Compromise Measures the Indiana Constitutional Convention of 1850 assembled. Excitement over the new slavery legislation was at fever heat. Robert Dale Owen did not believe that it lay within the real province of the convention or that it was the part of wisdom for the delegates to assume any attitude upon the Fugitive Slave Act or upon the conduct of those who were resisting its enforcement. When the introduction of a clumsily worded resolution made the question of the Compromise Measures an issue before the convention, Mr. Owen, recognizing that it would be necessary for the delegates to take some action, lest the real attitude of the State be misunderstood, with the readiness and diplomacy which made him more than the peer of all the members of that historical body, succeeded in securing the substitution of a resolution that breathed in every line a spirit of loyalty to the Union and submission to the law of the land.

The resolution declares that the common sentiment of the people of Indiana sustains and indorses the general features and intentions of the Compromise Measures and recognizes in their success " an earnest of security and perpetuity." After asserting the determination of " certain misguided individuals " to resist the fugitive slave law, the resolution, rising to a lofty plane of civic duty, maintains " that whatever may be the opinions of individuals as to the wisdom or policy of any of the details of the fugitive slave law, it is the duty of all good citizens to conform to its requisitions and to carry out, in good faith, the conditions of that compromise on the subject of slavery, which is coeval with the Federal Constitution."

The resolution mirrors the true attitude of Owen in the sectional strife that preceded the war. He was a partizan of neither the North nor the South, but of the Union. Though as the bitter opponent of slavery he regretted some features of the Compromise Measures before their enactment, yet he sustained and indorsed their passage " as the sole means of calming the wide-spread and pestiferous agitation which pervaded the land." Though he believed every phase of human bondage to be iniquitous, yet he deplored and censured the acts by which overzealous Abolitionists trampled upon the legal rights of the slaveholder and endangered the safety and perpetuity of the Union.

To the day on which Beauregard opened fire upon Major Anderson and his gallant little band, Owen, out of his great love for the Union, never abandoned hope that some way and some how it would be peaceably preserved and the threatened civil strife averted. After the six chief States had declared themselves out of the Union, Virginia, as the spokesman for seven border States, proposed certain additional compromise measures, the acceptance of which by the Northern States would be necessary in order to retain their allegiance to the Stars and Stripes. On the 13th of February, 1861, Mr. Owen, by invitation, delivered before the Indiana Legislature a pathetic appeal to the people of that commonwealth, urging them to support by memorials and petitions to Congress the measures whose enactment Virginia and her associates had demanded as a condition precedent to their continued loyalty to the National Government. " Up and be doing, ere it be too late! Yours is the power. There are constitutional means enough through which to make known your wishes to those who, if you but speak in numbers sufficient, must regard them. Speak, then! Memorialize. If you believe that in the Christian spirit of conciliation is our only safety, say so. If you believe that by compromise only can this Confederacy be held together, declare it. You have been called on by one in authority to act for yourselves. Answer the call! For myself, while the sword remains undrawn, while kindred blood remains unshed, never shall I despair of the Republic. While there is PEACE there is hope, for PEACE is the life of the Union."

The compromise proposals of the border States were suddenly terminated by the attack on Fort Sumter. One after the other all of them that dared joined fortunes with the rebellion, and memorial and compromise became alike fruitless. With the beginning of hostilities Mr. Owen's attitude underwent a radical change. Till the first gun was fired he had been essentially a man of peace, hoping against hope that the Union might without force of arms be preserved intact, even though slavery be perpetuated. At once he became a strenuous advocate of the war and of immediate emancipation as a measure of belligerency. With enthusiasm he entered into the defense of the Union cause. In southern Indiana, where sympathy for the South ran high in some communities, he was the most conspicuous and effective leader of the Union cause. He was commissioned by Governor Morton to purchase arms in Europe for the Indiana troops and performed his task with signal ability.

War afforded Lincoln the opportunity to make the emancipation of the negro a constitutional act. After the preservation of the Union, the liberation of the slave lay closest to the great heart of the President. Yet, because his paramount wish and duty was to save the Union, he hesitated to free the black man. He recognized that slavery was the real tap-root of the civil war. "Without slavery," he declared, "the rebellion never would have existed; without slavery it could not continue." But he

365

feared lest a premature emancipation might alienate the border States and "give fifty thousand bayonets" from them "over to the rebels."

On the 25th of July, 1862, the President issued a sixty-day notice calling upon the Southern soldiers to lay down their arms. Lee's reply was the invasion of Maryland. On September 17th he was repulsed at Antietam and retired across the Potomac to Southern soil. That same day, which was the sixth day previous to the expiration of the sixty-day notice, Robert Dale Owen penned a remarkable letter to the Chief Executive urging him to terminate the period of warning with the manumission of the negro. Emancipation seemed to hang in the balance. The Great Commoner apparently hesitated to take a course fraught with so much of good or ill to the sacred cause of the Union. Seizing the psychological moment, Owen through his letter confirmed Lincoln in the wisdom of the act that lay so close to his great heart.

With a diplomacy in keeping with the great mission upon which it was sent, the epistle begins with an assertion of the confidence of the writer in the one whom he purposed to rouse to action. How accurately Owen anticipates the true verdict of history!

Harsh opinions have been formed of you; even honest men doubting the probity of your intentions. I do not share their doubts. I believe you to be upright, single-hearted in your desire to rescue the country in the hour of its utmost need, without afterthought of the personal consequences to yourself.

Though from the beginning of the war an ardent advocate of the manumission of the slaves, Owen had not been disposed to increase President Lincoln's burdens by complaints concerning the seemingly slow progress toward that end. Better than his radical associates he had understood Lincoln's position and responsibility. Out of the greatness of a kindred soul he declares:

ROBERT DALE OWEN

If amid the multitude of contending counsel you have hesitated and doubted; if, when a great measure suggested itself, you have shrunk from the vast responsibility, afraid to go forward lest you go wrong, what wonder? How few since the foundation of the world have found themselves environed with public perils so numerous, oppressed with responsibilities so high and solemn as yourself!

Lincoln had undeniably been prudent in his conduct of the war—too prudent in the judgment of many over-anxious sons of the Northland. Did he possess the courage necessary to liberate the negro? Anxiously the letter argues that daring leadership is as essential as cautious maneuver. " Wisdom, prudence, forethought, these are essential. But not second to these is that noble courage which adventures the right and leaves the consequences to God. . . . There is a measure needing courage to adopt and enforce it, which I believe to be of virtue sufficient to redeem the nation in this its darkest hour, one only. I know of no other to which we may rationally trust for relief from impending dangers within and without."

In 1858, during his memorable debate with Douglas, Lincoln, preferring to be right rather than to be senator, proclaimed that " a house divided against itself can not stand. I believe this Government can not endure permanently half-slave and half-free. I do not expect the Union to be dissolved. I do not expect the house to fall, but I do expect it will cease to be divided. It will become all the one thing or the other." By these words, shrewd but sincere, the Great Commoner built a platform and upon it rode in triumph through the White House doors. Through him as the concrete exponent of its attitude, Lincoln's party advocated opposition to slavery because slavery and freedom can not abide together, no interference with slavery in the South but bitter resistance to the spread of the institution lest freedom be overcome, and ultimate abolition of the system as the only terms of permanent peace.

367

Craftily Owen's letter appeals to these well-known convictions of the President, and argues that war has strengthened the logic of the position which the Chief Executive assumed in his senatorial contest with the "Little Giant" and has made slavery and the Union forever irreconcilable.

"Can you look forward to the peace of our country and imagine any state of things in which, with slavery still existing, we would be assured of permanent peace? I can not. We can constitutionally extirpate slavery at this time. But if we fail to do this, then, unless we intend hereafter to violate the Constitution, we shall have a fugitive slave law in operation whenever the war is over. Shall the North have sacrificed a hundred thousand lives and two thousand millions of treasure to come to that at last? Not even a guarantee of peace purchased at so enormous a cost? After voluntary exertions on the part of our people to which the history of the world furnishes no parallel, is the old root of bitterness still to remain in the ground, to sprout and bear fruit in the future as it has borne fruit in the past? These questions are addressed to you. For upon you and your action more than any other one thing does the answer depend."

Declaring the institution of slavery to be not only morally wrong, but the one vulnerable point in the armor of the enemy, Owen maintains that the time has come when it is constitutional for the Chief Executive to strike at it.

"But the time has come when it is constitutional to redress it. The rebellion has made it so. Property in man, always morally unjust, has become nationally dangerous. Property that endangers the safety of a nation should not be suffered to remain in the hands of its citizens. A chief magistrate who permits it so to remain becomes responsible for the consequences. For he has the right, under the law and the Constitution, to take private property, with just compensation offered, for public use, whenever it is apparent that public exigency demands such appropriation.

368

Forgive what may seem curt speech if I say that, in my judgment, a President with a just sense of duty has no option in such a case."

Though convinced that Lincoln was unselfishly seeking the salvation of the country " without afterthought of the personal consequences to himself," Owen, in his overmastering desire to secure the immediate liberation of the negro, does not neglect to hold up before the eyes of the President the personal fame which, through the exercise of his power as military dictator, he may reap by the abolition of slavery.

" It is within your power at this very moment not only to consummate an act of enlightened statesmanship, but, as the instrument of the Almighty, to restore to freedom a race of men. If you are tempted by an imperishable name, it is within your reach. We may look through ancient and modern history, yet scarce find a sovereign to whom God offered the privilege of bestowing on humanity a boon so vast. Such an offer comes to no human being twice. It is made to you to-day. How long it will remain open—whether in three months or in one month from now it will still be in your option to accept it—God, who reads the hearts of men, alone knows."

Owen had purposely timed his written exhortation to the President so that it might come into his hands near the close of the sixty-day notice to the Confederates, which terminated on the 23d of September, 1862. The Southern States ignored the notice. No one expected them to do otherwise. There was much speculation both north and south of Mason and Dixon's line as to what measure, if any, Lincoln would adopt at the close of the period of warning in order to punish the Confederacy for the contempt with which his proclamation had been received. Owen, sharing in the general interest and anxiety, hopes that the Great Commoner may make the Emancipation Proclamation the weapon of punishment.

" The TWENTY-THIRD OF SEPTEMBER approaches—the date when the sixty-day notice you have given the rebels will expire—expire without other reply to your warning than the invasion of Maryland and a menace to Pennsylvania. Is it to rest there? Patiently we have waited the time. Is nothing to follow? Are our enemies to boast that we speak brave words—and there an end of it? "

With a prophetic soul, born of his own intense convictions upon all questions involving human rights, the younger Owen, looking into the future, describes to the Chief Executive the great day in the calendar which the act of manumission would establish. His description of Emancipation Day seems retrospective rather than prospective.

" What a day, if you but will it, may that twenty-third of September become! The very turning-point in the nation's fate! A day to the rebels of despair, to every loyal heart of exultant rejoicing! A day of which the anniversary will be celebrated with jubilee while the American Union endures! A day to be remembered not in our land alone, but wherever humanity mourns over the wrongs of the slaves or rejoices in their liberation! You are the first President to whom the opportunity was ever offered constitutionally to inaugurate such a day. If you fail us now, you may be the last."

Having demonstrated both the necessity and the present legality of the act of emancipation, Owen concludes his remarkable appeal to Lincoln by an eloquent exhortation so earnest as to be almost pathetic. How it must have touched responsive heart-strings in the tender soul of the Great Commoner!

" Lift then the weight from the heart of this people. Let us breathe free once more. Extirpate the blighting curse, a living threat throughout long years past, that has smitten at last with desolation a land to which God had

granted everything but wisdom and justice. Give back to
the nation its hope and faith in a future of peace and un-
disturbed prosperity. Fulfil—you can more than fulfil—
the brightest anticipations of those who, in the name of
human freedom, and in the face of threats that have
ripened into terrible realities since, fought the battle which
placed you where you now stand."

Some one has described this masterpiece of Robert
Dale Owen's as "an ever-enduring monument of dispas-
sionate, well-reasoned, perfectly poised deductions, at a
very critical time in the life of a great nation." To this
day the reader of his eloquent appeal finds himself stirred
by the simple power of this great paper. "Its perusal
thrilled me like a trumpet-call," said President Lincoln.
"It will be a source of satisfaction to you to know," wrote
Salmon P. Chase, Secretary of the Treasury, to Mr. Owen,
"that your letter to the President had more influence on
him than any other document which reached him on the
subject—I think I might say than all others put together.
I speak of that which I know from personal conference
with him." While it did not turn Abraham Lincoln to a
course upon which he had long been vaguely determined,
it strengthened him in his great purpose, and precipitated
the Preliminary Proclamation, which was issued five days
after the receipt of Mr. Owen's letter. After the lapse of
thirty years Providence had given to the two emigrants
from the Pocket an opportunity to strike the valiant blow
against human slavery which they had vowed. Gloriously
did they discharge that ancient resolution.

New England was the head and front of the antislavery movement during ante-bellum days. Before South
Carolina seceded, the Southern leaders proposed to recon-
struct the Union, leaving out the New England States.
"The South, abandoning her avowed intention to erect a
separate purely slaveholding Confederacy, is to consent
to receive into her fellowship a portion of the Northern

371

States. The Northern States in return are to abandon six of their number: those six in which the opinions against which the war is waged chiefly prevail."

When the entire North rose in arms after the firing on Fort Sumter this plan of reconstruction was temporarily abandoned. But when the congressional elections of 1862 seemed to result adversely to the administration; when the timid, discouraged by the prolongation of the struggle, cried out for "Peace at any cost," and the disloyal, emboldened by the stubbornness of the Southern resistance, gave increased encouragement and comfort to the enemy in arms, the leaders of the Confederacy, their cause already sinking, as a last desperate maneuver revived the scheme of reconstruction and compromise which hostilities had interrupted. Through secret emissaries the proposition to reorganize the Union was carried to every Northern State save the New England group, where it met with active support from the discouraged and the disloyal.

In Indiana the fall election of 1862 had placed all the State offices, save that of governor and both branches of the State Legislature, in the hands of the Peace Party. That legislature passed resolutions opposing the further continuance of the war, refused to receive Governor Morton's annual message, and sought to enact laws limiting his power to manage the militia of the State, to prevent which the Union members of the legislature retired to Madison, Indiana, where they remained until the term closed by constitutional limitation. Many members of the legislature, some of them openly—most of them, however, secretly—strongly favored the scheme of reconstruction of the Union with New England left out: a few because its adoption would aid the South; the rest because its adoption would consummate the peace for which they clamored.

Alarmed by the evident strength of the reconstruction sentiment in his native State, Mr. Owen, though prevented by his duties as head of the Freedman's Commis-

D. D. OWEN.

sion from visiting the object of his solicitude, printed for
gratuitous distribution and circulated among its citizens a
pamphlet dated March 4, 1863, entitled The Future of
the Northwest, in which with unanswerable logic he demonstrates the folly of dismembering the North and ac-
cepting the slaveholders' project.   In this pamphlet Mr.
Owen argues with irresistible force:

(1) That the Compromise plan for the reconstruction
of the Union was revived by the secessionists " as a specious
and daring device to uphold a sinking cause."

(2) That the Compromise, if consummated, would
create an alliance much more advantageous to the slaveholding States than either the old Union they were endeavoring to destroy or the present Confederacy which they
were seeking in vain to establish by force of arms.

(3) That Compromise would create an alliance completely dominated by slavery.   " Look at it, I pray you,
not vaguely or hastily but carefully and in all its practical
details.   In the Senate thirty Southern votes to twenty-two
Northern, in the House ninety Southern votes to one hundred and thirteen Northern.   One House hopelessly gone
while twelve votes changed would give a Southern majority
in the other.   And when has Congress seen the day when
twice twelve votes could not have been had from Northern
representatives for any measure the South saw fit to propose?"   "Just North enough in the scheme to afford
protection and support to slavery, and not North enough
to exert over it the slightest influence or control."

The invitation extended to the citizens of Indiana by
the scheme of reconstruction was given on conditions, some
of them expressed and some implied.

(1) " The first was that throughout this slave empire
no man shall be allowed to deny the great physical, philosophical, and moral truth upon which the new government
is founded; namely, that slavery is the natural and moral
condition of the African negro."

(2) The second was . . . that the North before it is admitted to Southern fellowship shall cast off six of her States; thus curtailing her power and her possessions by the surrender of nearly one-fifth of her population and more than one-fifth of her wealth.

(3) The third was that slavery would be practised on all the soil within the new alliance. " It is not more certain that the earth will continue to revolve around the sun, than that the South, while slaveholding, will persevere, whenever and wherever she obtains the political ascendency, in asserting and enforcing by law what she regards as her political rights in this matter."

(4) The fourth was that the new alliance shall shoulder the expense of the war which the proposed Compromise sought to dishonorably terminate. " The Southern insurrection will have cost its authors a thousand millions at the least. Can any man doubt that the North once entrapped into this base compact will be held to pay her full share of that stupendous sum?"

If Indiana accepted the proposed Compromise, the commonwealth must not only submit to the domination of the slaveholders, but she must repent every act committed by her brave sons in defense of the Union. Owen puts it thus: " If we take this step we must consent to repentance as well as submission. Before the world our acts must declare that from the first we were in the wrong and the South in the right. Before the world our acts must declare that a hundred thousand brave men have sunk from the battle-field to the grave—all in a disgraceful warfare, all in an iniquitous cause."

Declaring that the thinned ranks of a hundred Indiana regiments at the front would never submit to a compromise by which their achievements would be discredited and their loyalty degraded, Owen closes with a picture of the awful fate in store for the beloved commonwealth to which " he owed honorable station and a debt of

374

gratitude," should she out of either disloyalty or cowardice accept the proposition of the slave States. " Let Indiana, belying the courage she has shown on the battle-field, casting from her the last remnant of self-respect, false to her constitutional obligations, blind to a future of abject servility, deaf alike to the warnings of revolutionary wisdom and to the voice of civilization speaking to-day in her ears —let Indiana, selling Freedom's birthright for less than Esau's price, resolve to purchase Southern favor by Northern dismemberment and the world-wide contempt that would follow it—but let her know, before she enters that path of destruction, that her road will lie over the bodies of her murdered sons, past prostrate cabins, past ruined farms, through all the desolation that fire and sword can work. Let her know that before she can link her fate to a system that is as surely doomed to ultimate extinction as the human body is finally destined to death, there will be a war within her own borders to which all we have yet endured will be but as the summer's gale, that scatters a few branches over the highway, compared to the hurricane that plows its broad path of ruin, mile after mile, leaving behind in its track a prostrate forest, harvest crops uprooted and human habitations overthrown." Owen's pamphlet, circulated broadcast through Indiana and the Northwest, exerted a wide influence, especially in view of the fact that it came from one opposed politically to the party in power in all but the desire to preserve the Union.

Near the close of the war the Freedman's Bureau was established as a branch of the U. S. War Department and Mr. Owen appointed as its secretary and real executive officer. This new bureau controlled all affairs " relating to refugees and freedmen from any district embraced within the territory covered by the operations of the army." It provided work for the freedmen, established schools for their education, and guarded their rights. Mr. Owen's labors in behalf of the negro while connected with the bureau entitle him to the gratitude of the colored race.

Though he was the devoted friend of the black man, Mr. Owen strenuously opposed the scheme to bestow immediate suffrage upon the newly made freedmen at the close of the war. In the winter of 1865–'66 Mr. Owen was in Washington anxiously watching for legislation favorable for the negro, and he prepared a fourteenth amendment to the Constitution, providing for negro suffrage to begin July 4, 1876. Thaddeus Stevens, then chairman of the reconstruction committee, favored immediate negro suffrage, but he was persuaded to adopt Mr. Owen's views, and presented his amendment to the committee. It was adopted by the committee and ordered reported; but as Mr. Fessenden was ill with the varioloid it was deemed best to reconsider this action and postpone the matter until he could be present. In the meantime protest was made against the amendment, and the result was that the fourteenth amendment was adopted without any allusion to the question of suffrage, and nothing was done about suffrage till the fifteenth amendment was adopted several years later. Mr. Owen told the story in an article entitled The Political Results of the Varioloid.

Robert Dale Owen died June 24, 1877. For a period before his death " his mind was deranged by overwork— deranged, but not obscured—for during several months' residence in the hospital for the insane his mental powers were incessantly active and brilliant, though touched by grotesque shapes. Happily he regained his mental soundness, but did not long survive, dying at the ripe age of seventy-three."

" What was said of him in one of the newspapers," said Mr. John H. Holliday, in a paper written some years ago, " seems to me to hold good still: ' In scholarship, general attainments, varied achievements; as author, statesman, politician, and leader of a new religious faith, he was un-

376

questionably the most prominent man Indiana ever owned. Others may fill now, or may have filled, a larger place in public interest or curiosity for a time, but no other Hoosier was ever so widely known, or so likely to do the State credit by being known, and no other has ever before held so prominent a place so long, with a history so unspotted by selfishness, duplicity, or injustice.' "

With the death of Robert Dale Owen the last of the great figures conspicuous in the New Harmony communisms passed away, but the great movements to which they had given origin and direction still sweep onward in an ever-widening current.

APPENDIX

SOURCES

" THE New Harmony Communities " was taken as a research topic in 1893 by the author as a member of the seminarium of political science at DePauw University, and was followed during his senior college year under the direction of Colonel James Riley Weaver, Director of the seminarium, whose helpful suggestions have contributed materially to whatever success may have attended the effort to complete a thorough study of the social experiments at New Harmony. The initial work was done in the library of the Working Men's Institute at New Harmony during the summer of 1893, and a visit was made to the same library in 1896. The secretary of the institute, Mr. Arthur Dransfield, has for years been collecting with commendable care all the material obtainable with reference to the history of the Rappite and Owenite experiments, sparing neither trouble nor expense to make this collection complete. He has cooperated with the writer in his search for data, has made frequent corrections and suggestions, and under Mr. Dransfield's supervision the collection of photographs which form the basis for the illustrations in this volume was made. Considerable work was done in the Indiana State library at Indianapolis, where valuable material was found and rendered available through the courtesy of the former State librarian, Miss N. E. Ahern, and the present libra-

379

rian, Mr. W. E. Henry. The paucity of material in the Library of Congress at Washington served to emphasize the fact that the story of the New Harmony experiments had become a lost chapter in the history of American social reform movements. Through the courtesy of the Librarian of Congress, Mr. Herbert Putnam, and the librarian of Yale University, Dr. A. VanName, the Macdonald manuscript, which forms a part of the Yale collection, was temporarily transferred to the Library of Congress and used under the supervision of the manuscript division. The Macdonald manuscript is a history of the earlier communistic experiments in America, and the familiarity of the author with the Owenite communities rendered this material especially valuable.

In the New Harmony library, one of the most interesting book collections in the country, the files of the New Harmony Gazette, a weekly paper published throughout the lifetime of the Owenite experiment as the organ of the movement, was found the most prolific source of information. The scrap-books of Richard Owen and Mrs. Arthur Dransfield, the letters and papers of Josiah Warren, the community account-books, and the letters, wills, and deeds of William Maclure, were also found in the New Harmony library. From Dr. Aaron Williams's book on " The Harmonists," the author has drawn liberally, this being the only authoritative publication on the history of the Rappites. Acknowledgments are due to Mr. John Holliday, of Indianapolis, who placed at the disposal of the writer data collected in a study of the New Harmony communities some years ago.

The chapter on Josiah Warren, as shown by the footnote, is the production of Mr. William Bailie, of Boston, who has through several years prosecuted a study of the life-work of the founder of the philosophy of individualism. Mr. Charles A. Prosser, of New Albany, Indiana, collaborated in the preparation of the chapters bearing on the

APPENDIX

educational phases and relations of the New Harmony movement.

A list of the more important manuscript and book sources is appended. No attempt has been made to catalogue the great mass of fragmentary material found in magazines and newspaper articles:

The Harmonists, or The New Harmony Society.—Aaron Williams, D. D., 1866.

History of American Socialisms.—John Humphrey Noyes, 1870.

History of New Harmony, Indiana: The Rappites.—Dr. J. Schnack and Richard Owen.—Pamphlet, 1890.

Communistic Societies of the United States.—Charles Nordhoff, 1875.

Two Years' Residence in the Settlement on the English Prairie in the Illinois County, U. S.—John Woods, London. 1822.

Travels in North America.—Charles Lyell, F. R. S., 1845.

History of the English Settlement in Edwards County, Illinois.— George Fowler, 1882.

American Communities.—William Alfred Hines, 1878.

A Journey in America.—Morris Birkbeck, London, 1818.

Brief Sketch of New Harmony.—Library Catalogue of Working Men's Institute, 1845.

Visit to New Harmony.—William Herbert, London, 1825.

Life of Robert Owen.—Lloyd Jones, 1890.

Socialism, By a Socialist.—Charles P. Somerby, 1879.

History of Cooperation.—George Jacob Holyoke, 1878.

Speech at New Harmony, April 27, 1825.—Robert Owen.

Two Discourses on a New System of Society.—Delivered in the Hall of the House of Representatives.—Robert Owen, Pittsburg, 1825.

Twenty-three Lectures on the Rational System of Society.—Delivered in Egyptian Hall, Piccadilly.—Robert Owen, London, 1841.

Owen's Universal Revolution, With Supplement.—Robert Owen, London, 1849.

Lectures on the New State of Society.—Robert Owen, London, 1842.

New Religion.—Lecture.—Robert Owen, London, 1830.

The Addresses of Robert Owen, as Published in the London Journal.—London, 1835.

The Report of the Committee of the Association for the Relief of the Manufacturing and Laboring Poor to the Committee of the House of Commons.—London, 1825.

381

APPENDIX

New View of Society.—Lecture.—Robert Owen, London, 1842.

Social State of Man.—Robert Owen, London, 1842.

Manifesto of Robert Owen to Parliament.—London, 1840.

The Religious Creed of the New System.—Abram Combe, Edinburg, 1824.

The First Trumpet.—An Address to the Disciples of Robert Owen.—William Cameron, London, 1832.

Life and Last Days of Robert Owen.—George Jacob Holyoke, 1871.

The Town of New Harmony.—Proceedings of a Meeting of the Inhabitants held April 13, 1842.—Tract.

Memoir of William Maclure.—Samuel Geo. Morton, D. D., 1844.

Communism and Socialism.—Theodore D. Woolsey, 1888.

The Cooperative Movement in England.—Beatrice Potter, 1891.

The Cooperative Commonwealth.—Laurence Gronlund, 1890.

Richard Owen's Scrap-Book.

Letters and Papers of Josiah Warren.

New Harmony Community Account-Books.

Journal (MSS.) Proceedings of Meetings of Working Men's Institute.

Manuscript Copy of Community Dances.—Robert Fauntleroy

Scrap-Books of Mrs. A. Dransfield.

Letters, Wills, and Deeds of William Maclure.

The New Harmony Gazette. Vols. I, II, and III.—October 1, 1825, to March 1, 1829.

The Disseminator. New Series, Vols. I and II. Published at New Harmony, 1834–'35.—William Maclure, Editor.

The Free Enquirer. Vols. I–VI, inclusive. Published at Baltimore and New York.—Frances Wright, Robert Dale Owen, and Amos Gilbert, Editors.

The Crisis. Vols. I and II, 1832–'34, London.—Robert Owen and Robert Dale Owen, Editors.

The Beacon. Vol. III, Old Series, 1838. Vol. I, New Series, 1839.—G. Vale, Editor.

The Disseminator. "Containing Hints to the Youth of the United States." Old Series. Edited, Printed, and Published Semimonthly by the Pupils of the School of Industry, New Harmony. First issue, January 16, 1828.

The Indiana Statesman. May 13, 1842, to March 14, 1846.

The New Moral World. Vols. I to VII. London, 1834–'40. Edited by Robert Owen and Disciples.

The Cooperative Magazine and Monthly Herald. London, 1820.

Southwestern Sentinel. Vol. I, No. 1. Evansville, February 28, 1840.

APPENDIX

Millennial Gazette, London.—Robert Owen, Editor.
Practical Details of Equitable Commerce.—Josiah Warren, Evansville, 1835.
Equitable Commerce.—Josiah Warren, 1835.
Practical Application of the Elementary Principles of True Civilization.—Josiah Warren, 1873.
A Few Days in Athens.—Frances Wright.
Autobiography of Raffinesque.—Constantine Raffinesque.
A Brief History of Socialism in America.—Frederic Heath, 1900.
A History of the People of the United States, Vol. V.—John B. McMaster. New York: D. Appleton & Co., 1900.
Cooperative Communities in the United States.—Rev. Alexander Kent. Bulletin of the Department of Labor, 1901.
Education.—Joseph Neef, Philadelphia, 1808.
Neef's Method of Teaching.—Joseph Neef, Philadelphia, 1813.
American Conchology, or Description of the Shells of North America. Illustrated by Colored Figures from Originals, Drawings Executed from Nature.—Thomas Say, F. M. L. S. Engravings drawn and colored by Mrs. Say and C. A. LeSueur. Engravings by L. Lyon, C. Tiebout, and I. Walker.
Course of Popular Lectures.—Frances Wright.
Campbell and Owen Debate. Cincinnati, 1829.
Reise Durch Nord Amerika.—Alexander Philip Maximillian. Coblentz, 1838, 1843. London, 1843.
Travels Through North America.—His Highness Bernhard, Duke of Weimar, Saxe, and Eisenach. Philadelphia, 1828.
Method of Science Teaching in the Colleges and Universities of North America.—C. S. Raffinesque.
Self-Help a Hundred Years Ago.—History of Cooperation in England.—George Jacob Holyoke.
A History of Socialism.—Thomas Kirkup, 1892.
Socialism, Utopian and Scientific.—Frederick Engels, 1892.
Working Class Movement in America.—Edward and Eleanor Marx Aveling, 1892.
Socialism in England.—Sidney Webb.
Robert Owen and His Social Philosophy.—Sargent.
The Manufacturing Population of England.—Keel.
Stories of Indiana.—Chapters on New Harmony and Raffinesque.—Maurice Thompson.
History of American Education.—Richard Boone.
Pocahontas, A Drama; Hints on Public Architecture, 1840; Footfalls on the Boundary of Another World, 1859; Wrongs of Sla-

APPENDIX

very: The Rights of Emancipation, 1864; Beyond the Breakers, 1870; The Debatable Land Between this World and the Next, 1871; Threading My Way, or Twenty-Seven Years of Autobiography, 1874.—Robert Dale Owen.

United States Geological Reports. 1838-'59.—David Dale Owen.

Key to the Geology of the Globe.—Richard Owen.

American Entomology.—Thomas Say.

Account of the Doctrines of Charles Fourier.—Parke Godwin.

Recent American Socialisms.—Richard T. Ely.

Essay on Robert Owen.—Ralph Waldo Emerson.

Science Sketches.—David Starr Jordan. Chapter on Raffinesque.

Comparative Socialism. Chapter II.—Woodrow Wilson.

Letters and Lectures of Robert Dale Owen.—Richard D. Owen.

Twelve Months in New Harmony.—Paul Brown, 1827.

Higher Education of Women.—Lange. New York: D. Appleton & Co., 1890.

Journal Indiana House of Representatives, Twenty-second Session, 1836-'37.

Journal Indiana House of Representatives, Twenty-third Session, 1837-'38.

Journal Indiana House of Representatives, Thirty-sixth Session, 1851-'52.

Debates Second Indiana Constitutional Convention, two volumes.

Journal Second Indiana Constitutional Convention, two volumes.

History of Woman Suffrage, three volumes.—E. C. Stanton, S. B. Anthony, M. J. Gage, Rochester, N. Y., 1887.—Charles Mann.

Education in Indiana, a monograph prepared by State Superintendent F. A. Cotton for the Louisiana Purchase Exposition.—Indianapolis, W. B. Burford, 1904.

The History of Modern Education.—S. G. Williams. Syracuse, N. Y. C. W. Bardeen, 1903.

Education in the United States.—Edited by Nicholas Murray Butler. Albany, J. B. Lyon Co., 1900.

The Wrong of Slavery and the Right of Emancipation.—Robert Dale Owen. Philadelphia: J. B. Lippincott & Co., 1864.

Maclure's Opinions on Various Subjects, three volumes. New Harmony Industrial Schools Press, 1834.

A Proper System of Education for the Schools of a Free People.—Joseph Neef, 1807.

The Meaning of Education.—Nicholas Murray Butler. The Macmillan Co., N. Y., 1901.

APPENDIX

Pestalozzi: His Life and Work. De Guimps.—New York: D. Appleton & Co., 1890.

Pestalozzi: His Life, Work, and Influence. Cincinnati, Ohio: Van Antwerp, Bragg & Co., 1875.

A History of Education in Indiana.—R. G. Boone. New York: D. Appleton & Co., 1892.

Indiana Libraries, 1904, Monograph by W. E. Henry, State Librarian for Louisiana Purchase Exposition.

Pamphlet on the Maclure Libraries by Jacob Piatt Dunn, State Librarian, 1893.

Quick's Educational Reformers. New York: D. Appleton & Co., 1890.

Education in the United States.—R. G. Boone. New York: D. Appleton & Co., 1890.

School Law of Indiana, 1901.—F. L. Jones, ex-State Superintendent of Public Instruction.

Johonnot's Principles and Practise of Teaching. New York: D. Appleton & Co., 1883.

Thoughts.—Horace Mann. Boston: Lee, Shepard & Dillingham, 1872.

Synopsis Minutes Minerva Society.—Arthur Dransfield.

A Vindication of the Rights of Woman.—Mary Wollstonecraft. New York: Scribner & Welford, 1890.

Scheme for the Reconstruction of the Union with New England Left Out.—Pamphlet by Robert Dale Owen, 1863. New Harmony Library.

The Perils and Exigencies of the Present Crisis.—Address by R. D. Owen to Citizens of Indiana, State House, Indianapolis, 1860.

INDEX

INDEX

schools, 270–272; English, 218, 258; New Harmony, 93, 236, 243, 244, 246; provision for, in Preliminary Society, 89; self-supporting, 254, 269, 270, 281; Spartan system of education, 267–269, 282, 283.
"Boat load of knowledge," 81, 104, 236.
Bodmer, 315.
Bolton, 177.
Bolton, Samuel, chemist, 319.
Bonaparte, Prince Charles Lucian, Say edits publications, 76.
Boone, infant school, first, 286; technical schools, early, 245.
Borrowdale and Atkinson, Owen's partners, 48.
Boston, girls' schools in, 240.
Boston Women's Club, 196.
Botany, fossil, 318; researches of Raffinesque, 78, 79.
Boutwell, George, Pestalozzian movement, 292.
Braunberg, Baron. See Neuweid, Prince Maximilian Alexander Philipp.
Brentwood, Modern Times, later name, 303.
Brook Farm, life in, 134; Modern Times, unlike, 305; Nashoba similar to, 195; New Harmony compared to, 2, 3.
Brown, 177.
Brown, John, 197.
Brown, Paul, criticizes conditions at New Harmony, 147–149, 157, 158; criticizes Owen, 184; New Harmony, experiences at, 137–140; New Harmony Gazette refuses essays by, 149; opposes New Harmony management, 145.
Buchanan, infant school at New Lanark, 216, 217, 223; forerunner of Froebel, 286, 287.
Burkitt, Rev. John, 191.
Burt, C. W., New Harmony failure, 184.
Butler, Nicholas Murray, education, meaning of, 276; educational period, 282; religious instruction in the public schools, 228.

Cabet, 2.
Campanella, 2.
Campbell, Alexander, criticism of

New Harmony, 82, 83; debate with Owen, 307, 308.
Carnegie, Mr., Maclure compared to, 322, 323.
Celibacy, communism, rule of successful, 39; Zoarites taught, 39. See also Marriage.
Cemetery, Rappite, 28, 36.
Chappelsmith, John, 79; artist, 318.
Chappelsmith, Mrs. John, entomologist, 318.
Character, how formed, 61, 106, 210–213; motto concerning, 210; studies at New Harmony, 82.
Chase, Salmon P., Owen, R. D., effect of letter to Lincoln, 371.
Child labor, age limit, 119; in England, 48; legislation, campaign for 53, 55; Owen's speech, 54; Peel's factory act, 48.
Children, age when received by community, 132, 241; behavior, 119; belonged to community, 132; Brown criticizes New Harmony, 145, 149; Community of Equality, members of, 108, 111; dancing at New Harmony, 131; education in one family, 154; education of, 65, 66, 152, 259; fear, effect upon, 258–260; lectures for, 149; Lyell's impressions of, at New Harmony, 321; Maclure's educational methods, Owen disapproves of, 167, 251–253; mechanics' and farmers', 150; New Harmony schools, ages prescribed, 238; New Harmony schools, tuition in, 239; Owen's ideas as to treatment of, 64, 66; Owen's schools, purpose of, 213–216; parents, seldom seen, 243, 246; poor, discrimination against, 341; Preliminary society, provisions for, 89; punishment of, 229–231; reading of, 224; religious teaching of, 226–228; school republic, 277–279; schools, centralization of, 270–272; schools, self-supporting, 254, 269, 270, 281; Spartan system of education, 267–269, 282, 283; spiritual inheritances, 284, 285; war, teachings regarding, 90.
Choate, Senator, Smithson bequest, 339.

388

INDEX

389

INDEX

Dorsey, Mr., Owen's school system, in charge of, 165, 252; Owen's steward, 173.
Dransfield, 177.
Dransfield, Arthur, librarian of New Harmony Working Men's library, 27, 328, 332.
Drawing, Maclure's course of study, 237.
Dreidoppel, 315.
Drinkwater, Mr., cotton mill, of 47.
Duclos, 177.
Dunn, Jacob P., Maclure estate, 324.
Duss, John, career of, 34, 35; Economy (Pa.), trustee of, 34, 35; Rappite estate, 35.

Economy (Pa.), 24; last years of the community, 34, 35; Leon's followers withdraw from, 33; Rapp buried at, 36; Rappites build, 32; secession at, 32.
Edinburg, "Practical society" of, 112.
Education, centralization of schools., 270–272; children, 151, 152, 154, 259; classical opposed, 279, 280, 287; Community of Equality, 108; cramming system attacked, 218; environment a factor, 212; free and universal, 4, 264–267; Indiana, State Board of, 357; infant, 64; interest, value of, 260; lectures on, 149; legislation for, in Indiana, 340–359; love a principle in, 221; Maclure's efforts after Owen's defeat, 254; Maclure's interest in, 74, 75, 234; Maclure's method, dissatisfaction over, 167, 251–253; meaning of, 273–277; New Harmony Educational Society, 251; New Harmony schools, course of study in, 236–238; New Harmony schools, factors in, 79, 81; New Harmony schools, superintendent of, 113; New Harmony schools, to be center of, 75, 99; New Lanark Schools, subjects taught, 223; R. D. Owen's creed, 342; Pestalozzian movement, second, 292, 293; Rappite agreement on, 12; reading, importance of, 224; religious element in, 226–228; self-

supporting schools, 254, 269, 270, 281; sexes, equal privileges for, 4, 100, 239, 240, 287; Society of, jealousy toward, 148; Society of, opposes reorganization of the community, 151; Spartan system, 267–270, 282, 283. See also Boarding schools; Infant schools; Kindergarten; Pestalozzi; Schools.
Edwards county (Ill.), settlement in, 17, 23, 30; slavery opposed by settlement, 30.
Elderhorst, Dr., 4, 319.
Elliot, James, New Harmony property, 176.
Emerson, Ralph Waldo, 3; Owen and socialism, 309–311.
Engelman, George, visited New Harmony, 320.
Engels, Frederick, tribute to Robert Owen, 43, 46.
England, coöperation in, 5, 308; Flower's arrival in, 57; industrial revolution in, 43–52; labor legislation, 55–57; labor trouble, 53; New Lanark best community in, 51; Sea island cotton introduced, 47; slavery rare in, 360.
English Prairie, colony on the Wabash river, 128.
Environment, importance attached to, 61, 211, 212.
Equality, New Harmony community of, 104–111; not agreeable to all, 124, 126, 129, 130; of labor not a success, 119, 120.
Equity, stores, 296, 297, 300; village in Tuscarawas co. (O.), 298; village of Modern Times, 302–305; village of Utopia, 301, 302; villages did not fail like New Harmony, 305.
Evans, 177.
Evans, Frederick W., political movement organized, 337.
Evans, George H., political movement organized, 337.

Factories, child labor in, 48; conditions in English, 47–54; legislation, 53–56; Owen as superintendent, 47, 48; Peel's factory act, 48.
Family, Amana society, 39; children surrendered under Spartan system, 267–269, 282, 283;

INDEX

legislation for women, 204–208; legislature of 1862, 372; libraries, Maclure, 325–327, 333, 334; libraries, township, 333, 357; Lincoln reared in, 361; mounds in, 77, 318; R. D. Owen in politics of, 337; pioneers in, 16–18; Rappite community, 15, 16; rebellion, conditions during, 365, 372–375; school fund, 354, 357; school legislation, 290; 340–359; slavery legislation, 363; Union reconstruction, southern plan for, 372–375; State geologists, 319, 320; Superintendent of Public Instruction, 355; surplus revenue fund, 344–347; wealth in, 28.

Indiana Constitutional convention, 25; free schools, fight for, 340, 347, 351–354; R. D. Owen's tribute to woman, 190; slavery question in, 363; women, property rights of, 205–207.

Indiana State University, Owen geological collection, 317; Richard Owen professor in, 319.

Indianapolis, capital located, 25.

Indians, burying ground at Harmonie, 28; Gabriel's Rock attributed to, 20; mounds described, 77, 318.

Individualism, origin of, 5.

Infant schools, age admission to, 216, 238; games used at New Lanark, 222, 223; first, 214, 286; New Harmony, 4, 238, 241; New Lanark, 214–223; purpose of, 218; Spartan system for, 267–269, 282, 283; teachings in, 219–223. *See also* Boarding schools; Education; Kindergarten; Pestalozzi; Schools.

Infidelity, at New Harmony, 82, 83, 101; Owen charged with, 51. *See also* Religion.

Inventions, divital, by Raffinesque, 122; Owen's, 132.

Iowa, Amana society in, 39.

Iverdun, Pestalozzi's school at, 79.

Jackson, President, friend of Owen's, 308.

Jacobi, leadership in communism, 40; marriage sacrificed to communism, 41.

Jardins des Plantes, Lesueur's connection with, 77.

Jefferson, Thomas, U. S. constitution, opinion of, 66.

Jennings, R. L., Community of Equality constitution, 105; Saxe-Weimar's account of, 125.

Jennings, Robert, Nashoba, trustee of, 195.

Johnson, 177.

Jones, partner of Owen's, 46.

Jones, Lloyd, tribute to Owen, 311–313.

Jordan, Dr., Raffinesque, 77–79.

Just, Baron, visits New Lanark, 232.

Keil, Dr., Philipsburg colony, 33.

Kelly, Abby, 197.

Kendal (Ohio), community, 177.

Kent, Duke of, Owen acquitted of infidelity charge, 51.

Kentucky, State geologist of, 319.

Kindergarten, methods of Froebel and Owen compared, 216–223; Owen founder of, 214, 215, 218–220, 286, 287; part of the public school system, 287; a preparatory school, 219; purpose of, 217; teachings of criticised, 58. *See also* Boarding schools; Education; Infant schools; Pestalozzi; Schools.

Kingsley, J. S., tribute to Say, 76.

Labor, coöperative, 5, 38, 43, 185, 301, 308, 312; factory, 44–52; "labor notes," 5, 296, 297, 301; motive necessary, 118; not equally shared, 120; occupational communities, 144; riots, 53; shorter hours advocated, 54. *See also* Child labor.

Laboring class, condition in England, 44–52; legislation for, 55, 56, 212; Maclure's regard for, 324, 325; New Lanark mills, 49–52; Owen's speech concerning, 53, 54; Peel's factory act, 48; riots of, 53.

Lafayette, Gen., 193; solitary confinement cruel, 200; trustee of Nashoba, 195.

Land, disposal of, at New Harmony, 175, 176; dissatisfaction among societies over, 154; for Mechanics society, 147, 148;

393

INDEX

for School society and Pastoral
society, 148; secured by Macluria
and Feiba Peveli, 144; terms
upon which Owen granted, 183.
Lane, Charles, family life, 41, 42.
Languages, in Maclure's course of
study, 238; opposition to classical education, 279–281, 287, 288.
Latin, study of, opposed, 279–281.
Latitude, Whitwell's scheme for
geographical names, 114, 115.
Law, concerning slavery, 362, 363;
in New Harmony Community
of Equality, 108; labor legislation, 56; libraries, in Indiana,
333, 357; liquor traffic, prohibition of, 5; Peel's factory act, 48;
school legislation in Indiana,
340–359; women, legislation for,
5, 186, 200, 204–208.
Lee, Gen., invasion of Maryland,
366.
Lentz, Jonathan, mission to New
Harmony, 36.
Leon, Count Maximilian de, ab-
sconds, 33; death of, 33; marriage permitted by, 33; Philipsburg colony, 33; secession among
Rappites, causes, 32, 33.
Leonard, L. R., New Harmony
failure, 184.
Lesquereux, Leo, 4; fossil botanist,
318.
Lesueur, Charles Albert, 4, 314;
accompanies Prince Maximilian
von Neuweid, 315; curator at
Havre, 318; engraving by, 76;
painter, 337; Saxe-Weimar describes, 132, 133; scientific work,
318; sketch of, 77; teaches drawing, 242.
Lewis, Warner W., 124; Community of Equality, 105; secretary
of New Harmony, 113.
Liberty Land Co., purchased Rappite estate, 35.
Libraries, local historical collections for, 332; Maclure, disap-
pearance of, 333, 334; Maclure,
established by, 5, 256, 322–328,
330–334; Maclure gifts, effect
of, 289, 333, 334; Maclure, list
of, 325–327; A. Maclure, 321;
New Harmony Workingmen's,
1, 36, 76, 256, 323, 327–332;
township, in Indiana, 333, 357.
Lichtenberger, 177.

Lincoln, Abraham, 5; Indiana,
reared in, 361; hatred of slavery,
362; R. D. Owen compared to,
360–362; R. D. Owen's letter
to, 366–371; sixty day notice
to the south, 366, 369.
Linton, Edward, cares for Warren,
306; Modern Times, success of,
303; tribute to Warren, 304.
Liquor traffic. See Temperance.
Literature, Pietistic fervor destroyed by, 8, 9; superintendent of, 113.
Locofoco party, 337.
London, attempt to establish
colony in, 232.
Long, expedition to Rocky Mountains, 75.
Long Island, Modern Times site
of, 302.
Longitude, Whitwell's scheme for
geographical names, 114, 115.
Lundy, 197.
Lycoming county (Penn.), 11.
Lyell, Sir Charles, 4; New Har-
mony, impressions of, 320, 321.
Lyon, L., engraver, 76.
Lyon, Sidney, geologist, 319.
Lyons, 177.

McDonald, Capt., presents community model, 101, 102.
Macdonald, A. J., American communities, 177; New Harmony
community failure, 178–183;
Owen, Maclure quarrel, cause of,
165.
McDonald, Donald, Community
of Equality constitution, 105,
112; Macluria, 113; sketch of,
112.
Machinery, crusades against, 53;
labor saving, 56; supplants manual labor, 44.
Maclure, Alexander, 318, 321; W.
Maclure's will, executor of, 325.
Maclure, Mary, W. Maclure's will,
executor of, 325.
Maclure, William, agricultural
school, 74; centralization of
schools, 270–272; classical education opposed, 279–281; collection of, 4, 317; communistic
failure, charged to, 252, 253;
death of, 323; education, free
and universal advocated, 264–
267; education, impetus to, 314;

394

INDEX

educational efforts at New Harmony, 236, 254–256; estate, 324; fails to do educational work guaranteed to Owen, 251, 252; hatred of non-productive class, 324; in Mexico, 255, 322; investments at New Harmony, 75; libraries, 5, 256, 289, 322–328, 333, 334; manual training, champion of, 4, 242, 261; Nashoba, trustee of, 195; natural science as a study, 262; New Lanark, visit to, 232; "Opinions on various subjects," 234; Owen, opinions in common, 233, 244; Owen, quarrel with, 163–165; Pestalozzian school in Pennsylvania, 235; Pestalozzian system, introduced by, 3, 235, 287; Pestalozzian system, opinion of, 234, 235, 283, 284; Philadelphia Academy of Natural Science, 4, 74; philanthropy, effect of, 334, 335; punishment, 258–260; Rapp mansion, 124; religion, opposition to, 257; Saxe-Weimar visits, 129, 130, 131; schools, course of study, 236–238; schools, withdraws support from, 255; security for sums due, 129; self-supporting scheme for schools, 254, 269, 270, 284; sketch of, 73–75; Spartan system, 267–269, 282, 283; will, 324, 325; Workingmen's Institute and Library, 256, 323.

Maclure's Seminary, announcement of, 254.

Macluria, breaks up, 151, 162, 163; establishment of, 113; failure, cause of, 185; government, 113; land, conditions of securing, 144; Owen's retrospect of, 142, 143; Saxe-Weimar visits, 127, 128; success of community Number 2, 120; women, treatment of, 113.

McNamee, Dr., conducts Saxe-Weimar, 127.

Madison, opinion of U. S. constitution, 66.

Madison, Union members of Indiana legislature retire to, 372.

Maidlow, James, New Harmony property, 176.

Manchester, literary society, 48; Owen's business in, 47–49.

Mann, Horace, 351; in Pestalozzian movement, 292.

Manual training, colonies for poor, 56; criticism of, 139; first school, 244; in Maclure's course of study, 238; Maclure's schools after the community failure, 254, 255; school at New Harmony, 4, 241–244; self-supporting scheme, 242, 254, 269, 270, 281; value of, 261; Warren's experiments in teaching, 298.

Manufacturing, buildings for, 16, 17; legislation governing, 55, 56; market for, 38; New Harmony, 94–96; Owen's career in, 47–56; success of New Lanark mills, 50–52; superintendent of, 113; woolen factory, 13.

Marriage, agreement concerning, 12; civil contract for, 191, 192, 202; evils of, 146; Leon permits, 33; New Harmony, first at, 100; not practiced, 13; Owen's 48, 49; Owen's ideas on, 132, 190, 191; R. D. Owen's opinion of, 201; Rappites renounce, 10; sacrificed for communism, 40–42; successor to Rapp a married man, 34; Zoarites permit, 39. See also Celibacy.

Mason, Dr., Warren's musical notation, 300.

Mason, Lowell, Pestalozzian movement, 292.

Masons, lodge at New Harmony, 99, 100.

Massachusetts, wealth in, 28.

Mathematics, in Maclure's course of study, 237.

Maximilian, Prince Alexander Philipp. See Neuweid, Prince Maximilian Alexander Philipp.

Maximilian, Prince John, visits New Lanark, 232.

Mechanics society, land secured, 147, 148; trouble in, 149.

Meek, Rev., performs marriage ceremony, 100.

Meek, F. B., 4; paleontologist, 318.

"Mental independence, Declaration of," 146; importance of, 153, 155.

Metcalf, Kate, nursed Warren, 306.

Mexico, communistic colonization of, 307; Maclure in, 255, 322.

Mills, Caleb, credit for Indiana

395

INDEX

INDEX

New Harmony, 82, 83; Germany, state of, 7, 8; Macluria, cause of formation, 112, 128; Macluria disrupted by, 151, 162, 163; Mexico, toleration in, 307; New Harmony failure, 183; New Harmony, services at, 101; opposed at New Harmony, 5; Owen accepts, 311; Owen and Maclure reject, 257; Owen-Campbell, debate 307; Owen's, 57, 65, 66; Rappites, observances of, 21, 22, 24, 26; spiritual inheritances of the race, 284, 285; teaching, omitted by Owen, 226–227. *See also* Infidelity; Spiritualism.

Rensselaer Institute, compared to New Harmony, 244, 245.

Republic, Plato's, 2.

Richardson, James, Nashoba, trustee of, 195.

Riots, in 1811, 53.

Robinson, Mary, marriage of, 201, 202. *See also* Owen, Mary.

Robson, 177.

Robson, Robert, marriage of, 191, 192.

Rose, Ernestine L., woman's rights advocated, 187; Frances Wright, tribute to, 197, 198.

Runcie, Mrs. Constance Fauntleroy, Minerva society, founder of, 196.

Rush, Richard, Smithson bequest, 338.

St. Louis, kindergarten in public schools, 287.

St. Simon, 2; socialism advocated, 45.

Salmon, Alfred, marriage of, 100.

Sampson, 177.

Sampson, James, scientific collection, 318.

Sargant, Owen's infant school system, 220; Owen's religious acceptance, 311; religion at New Harmony, 183.

Satterfield, Mr. 46.

Saxe-Weimar, Duke of, Gabriel's Rock, theory of, 21; New Harmony schools, 243, 244; New Harmony visited, 123–133.

Saxony, presents medal to Owen 232.

Say, Thomas, 4, 314; collection of,

4, 317; New Harmony schools, in charge of, 251, 255; Saxe-Weimar's impressions of, 126; scientific work, 75, 76; sketch of, 75, 77; teacher, 236, 242; tributes to, 76, 77.

Say, Mrs. Thomas, draws plates for Say's books, 76.

Schmidt, 131.

Schnack, Dr., New Harmony family names, 177; New Harmony theatre, 36; D. D. Owen's geological work, 317; owners at New Harmony, 176; Prince Maximilian von Neuweid's book, 315; Rappites gave library building, 36; scientists, 318.

Schnee, 177.

Schnee, Jacob, New Harmony property, 176.

School republic, Neef's scheme for, 277–279.

Schoolcraft, H. R., Gabriel's Rock, 20, 21.

Schools, centralization of, 270–272; common school fund in Indiana, 354, 357; common school system at New Harmony, 4, 239; course of study at New Harmony, 236–238; free, 264–267, 287; free, legislation for in Indiana, 265, 266, 340–359; higher at New Harmony, 241, 242; in shoe factory, 150; Indiana, 347–351; industrial, 287; kindergarten in public, 287; legislation urged, 55; Maclure's belief in, 234; Maclure's efforts after Owen's defeat, 254, 255; mission of, 273–277; New Harmony, 91, 93; New Harmony, results at, 288–293; New Lanark, 50, 51, 213–233; New Lanark, difficulties at, 231; Owen's gift to New Harmony, 173; Owen's system, 165, 252; Pestalozzi's, 234, 235; Preliminary society's plans for, 89; punishment at New Lanark, 229, 230; religious prejudice against New Harmony, 101; religious teaching in, 226–228; self-government of, 277–279; self-supporting scheme, 254, 269, 270; sleeping arrangement at New Harmony, 243, 244, 246; Spartan system, 267–269, 282, 283; subjects taught at

INDEX

New Lanark, 223; surplus revenue fund, 344–347; teacher in, 135; tuition at New Harmony, 239. *See also* Boarding schools; Education; Infant schools; Kindergartens; Pestalozzi.

Science, at New Harmony, 314–321; Lesueur's activity, 318; Maclure's course of study, 237; D. D. Owen's work, 316, 317, 319; researches in, by Prince Maximilian von Neuweid, 314, 315; Sampson's collection, 318; study of, 262; superintendent of, 113.

Sears, Barnas, Pestalozzian movement, 292.

Separatists, asylum in Russian Tartary, 8.

Shakers, land, value of, 38; near Vincennes, 126; religious basis, 2, 40.

Shawneetown (Ill.), Rappite store, 31.

Sheldon, E. A., Pestalozzian movement, 292.

Sicily, 78.

Silliman's Journal, 236, 238.

Sistare, Lucy, 81, 130; wife of Say, 76.

Slavery, abolition favored at New Harmony, 5, 188; Compromise of 1850, 362; emancipation proclamation, 371; English, 360; English colonists oppose, 30; legislation in Indiana, 363; Nashoba solution, 194–196; R. D. Owen opposed, 360–376; women oppose, 188.

Smith, F. W., New Harmony failure, 184.

Smithsonian institution, legislation, for 4, 338, 339.

Snelling, 177.

Social Science Association of Birmingham, 312.

Socialism, advocated, 45.

Society, Owen's ideas for betterment of, 59–68.

Society for mutual instruction, 255; libraries modeled after, 289; results of, 256.

Soper, 177.

Sorosis, 196.

Spiritualism, books on, 360; R. D. Owen accepts, 359, 360.

Squatters, 17, 27.

Stanton, Elizabeth Cady, woman's suffrage, 187, 188.

Stanz, Pestalozzi's school at, 218, 219, 224.

Stevens, Thaddeus, negro suffrage, 376.

Stillwell, William, 342.

Stocker, Jonathan, New Harmony property, 176.

Stone, Lucy, 197.

Suffrage, Feiba Peveli, 115; negro, 376; women granted, in Community of Equality, 108; women not granted, at Macluria, 113; women, why demanded by, 186–188.

Sumter, Fort, 365, 372.

Sunday, Community of Equality, 105; meetings on, 158; observance at New Harmony, 101, 129, 130; women's attendance at meeting, 192.

Superstition, among Rappites, 19, 20, 24.

Tariff, on cotton, 53.

Taylor, William, Owen, dealings with, 156, 182.

Teachers, training school for, 291.

Teaching, methods at New Harmony, 257; methods at New Lanark, 51; methods in infant school, 221, 222; object method, 224, 257; Pestalozzi's methods, 225.

Technical education. *See* Manual training.

Temperance, distilling forbidden at Macluria and Feiba Peveli, 144; not practiced at New Harmony, 179, 184; Owen forbids distilling, 126, 144; prohibition, 5; Rappites practice, 12; Taylor's distillery at New Harmony, 156, 182.

Tennessee, communistic colonies in, 177, 178; Troost, State geologist of, 79, 319.

Terre Haute, site owned by George Rapp, 38.

Texas, communistic colonies for, 307; school funds, 357.

Theatre, at New Harmony, 36.

Thrall, Mrs. Sarah Cox, pupil in New Harmony schools, 245, 246.

"Threading my way," Harmonie, 28, 29; New Harmony, 134–137.

INDEX